Making a Priest in the 'Fifties

◆

Memoir of a Nervous Seminarian
Or: How Your Elderly Pastor Got That Way

James M. O'Brien, Ph.D.

iUniverse, Inc.
New York Lincoln Shanghai

Making a Priest in the 'Fifties
Memoir of a Nervous Seminarian

Copyright © 2006 by James M. O'Brien

All rights reserved. No part of this book may be used or reproduced by any means, graphic, electronic, or mechanical, including photocopying, recording, taping or by any information storage retrieval system without the written permission of the publisher except in the case of brief quotations embodied in critical articles and reviews.

iUniverse books may be ordered through booksellers or by contacting:

iUniverse
2021 Pine Lake Road, Suite 100
Lincoln, NE 68512
www.iuniverse.com
1-800-Authors (1-800-288-4677)

ISBN-13: 978-0-595-40853-5 (pbk)
ISBN-13: 978-0-595-85217-8 (ebk)
ISBN-10: 0-595-40853-2 (pbk)
ISBN-10: 0-595-85217-3 (ebk)

Printed in the United States of America

Contents

Foreword... ix
Prologue.. 1

1957–58
Chapter 1   Arriving............................. 7
Chapter 2   Classes Begin....................... 35
Chapter 3   A Busy Place........................ 76
Chapter 4   A Summer in Sterling............. 108

1958–9
Chapter 5   Second Year....................... 127
Chapter 6   Seminarian Steelworker............ 161

1959–60
Chapter 7   Third Year........................ 175
Chapter 8   Summer in Prison: St. Charles School for Boys.... 209

1960–1
Chapter 9   Deacon Year....................... 223

Author Biography................................. 251

Acknowledgements

Where to start? Years ago, I was laboring over an Introduction to Television text I was trying to write when my colleague Teri Gamble, a much-published textbook author, said, "Forget about that television book. There are dozens already. You should write those seminary stories you're always telling."

She was right! And here they are.

The stories have benefited from the keen eye and encouraging pen of Marnie Schulenberg, a friend and published author in her own right. And from the supportive laughter and occasional questions from my PLATO reminiscence writing group. And from the patient but relentless gaze of my good wife, who won't let me get away with my casual approach to spelling, grammar and good sense.

I acknowledge too, my classmates and schoolmates at St. Mary's, a few of whom have made it, all unbidden, onto these pages. Also the faculty, who may come across as caricatures as seen through the adolescent eyes of my central character, but whose selfless dedication to their task now seems awesome from the perspective of a life-long teacher. Also the staff, who made available some pictures for the book.

I acknowledge finally, that this is a memoir, subject to the vagaries of my recollections as filtered through the past fifty years. I have followed the journalistic dictum laid down in *The Man Who Shot Liberty Valance* (1962): "If the facts and the legend are in conflict, print the legend." If my stories have slighted, distorted, or downright damaged the facts, you have only myself to blame. But these vivid memories are 100% accurate, mostly, and I'll stand by that, pretty much.

—Jim O'Brien

Foreword

I took my place in front of the catechism class, robed as usual in the long black rayon cassock, buttoned neck to ground. They taught us always to teach wearing the cassock—a testament to the fact that we were "in the world but not of it."

I began, also as usual, by asking for questions. After the typical long pause, one of the boys raised his hand.

"Father, why are you wearing that dress?"

Ouch! Of COURSE it looked like a dress. It WAS a dress. How could I not see that?

Simple. I had just lived in such a "dress" for four years of seminary, and so had everyone else there. The utter strangeness of the outfit I had come to take for granted.

A Catholic seminary in the fifties was a strange place, too, now that I look back at it over a span of fifty years. I didn't think so then, because I had spent all my institutional life in Catholic settings: St. Mary's grade school; St. Edward High School—both in Elgin, Illinois; then the University of Notre Dame in exotic South Bend, Indiana.

St. Mary's Seminary and University in Baltimore in the pre-Vatican II Catholic Church isolated me from the world for the most part, just what I needed at that stage in my life (although I didn't know it then!) and plunged me into an intense process intended to shape me into a priest.

Though I loved my years at Notre Dame, then all-male and more than a little seminary-like, I remember my years at St. Mary's even more vividly, though not necessarily accurately. I think most of us felt that a lot was at stake and we needed to get with the program.

At the same time, high seriousness and high intensity often lead to high absurdity, and we had plenty of those moments, too, as you may read. Human endeavors are fallible and this requires a sense of humor for survival. This I had in spades!

We had no idea at the time that our class of 1961 would be the largest class St. Mary's would ever see; that both the Church and American society were at a turning point in contemporary culture; that the unchanging Church which had filled our Catholic lives was about to undergo "a sea change into something rich and strange" to quote the Bard. The Church today is still trying to recover from that change but, in many ways, there's no way back.

But this book won't be a heavy sociological treatise. It's a cheerful and affectionate (if not uncritical!) memoir of a past time and place, still living in the minds of its participants.

In this writing and re-writing, I've learned some things about that kid I thought I knew, and not all the learnings have been pleasant. But I wouldn't have missed it for the world.

—Jim O'Brien

Prologue

Major Orders.

Ordination to the Roman Catholic priesthood comes at the end of a series of ceremonial steps, beginning with Tonsure, which admits the candidate to clerical status; the four minor orders: Exorcist, Acolyte, Porter, Lector, (the names represent minor liturgical functions) and three major orders: Sub-Deacon, Deacon, and Priest. Only the latter two date to the apostolic age. Ordination to the Deaconate empowers the Deacon to preach from the altar, to bless, and to perform other ceremonial roles. Deacons make solemn promises (not vows) of obedience and perfect celibacy.

Getting the Call

What am I *doing* here?
What am I doing *here*?
What am *aye* doing here?

    I find myself lying face down on the cold terrazzo center aisle of the chapel at St. Mary's Seminary, Baltimore, robed in long white alb and cincture, along with some eighty of my classmates; my head pillowed on my left forearm; my right arm curved gently around the top. A posture of profound submission. My shoulder hurts and my wrist hurts as the long Latin ceremony proceeds, but my real discomfort is largely spiritual. What am I doing here? Am I perpetuating a fraud which can never be undone? For my ordination to the Deaconate is eternal, but my worthiness is profoundly uncertain.

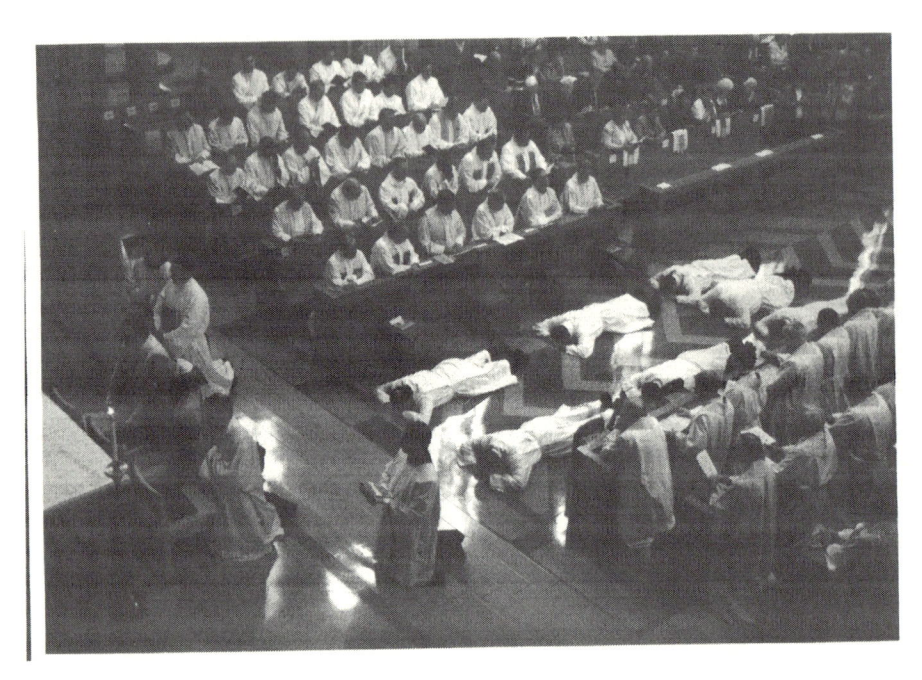

Deacons-to-be lying prostrate at St. Mary's Seminary. Undated.

"Jacobus Robertus O'Brien." The Bishop's expected call nonetheless startled me.

"*Adsum.*" I answered, meaning "present." I tried to pitch my voice to reflect my confidence. After all, I *was* present. I had taken my place about half way down the long center aisle of the chapel, moving solemnly in a measured pace and lowering myself humbly to the prone position. Nothing within me urges flight down the aisle and out the door. Some tiny part of me wants to yell out "Wait!" But most of me, including my skinny, 26 year old body, plays it safe and goes along with the elaborately choreographed and ancient ceremony.

Among my high school and college peers, I must have seemed an unlikely candidate for the priesthood. Nancy Bonnike, a classmate and close neighbor through grade and high school, burst out laughing upon learning the news. "Jimmy O'Brien?" she screamed, "You must be kidding." She saw it as the latest in a long series of escapades and practical jokes that marked my adolescent life.

And hey, I was no kid (at least in my own mind.) I had graduated from Notre Dame, worked for a year in Chicago, dated both seriously and slightly all that time (including Nancy Bonnike!), and, while a faithfully practicing Catholic youth, not particularly noted for my piety and devotion. Better description: a skeptical, smartmouth wise guy, whose general attitude toward life might easily have been described as irreverent. I'm sure many of my nun teachers would confirm this.

I had no particular illusions about priests, either. Although never personally exposed to the least sign of pedophilia, the scandal which continues to wrack the Church at the present time, I had a wide personal acquaintance with members of the clergy, from the hotshots to the flat tires, and I knew far more of the latter than the former.

Even as an altar boy in grade school, I sensed something wrong about the pastor, Father Ouimet, taking two full cruets of sherry for the celebration of Mass. Most priests barely used half the first cruet. And Assistant Pastor Mike Shanahan, a shy man who hated to preach and mumbled his way through incomprehensible but mercifully brief sermons, didn't inspire thoughts of vocation.

Speaking of preaching, Father Ouimet held forth for a solid 20-30 minutes on any given Sunday, exploring the various ramifications of his two sermon themes: his trip to Ireland, taken many years before, and the fact that St. Mary's did not have a coal collection, an obvious incentive for the congregation to increase its contributions. We, the congregation, hunkered down and took it. A part of our penance.

For years before that time, I came to know the assistants at St. Mary's up close and personal. My father, a paraplegic, received Communion once a month at home and, because my parents welcomed the priest as an honored guest, and provided him breakfast afterwards, I came to know them on a first name basis (Their first name being, of course, "Father.")

In Catholic grade school, vocations to the priesthood and religious life got pushed hard. We were challenged to "hear the call" and consider giving our lives to God. (Of course, the nuns who made the pitch had *already* given their lives to God, and this was a subtle reminder of that, too.) A dramatic choice, doubtless considered briefly by many of the students but quickly dismissed by most as the urgings of puberty became a primary preoccupation. I had thought about the priesthood, off and on, during my sixteen years of Catholic schooling, but for one reason or another, kept making other plans. But now, after three years of theological study, I found myself on the brink, of much more than I could know.

1957–58

o o o o o o o o o o o o o o o o o o o o o o o o o o o o o o
"A time of innocence…………….."

—*Paul Simon*

1

Arriving

Baltimore, Maryland, hot and humid on an early September morning. A young man steps off a city bus at the corner of Roland Park and Northern Parkway. He carries a brown Samsonite suitcase, a tennis racquet, and a paper bag. A skinny 5'10, maybe 125 lbs with his shoes on, light brown hair crewcut in the style of the times—it is l957. Twenty-three years old, he looks barely eighteen, more like a particularly green college freshman than the cool, sophisticated college graduate that he likes to think he is. Filled with illusions, exhausted from lack of sleep, and a long way from home, he is about to enter St. Mary's Theological Seminary to embark on four years of preparation for the Roman Catholic priesthood.

Checking in

That all-night jam session in D.C. seemed way cool at about 2 a.m. Right now I was beginning to have my doubts. But who could pass up the glamour of an after-hours jam session with noted jazzman Zoot Sims and a bunch of local musicians, some of whom I actually knew? I couldn't and I didn't. My piano-playing buddy, Gene Bonnike, dropped me off at the bus station in time to catch the six a.m. Greyhound to Baltimore and points North.

I climbed aboard the bus and dropped into the nearest seat. I told myself that I must not fall asleep or I might end up in New York. My head hit the seatback, and that was my very last thought 'til I woke in panic as the morning sun slanted through the windshield. We were just coming to the outskirts of Baltimore. I wandered around downtown Balto until the stores opened, found a clerical clothing store and bought myself the cheapest plastic version of the Roman collar that I would soon have to start wearing.

Then to the metro bus station, where I ignored the bums and the general grunginess, located schedules and found my ride to the seminary.

Jolting along on the nearly empty bus, I spotted a set of stone pillars marking a blacktop driveway. The brass plaque read: St. Mary's Seminary and University. Steamy heat, typical for Baltimore, enveloped me as I dismounted. I plodded wearily along the winding blacktop driveway toward the still-invisible seminary, my nervous anticipation pretty much buried beneath layers of exhaustion and the melting heat. I shifted the heavy suitcase and my tennis racquet back and forth from one hand to the other, as I made my way through the huge trees toward a place that I had never seen, too hot and tired to be nervous.

As I approached the wide front steps of the large grey building, I noticed seminarians scattered around in small groups. It didn't hit me that they were all in black suits or cassocks, nor that my "Joe College" sport coat and grey flannels stood out in any way. But then, a lot of stuff didn't hit me till later....much later!

Jim as "Joe College," 1957

I climbed the long concrete front steps, made my way through the heavy oaken doors and into the little office on the left. "Hi," I said cheerfully to the seminarian sitting behind the counter. He wore a black cassock and roman collar, but it didn't send me any signal.

"I need to check in with somebody." Oblivious to the odd look he gave me, I got directions to the rector's office on the second floor. Still schlepping the heavy suitcase and the tennis racquet, I mounted the stairs and fell into the short line outside the rector's office. Nobody spoke, so neither did I.

Father Laubacher.

Now, I didn't feel at all intimidated by priests. I felt respectful, basically admiring of them, and anticipated some kind of approving, pastoral response upon meeting them. (The fact that I was often disappointed did not affect my expectations.) I was, after all, here to become one of them, and I assumed that they would both approve and even esteem me for my choice. I had not yet met James Laubacher, S.S., Rector of St. Mary's Theological Seminary. Despite the German name, and the ominous initials (which actually stood for Society of Saint Sulpice), I had no reason to tremble. I did not yet know that the Rector's nickname in the seminary was "Jahweh" nor that the seminarians, somewhat blasphemously, would say about his office, "The tabernacle door is open." A warning to the unwary.

The guy in front of me had gone in, closing the door. Now he departed, expressionless, also closing the door. I hesitated, then knocked. "Come in."

As I opened the heavy door and stepped through, I formed an instant impression: square face, steel-rimmed spectacles, steel-grey hair, a very firm manner, totally serious. Perhaps just a trace of impatience?

"Yes?"

"Hello, Father," I said, confidently, striding across the room, dropping my bag, stretching out my hand like some sort of salesman. "Jim O'Brien. Rockford diocese."

"Yes." The rector took my hand briefly, sat down, consulted a list, made a check mark, then said, without any preliminary chat, "Mr. O'Brien, do you have a black suit?"

"Yes, Father. Well, that is, it's on order. I should get it in a few days." No "Welcome to St. Mary's?" No "How was your trip?" I felt a little let down.

"Do you have a cassock?" The Rector seemed quite preoccupied with my clothing.

"Yes, Father, in my suitcase." I gestured vaguely. Did he want me to show him? To put it on right there? I hesitated.

"Well, put it on, as soon as you get to your room. The dean, Father Cerny, will give you your room assignment. You should see him now."

He looked down at the papers on his desk, and I gathered that the "welcome" was at an end. Uncertainly, I gathered my suitcase and tennis racquet, and made my way to the door.

"Uh, well, nice meeting you, Father." I offered lamely. Father Laubacher raised his head and gazed through me. "Yes," He said. "Put on your cassock." I got out of there.

The next guy in line told me that the dean's office was at the end of the corridor. Still lugging the suitcase and racquet, I made my way to the Dean's office, and got in another line. The usual odd glances and the silence which seemed to be the rule didn't bother me by now. All I wanted was to get to my room and lie down for a while.

Father Cerny

When I entered, the dean, a tiny, ancient, bespectacled figure, sprang up from his desk, and speaking in an excited, breathless series of bursts that I would come to know well, fired off a series of phrases. "Come in, come in. What's your name? Where's your black?" He didn't wait for me to answer but rushed ahead with the questions. I was beginning to get rattled.

"Jim O'Brien, Father." Tentatively, I put down the suitcase, but somehow kept clinging to the racquet.

"O'Brien. O'Brien...." He muttered, shuffling a list of papers. "Yes, yes, I have it right here. O'Brien. Say, you're from the Rockford diocese." The word "Rockford" sprang from his lips as if it were hot.

"Sit down. Sit down," he insisted excitedly. "Tell me all about the diocese. Do you know Father Larry Murtaugh? Where are you from? Who was your pastor? How is Monsignor O'Neill?" I hardly knew where to start. Clearly he had forgotten about my lack of black, which was just as well, I figured.

"I'm from Elgin, Father," I began.

"Elgin, Elgin. Yes, Yes, I know it. Know it well. I'm from Aurora, myself, but that was a long time ago." He launched into a torrent of reminiscences, mentioning priests I knew, others I didn't. His manner of speaking was wholly unique, inspiring dozens of impressionists among my classmates, myself included. I couldn't really follow what he was saying, and he didn't seem to need encouragement. I began to feel aware of the line waiting in the hall. Surely these guys would hold me responsible for the time I was taking. But what could I do about it?

Father Cerny did not look like an "Aurora boy" or even like an American. He was ancient, wizened, with tiny slitted eyes, like some wise man from the Himalayas. The face of *Star Wars'* Yoda springs to mind. I listened, uncomfortable but fascinated. However, none of what he was telling me seemed to have anything to do with my seminary career. Finally, he began to wind down, gathered up a packet of papers and thrust them at me, pointed out my room number written at the top, and swept me to the door, insisting that I come back and chat with him about the good old days in the Midwest.

Sure enough, the line was now around the corner, as I once again lugged my suitcase and racquet. Ignoring the stares and glances I received, I made my way down the long corridor to the room, found it empty, picked a bed and fell on my back into something like instant sleep.

Ed Kehoe.

I woke with a start to find my new roommate had entered the room. Roommates were no big deal to me, but they were a rarity in the seminary, for reasons I later would be learning.

"Hi, I'm Jim O'Brien." I rolled off the bed and extended my hand.

"Ed Kehoe." My roommate was about my size, but more rawboned and angular. As I quickly learned, he hailed from far-distant upstate New York, almost at the Canadian border, and had attended a tiny diocesan minor seminary known as Wadhams Hall. He was much impressed, (as was I) that I had gone to Notre Dame. On the other hand, he knew a lot more about the way a seminary worked. For example, he was wearing the regulation cassock and roman collar, a sudden reminder to me to get into my "black."

As I dug through my meagre possessions and pulled out the cassock—the "Roman style" with buttons all the way down the front to the floor—I couldn't afford (and didn't even know about) the classier and more expensive "semi-Jesuit" style with the sash—Kehoe chatted about the seminary. I struggled to get the single-ply plastic Roman collar to stay down as it rose implacably up my long, skinny neck and cut viciously into my chin. Kehoe watched the process a bit curiously, but offered no comment. I finally managed to bend and twist the collar till it stayed somewhat within the top of the cassock, and I left well enough alone.

From Kehoe, I learned that most of the first year men were on the fourth floor in single rooms, but we were on the deacon corridor in one of the very few doubles, just a couple of doors from the Rector's apartment. A dubious privilege, as it turned out!

After we exchanged information in a friendly fashion, Ed pointed out to me that we were free to wander until lunch time, when the routine of the seminary would begin. We agreed to go down and meet some of the guys, who were hanging out on the front steps.

We walked down the steps to the outer atrium and into the steamy morning. We split up. I joined a group at the foot of the stairs, knowing nobody. One guy was excitedly describing an earlier event. "Yeah, this guy showed up, wearing a sport coat and carrying a tennis racquet!"

"Ooooo." The group murmured, and I oooed along with them. Clearly, the violation of custom had been serious. Now my cassock made me invisible, and I was very willing to keep it that way.

"Cerny kept him in there for almost a half hour," the speaker continued, as evidence of the transgression.

"Another Al Lingus," Someone else volunteered, and the group murmured again. Who was Al Lingus, and why was I like him? I had the sense not to ask anyone. At a break in the conversation, we exchanged names and shook hands, but the bell rang before I could elicit any further information. Virtually instant silence followed.

Prayer Hall

All the seminarians outside immediately headed for the front doors and joined others streaming down from upstairs and along the adjoining halls. A total population of about 350 counting the four classes. (Our first-year class, the ordination class of 1961, stood at 131 strong, forming the largest St. Mary's had ever had, or would ever have! Some fifty of us would leave over the four years!)

We poured into a large lecture hall with a wooden dais, large desk and microphone at the front. The first year men, myself among them, assembled way in the back. Someone managed to find my assigned place for me, and I fell into the folding wooden theatre seat with a well-worn wooden kneeler attached to the seat in front. I felt my infernal plastic Roman collar again mounting up my neck and I scrabbled fiercely to force it down, without much effect.

I noticed that no one else was sitting. I slipped to my knees as Father Laubacher took his place in the front, and began reading a long sequence of prayers in Latin. The seminarians, myself excepted (as far as I knew), answered together, also in Latin, and I mumbled along, trying to pick up the occasional word.

Excursus (whoa!) on Latin

Let me wander a bit here on the subject of Latin. My greatest fear in entering the seminary arose not from the demands of celibacy, not the rigors of a semi-monastic life, not the demands of the classroom. I felt my ignorance of Latin. A hotshot Latinist as a freshman in high school, I won the district competition in the state contest and almost placed to go "downstate" for the finals. During the following summer, I spent not one minute with my Latin books and at the beginning of sophomore year, I discovered to my shock and dismay that I had forgotten everything I learned. Caesar's *Gallic Wars* would not be a snap. I never even considered taking third year Latin.

During my sophomore year at Notre Dame, having switched to Liberal Arts from Chemistry, the dean's secretary informed me that I would have to take a language. I didn't realize that she had no authority to advise me.

"You should take the language you had in high school." she stated authoritatively.

"But I took Latin in high school." I whined. I was hoping to take French. It didn't occur to me that I could just do it.

"Then you should take Latin," insisted the secretary. "What year?"

"I had two years in high school." I mumbled, hoping that this lame response would change her mind.

"Then you should take third year Latin." she decreed, and so I found myself, totally unprepared, in Father Hebert's 300 level Cicero class.

Father Hebert, a Holy Cross priest in his mid-eighties who had spent his entire life from age six at Notre Dame, announced to the smallish class, "Gentlemen, you are classicists in an age of engineers. Your grade for this class will begin at 90, and go up from there, depending on your performance. (I should report that I received a grade of 91 for my efforts in Cicero.)

As my undergraduate career proceeded, I had class after class with Father Hebert. ND didn't offer many classes in Latin, particularly in advanced Latin, and Father Hebert taught all of them. My grades gradually rose as my face became more familiar. Father Hebert, sickly but trying desperately to hold on to his teaching position, missed many classes, but no complaints came from the students. I graduated with a minor in Classics and a 95 average in Latin.

When the Bishop of Rockford met with me to determine at what level I should enter the seminary, he looked at my transcript and said, "Well, Jim, I see you have no difficulty with Latin."

I gave the traditional and expected answer, "No, Bishop," secretly fearing that he might continue the interview in the ancient tongue, but he didn't. As a result of that interview, and my major in Philosophy, I now found myself kneeling in the prayer hall, stunningly ill-equipped for my theological studies, but hoping that God or some other stroke of luck would provide.

The Dining Hall

After some ten minutes of clear, solemn, (and, to me, largely incomprehensible) Latin, the Rector closed the book, blessed himself and passed from the room. The seminarians rose in total silence and followed him through various doors, and into the long dining hall Dozens of golden maple picnic tables butted two together and flanked by matching benches stretched the long way down the room. Lengthwise along one wall of the room ran the faculty table facing the students, with some twenty places laid. A pulpit towered at one end.

If you can remember the banquet hall scene from *Chariots of Fire*, or even the dining hall in the Harry Potter films, you have the picture. At Ed Kehoe's recommendation, I had already located my seat, and, though I hadn't had assigned seating since grade school, I found my place and stood awaiting what I correctly assumed would be more prayers.

The grace for lunch was mercifully short: *Mense caelestis faceat nos, Rex Aeternae Gloriae.* (Make us participants at the heavenly banquet, King of Eternal Glory.) The Rector followed with a *Tu Autem....*, aloud, which meant we were permitted to talk during lunch—a rare privilege, it turned out.

(Note to the reader: There won't be a lot of Latin in this tale, because I don't remember that much. But I like to pop in the odd phrase, just to give the whole thing a kind of authentic flavor. So *mea culpa*! You got a problem with that?)

After the savagely rapid meals I was used to in the Notre Dame Dining Hall, (on similar tables, now that I think of it!) the seminary meal was relatively decorous—family style, dishes passed along, everybody (almost) careful to take an appropriate helping. We exchanged names and dioceses. "Rockford" produced a little extra interest, which I was yet to understand.

St. Mary's, the nearest thing to a national seminary in the U.S., served many dioceses, mostly from the East coast, but had a smattering of Midwesterners and Southerners. To the Easterners, we seemed colorful, I guess. Curiously, the small rural diocese of Rockford, Illinois, had developed a special reputation at St. Mary's.

The faculty sat at the head table facing the students, seated in rank order, with the Rector in the center, the Assistant Rector to his right, the oldest faculty member to his left, and so on. As I thought more about this, it must have been a surpassingly dull arrangement for the faculty, stuck with the same people on each side for the year.

We seminarians had it a little better. We rotated around our tables, clockwise, in groups of eight, so that, as you got into position #4 and #5, you were seated next to #5 and #4 at the abutting table. Also, you continually sat across from someone else, so we gradually got to know a wide spectrum of the seminarians. "Got to know" is a bit relative, since we usually ate the noon and evening meals in silence to the accompaniment (having very limited entertainment value) of practice sermons from the seminarians.

Neil Parado

I should note here that most of the theology students had done "seminary time" before, and generally knew what the customs were. But they were delighted when someone from "the outside" joined the ranks, because we didn't know what to do, or what was considered appropriate.

For example, the previous year (as I learned later), an exotic seminarian showed up from the Phillipines, who shall be known here as Cornelio Parado, since that was his name. His family had diplomatic connections and Neil, as we called him, had been transported to the U.S. aboard a

Naval vessel, where he had learned certain American customs not quite appropriate for the seminary.

At his first meal, after the usual *Tu autem*...had been granted, and everyone had introduced themselves, the meal began, and Neil spoke up in his melodious, somewhat accented voice.

"Pass the f**king butter, please."

Neil's tablemates froze. Somebody said, "What?"

"Pass the f**king butter." Neil reiterated calmly. It was what he understood to be the polite form of the request. I don't know who explained the term to him, but Neil was quick on the uptake and the familiar adjective quickly passed from his active vocabulary.

After lunch (and a Latin grace) we poured into the long hallway, most of the guys talking animatedly. Since I hardly knew anybody, I headed for shopping. I had learned during lunch that the bookstore would be open and that a clerical apparel retailer would be setting up shop in the large front parlor. A tailor fully equipped with tape and chalk, offered a line of patter for those who could afford made-to-order clothes, and a full line of standard, off-the-rack cassocks, surplices, rabats, collars, and various other doo-dads of clerical attire.

I had a cassock, what need for another? I had a black suit, ordered in Chicago from some clerical outfitter, which had not yet arrived. But what I didn't have was a roman collar which actually fit and stayed down on my skinny neck.

I steal a collar

A table with rabats caught my attention. (A rabat is a kind of black shirt front with a collar slot which showed the thin strip of white typically associated with the Roman Catholic priest, as in *Going My Way*. In my day, they called these, for no reason that I have ever learned, "go-to-hell" collars. The rabat could be fastened over a regular white shirt with the collar turned under or, more commonly, over a t-shirt. They also had rabats which mounted the full-round white collar, associated in my day and mind with the protestant clergy. In the fifties, only the most rebellious or most ecumenically-minded Catholic clergy wore them. (I wore them.)

In any case, as I studied the scattered pile of collars, I began to see what it was that I needed. What I had were several, high (#3) single-ply, plastic collars. Very cheap, and totally unsuited to my neck. What I needed was a #2, double-ply plastic collar. They had plenty available, but unshaped and cylindrical, the collars rose right up my neck like the one I had.

However, I noticed one in a display rabat, where the rear ends of the collar curled down in the back and held itself in place. The clerk being elsewhere, I plucked the collar out of the rabat, snatched my own collar off my neck and slipped in the curled one. Miracle of miracles, it sat in place, and didn't cut into my neck.

But now, an ethical dilemma. The magical collar was part of the rabat display, and not for sale. The collars for sale didn't have the wonderful curl which held the collar in place. How could I persuade the clerk to sell me the "used" collar without an elaborate explanation involving a display of my total ignorance of the technology of the collar. Since I was desperately trying to pass for someone who knew what was going on, I made an instant, guilty, irrational, impulsive decision. I forced the evil, single-ply collar into my pocket, left the magical, two-ply collar in place around my neck, and blended into the crowd. I had stolen a Roman collar (value: $1.89) in my first full day of the seminary. It would haunt me during the coming days of retreat.

The Book Store

On to the bookstore, a closet-like room in the basement, where I found lists of required books posted for each class. I loved books, but these looked heavy! *Theologica Dogmatica* by Rev. Adolph Tanquery, S.S. *Theologia Moralis* by Rev. Adoph Tanquery, S.S. (Who was this guy?) *Liber Usualis*, a 1,900 page collection of liturgical Gregorian chant; *Codex Juris Canonicis*, hundreds of pages of legal Latin which would govern my life as a cleric in the Church. Finally, *A Path through Genesis*, by Bruce Vawter, in blessed English, and the Chicago University version of the Bible, also in English and a mere three dollars, a relief for my straitened finances

I toted my load of largely incomprehensible future studies up to my room, paged through a few of them, wondered vaguely why we didn't get a Catholic version of the Bible, then fell into my bed for another nap. I didn't even have the energy to explore the huge building which was to be my home for the next four years.

I spent the rest of the afternoon talking to Kehoe, organizing my possessions, getting a feel for the room. It was a large square room equipped with two closets, two twin beds, two desks, one standing lamp and a sink against one wall. Spartan, I guess, but just like my college rooms at Notre Dame, so I was neither surprised nor dismayed. As I remember, the room layout previously existed, so Kehoe and I went with the obvious.

"You were here first, which bed do you want?" I offered magnanimously.

"I'll take this one, since my stuff is already there." Kehoe observed.

"OK, then. Your closet, your desk, your bookcase."

"Right." "Guy" decorating—equality, symmetry, regimentation, clarity—boring. Our two desks stood out from the wall, backs to the window for the sake of the light. We placed the standing lamp between the desks and there everything remained for the rest of the year.

Spiritual Reading

At 5:20, the bell rang fiercely in the corridors. I looked at Kehoe wonderingly.

"It's time for Spiritual Reading before dinner." Kehoe explained. "Just cassock."

Spiritual reading? I thought we did that privately. Did we read to ourselves, together? Since Kehoe didn't have a book, I didn't bring one. I threw on my cassock (and the purloined collar) and headed down to the Prayer Hall.

The exercise turned out to be somewhat different than I had envisioned. The rector made announcements, called attention to issues and, most importantly, explained the Rule. By this, I don't mean that he rationalized or justified the rule. The Rule required no justification. The Rule stood alone. It provided not merely a set of regulations by which the community would operate; it represented a visible test of each individual's sense of obedience—the key virtue in a 'good' seminarian. I must admit that I never quite "got" this, but my innocence was my armor.

When the rector was not using the time, the 30 minute period was spent listening to one of the underclassmen read, often ploddingly, from a book chosen by the faculty. Many of us had not read aloud to anyone since about the fourth grade. So we called it Spiritless Reading, out of hearing of the faculty.

I found my seat, the same as earlier and the same every day and every exercise for the next nine months. Since we were not in silence, I introduced myself to the guy on my left, Dan O'Connor, but suddenly the room fell quiet.

The rector seated himself deliberately at the desk in front, arranged some papers, glanced over the full hall, then rang a bell which produced instantaneous silence. After the prayer, *Veni Sancte Spiritus*, (Come, Holy Spirit) which began every exercise, the Rector went through the schedule for the rest of the evening and the following morning when the opening retreat would begin. Following his remarks, timed to the minute, he read a closing prayer, we rose in silence and passed to our seats in the dining hall for supper.

Apart from the strangeness of the setting and the regimentation, I found the first day not that much different from the first day of college. Moving around in crowds, meeting a lot of new people; following the herd, and trying not to stand out. Apart from my arrival in civvies, (and my grotesque roman collar) I had managed fairly well to blend in. After a long recreation period (till 9) during which I met more of my classmates, we returned to the Chapel for Compline and then to our rooms in the Grand Silence which would last until after breakfast the following morning.

First Full day.

I began my first full day in the seminary horrendously.

As a first year man on a Deacon corridor, I was appointed Exhortator, the "price" of my privileged, second-floor room location. The appointment appeared on an announcement sheet, and Bill Peterson, a third-year student from the Rockford diocese, pointed it out to me. That, as it turned out, should have been warning enough.

Peterson "explained" the Exhortator's responsibilities. I would rise before the wake-up bell at 6:00 a.m., vest myself in cassock and surplice, and proceed quickly down the corridor, knocking at each door and intoning, "*Benedicamus Domino.*" (Let us bless the Lord.") The inmate was to answer, "*Deo Gratias.*" (Thanks be to God.) If I received no answer, I was to sing out again, louder. If I got an answer, I should move to the next door. (There were about 30 rooms on the corridor I was to cover.)

"Oh, one more thing," Peterson added, seriously. "Be sure and knock on the Rector's door. That's how he knows you are doing your job."

Despite my total innocence of seminary procedure, that last directive seemed like a bit much, and I waited after night prayer to speak to the Rector, who waited to receive acknowledgement of faults (a kind of minor confessional) and to grant small permissions such as telephone use.

Nervously, I waited in line, and when my turn came, I informed the Rector that I had been appointed Exhortator for my corridor. This came as no surprise to Father Laubacher, since he had appointed me.

"Yes," he said, a bit impatiently, glancing at the line behind me.

"One of the senior men told me that I should be sure to knock on your door, Father."

He looked at me oddly, not for the first time. "That won't be necessary." he said, with a touch of irony that I failed to notice.

"He also said that I should be vested in cassock and surplice," I pressed on, nervously. "That, too, will not be necessary." The Rector added, doubtless making a mental note about my gullibility. "Thank you, Father." I eased away down the corridor, my mind only partially at ease.

The next morning, my alarm went off at 5:30. I had not slept well, waiting for the clock to go off, and anxious that I perform my first assigned duties perfectly. Rolling out of my bed, I staggered off to the jakes (toilets), dressed and prepared for my Exhortator duties. The instant the bell began clanging, I charged down the corridor, knocking at doors and singing out, in a raspy early-morning voice, "*Benedicamus Domino.*"

The responses were various. Some answered, sleepily, "*Deo Gratias.*" Some called, "What?" Some shouted, "Get the hell out of here," which surprised me more than a little.

It took me a good fifteen minutes to reach all the doors, and by the time I was finished, the Deacons were pouring out into the corridor in bathrobes, clutching towels and bars of soap, and favoring me with opaque glances, but silently.

After breakfast, a delegation of Deacons from my corridor approached me, and asked me, nicely but very firmly, what did I think I was doing.

"I was told to knock on every door, sing out the exhortation, and wait for an answer."

"Who told you," one of the Deacons asked, impatiently.

"Bill Peterson." I answered, innocently. The Deacons all laughed.

"That explains it," my interlocutor said, without elaborating. "Listen," he continued, more kindly, "Forget about all that. Just sing the *Benedicamus* two or three times as you go down the corridor. Forget about knocking. Forget about the answers."

"Thanks a lot." I said, sincerely. This would make it a lot easier. I also made a mental note not to listen to Peterson. It didn't help.

Opening Retreat

Retreats formed a staple of Catholic life for many years. Those literarily inclined will remember the detailed accounting of the classic Jesuit retreat in Joyce's *Portrait of the Artist as a Young Man*. Retreats served as the RC version of "hellfire and damnation" preaching so famous in an earlier America. Typically an 'order' priest particularly gifted in preaching would come in to the parish or school and lay it on us hard and heavy. The retreats were surrounded by silence (for reflection and meditation) alternating with "conferences" and various religious exercises.

In high school, we usually started out taking the retreat pretty seriously, but by the second of the three days, the rule of silence quickly turned into a kind of game, with glances, hand signals, whispers, laughter and then a kind of "school-is-out" party. The high point of the school retreats—the "sex" lecture, boys and girls separated and our intense hope for some "straight talk" about our absolutely favorite subject.

But here in the seminary, the retreat would be a full seven days; a time of high seriousness; of intense personal reflection; and a time to ponder thousand doubts about my vocation, my worthiness, my general piety, my faith itself. Everything on the line. Major stress!

The retreatmaster faced a heavy challenge. Confronting a serious and pious group, respectful (generally) and orderly, inclined to go along with the program, open to new ideas, and old ideas newly put, many of us, particularly the older seminarians, had fixed ideas about a number of issues.

Most of us thought of ourselves as religious professionals (almost) and we had heard a lot of preaching. We were deeply divided, as I was later to learn, along liberal/conservative lines. Anyone attempting to communicate with the whole body of seminarians had to tread through a minefield of ideological traps, including the way he pronounced his Latin, the sources he cited, and even the way he held his hands at Mass.

I was blessedly ignorant of these divisions at the time, having enough to deal with in my own soul without solving vast problems of Church polity. And I was beginning my spiritual journey as a confirmed thief, vain and a liar, and so embarrassed by the triviality of my crime that I could not bring myself to confess it.

(Technically speaking, this particular sin of theft would be rated as venial, that is to say, not worthy of hellfire, by reason of lack of matter. You don't get eternity for a two dollar collar, if I may put it that way. On the other hand, the pride and vanity which underlay the act hinted at more serious spiritual problems apart from the shame of it all. At this cusp moment in my religious journey, I felt highly sensitized to these issues.)

My memory of the retreat at this fifty year distance is limited to the Latin phrase, *Ad Robor*, meaning something like "rigorously" or "vigorously," that is, the way we were to obey the rules and engage in the seminary process.

The weeklong retreat was conducted largely in solemn silence, apart from the long recreation in mid-afternoon. This was both a plus and a minus for me. I really couldn't get to know anyone, but my natural shyness was protected from challenge. Ed Kehoe and I respected the rule of silence in our room, so there was no chance for me to pick up the million things I needed to know in order to "engage in the seminary process." Fortunately, he did break the rule to tell me that we had been appointed to the ceremonial crew for the solemn Vespers which ended the retreat. Serving as Acolytes, literally, we would report to Father Meyers the afternoon before the service.

I felt a jumble of emotions at the news. I was pleased, embarrassed, nervous, excited, threatened, rattled. I guess 'rattled' comes closest. I had no intention of confiding this to Kehoe, though I very casually asked him what was involved.

"I have no idea," he murmured. "I guess Father Meyer'll tell us."

"Yeah." I said, faking an unconcern. I excelled at that.

Why should I be threatened at this minor liturgical exercise? I had been a Mass server (read "altar boy") since the sixth grade.

Ceremonies

I'm going to guess with confidence that every seminarian began his liturgical career as an altar boy or, technically, acolyte. At St. Mary's in Elgin in the late '40s, it was one of the very few things a boy could do to gain any status. Basketball and Patrol Boy were the other two status activities, and I was too small for effectiveness in either area.

For that matter, I was very nearly too small to be an altar boy. The first responsibility of the server involved lighting the six tall candles lit before a high (that is, chanted) Mass. All Sunday Masses at St. Mary's were high Masses. The worst moments came when the candles had been replaced and the new ones towered at their full height.

Boys
Clockwise from the top: Charlie McBriarty; Dick Jacob; Ed Joyce; Jim O'Brien, robed in our fanciest outfits, fall, 1948.

I would take the seven foot wooden candle lighter, which held a lighted waxen taper at the end, climb to the altar, cling to the lighter at its very end, making it hard to control, and attempt to bring the flame to the top of the candle. As the candle lighter swayed back and forth, threatening to topple the candlesticks, the congregation held its collective breath at the mini-drama, and I gritted my teeth, fiercely determined to get the candles lit so that the Mass could begin. On a couple of occasions, the celebrant himself would come out, seize the lighter and finish the job, as I stood by, humiliated.

In server training, we had to learn the Latin responses to the priest during the Mass. We didn't need to understand the Latin, only to pronounce the words correctly. The Mass began with the Prayers at the Foot of the Altar. (These prayers were dropped from the ritual of the Mass many years ago, even before Latin itself was dropped as a requirement.) In my day (the forties), learning and saying the Latin prayers became the first step in moving beyond the ranks of the laity into the exalted realm of the clergy.

The real clergy were not always that sharp in their Latin, either. I vividly remember serving a funeral Mass celebrated by a priest related to the deceased, that is, not one of our own parish priests. He seemed like a good enough guy and Ed Joyce and I, by this time experienced servers in the 8th grade, took our places, cool and confident as the priest began the prayers.

"Innommmennebubbba," he began, "Inrabbbblbablble." Ed and I both paused. We had no idea what he said or what our response should be. After a fair pause, we simply said our first response, *"Ad Deum qui laetificat...."* and so on. We continued to alternate our responses to the priest's incomprehensible mutterings until he had apparently finished and mounted the altar. Ed and I studiously avoided looking at each other.

The priest reached the top of the altar, where he bowed, kissed the altar and turned to greet the congregation. We expected *"Dominus vobiscum,"* (the Lord be with you.) What he sang was: *"Daaaawwwm."* Loud and clear. We totally could not respond. As he turned to continue the prayer, I stole a sideways glance at Ed, kneeling a few feet away. His head was bowed, his folded hands were pressed against his face, he was struggling to suppress a laugh. Seeing this, I lost it completely, and the Mass progressed without any audible Latin responses from either of us.

The situation became worse after the Funeral Mass, when we had to stand alongside the priest facing the coffin (and the congregation) and engage in further prayers, incensing and blessings. There was no way to hide our faces. Fortunately, we had gotten somewhat used to the bizarre sound of the chanting, and managed to keep from laughing aloud, tho our faces were red and our eyes tearing. We could only hope that the congregation took these as signs of grief.

Apparently this was the case, for, when we returned to the sacristy to begin unvesting, the priest thanked us kindly, and seemingly without irony. We slunk away to the boy's vestry, still embarrassed and still on the edge of hysterics. What this may or may not have had to do with my vocation, I do not, to this day, know.

Carrying a Torch

Performing at seminary Solemn Vespers would not be the same. I knew that every single seminarian would be focused on the liturgical "action," very many of them judgmentally. So I was already on edge and defensive when I presented myself to Father Meyer in the sacristy.

I knew that the Faculty Master of Ceremonies was a martinet, much feared by the seminarians for reasons which I will make clear later. I had heard that he had zero tolerance for error. Swell.

Father Meyer looked us over, quite unimpressed. "Mr. Kehoe?"

"Yes, Father."

"Mr. O'Brien."

"Yes, Father." So far, so good.

"Your function in the service will be to act as torchbearers for the Celebrant, and accompany him during the service." Father Meyer's voice was quiet, even gentle. Didn't make it any less scary.

Torch-bearers! Hmm. I had a sudden image of the mob marching against Frankenstein's castle, waving flaming torches in the air. But these torches turned out to be five foot poles topped by candles. Somewhat less dramatic and more controllable.

"You will report to the sacristy wearing cassock, surplice and biretta. You will vest yourselves in copes, acquire your torches, light them and await the celebrant. In silence, of course." Father Meyers dismissed us. He didn't ask for questions, and we didn't volunteer any.

The biretta: a ceremonial black hat-like thing, had three black wings and a fluffy black pom-pom at the crest sticking up about an inch from the top. Devised in Rome, centuries ago, perhaps by the Medici, it may have been cool-looking in those days. By the mid-twentieth century, I fear the biretta appeared genuinely ludicrous. I only think of them now when some movie mentions the similar-sounding Italian handgun, the Beretta. I think James Bond occasionally used one.

But I digress.

Kehoe and I arrived in the sacristy, finding a bustle of purposeful but silent activity. We acquired our copes, long, elaborately decorated capes which, with my height and narrow shoulders, reached almost to the floor. The Retreatmaster acted as the Celebrant. Father Meyer as Master of Ceremonies would be flowing around the service as if invisible, but very much present.

After genuflecting at the high altar, we processed down the length of the chapel to the faculty stalls in the back, where the celebrant would incense (that is, wave incense at, not irritate) the faculty, then pass back up the aisle, incensing the student body, one side and the other. No big deal, right?

Fully focused, not to say near panic, I made my way down the aisle, clutching my torch in sweaty palms, repeating like a mantra to myself, "Must not fall. Must not drop torch. Must not look at anybody."

I have no recollection of the rest of the service. We didn't have much to do, and we made no evident blunders. After unvesting, Kehoe and I fled to the front steps for some much-needed air and relief.

The steps were crowded with seminarians celebrating the end of the restrictions of the retreat. One of my tablemates greeted me enthusiastically.

"Hey, O'Brien. Nice job." The traditional response as I was to learn, despite the fact that my 'job' had been of the most minimal, liturgically speaking.

"Yeah," added one of the deacons., "With that cope on, you looked just like the Infant of Prague." He referred to a well-known image of Jesus as a baby, wearing a crown and a long cope. Everybody in the group laughed, confirming the accuracy of his observation.

Spiritual Director

(From The Rule.) Each seminarian is required to select a member of the faculty as his confessor and Spiritual Director. He will confess to the Spiritual Director once a week, and confer regularly for a half hour on matters both spiritual and academic.

My first (and almost only) decision required me to choose a Spiritual Director, since the relationship would be highly personal and completely confidential. The Spiritual Director, apart from religious counselling, could and did communicate the faculty's concerns about the student by suggesting improvements and strategies.

I didn't realize at the time how important this decision would be. I had never experienced a relationship equivalent to what the Rule envisioned—not from my Father; not from my (non-existent) older brother; not from any priest or relative. I understood the concept of a Spiritual Director but not the process. I only knew that I had to pick someone.

During that first week, the older seminarians offered abundant adivice about choosing a director. The range of choices included the entire faculty excluding the Rector, and the reasons for picking one man or another were multiple and confusing. Recommendations were usually followed by the warning, "Whatever you do, don't choose Father So-and-so." All the advice well-meant, but meaningless to me, since I knew hardly any of the faculty as yet. I listened carefully, however, and jumbled the names around in my mind.

At the end of the retreat, we first year men waited in a long line outside the Rector's door, to tell him of our selection. As I entered, I tried desperately to pull out a name from the many recommendations. The Rector looked at me, already with some recognition, I feared.

With the now-familiar head tip, the grey eyes, the steel-rimmed spectacles, Father Laubacher said firmly, "Mr. O'Brien, have you decided on a Spiritual Director."

I panicked and blurted out the first name that occurred to me. "Father Newman, if you please, Father."

The Rector paused and picked up the list of the faculty (as if he had to check it.) After a glance, he turned to me and said, a bit wearily (or maybe warily), "We have no Father Newman on the faculty, Mr. O'Brien."

"Oh, well, then…..uh." Nothing came to mind. "Anyone you would choose, Father." I figured my answer was safe.

"Perhaps….." The Rector scanned his list again, "….I think Father Dukehart will do."

"Yes, Father. Thank you, Father." I rose and slid out of the room, wondering who Father Dukehart might be. I was soon to find out. I was to report to him within the week and thus identify myself as his responsibility.

That evening during rec, Frank Miller, a classmate and long-term seminary inmate who I took to be an oracle, asked me casually, "Who'd you get for Spiritual Director, Jim?" A standard question. No need for evasion.

"Dukehart," I answered.

"You picked *Duke*hart?" Frank exclaimed, making no attempt to conceal his incredulity?

"Well, no," I assured him. "Actually, the Rector picked him for me." I didn't go into the details of my choosing process.

"Well….." Frank paused, trying to find something reassuring to say. "I guess it'll be all right. At least you have him silenced in the faculty council."

Silenced? Council? What?

The System

Miller knew the system. He entered St. Charles Preparatory Seminary at age 14, passed on to the Philosophy house at Paca Street at age 20, and arrived at St. Mary's at 22. After eight years of seminary, he knew the names, the faces, the chinks, the flaws and the flat tires. Deeply cynical about the system, he had become heartily sick of the seminary process, but was still determined to be a priest.

I didn't share his cynicism, having only a week's seminary time under my belt, but I respected the authority of his experience.

"The faculty meet every week to discuss the students." Frank explained. They have copies of your folder. They go round the table and anyone who has something to say about you, does. The only one who can't talk is your Spiritual Director. Your relationship with him is absolutely confidential."

"I didn't know any of this," I admitted. "They talk about us?" A whiff of paranoia had crept into the conversation.

"You better believe it." Frank announced firmly. A small group of first year men had gathered and listened attentively. "That's how they decide who gets clipped and who gets tailed." The others nodded.

I didn't like the sound of it. Seemed like a fraternity hazing process. I asked for explanation.

"Being clipped means that you don't get called for orders with the rest of your class. Being tailed means that you get called in for a talk with the Rector. And it's all reported to your Bishop."

I could feel my paranoia developing rapidly. Frank warmed to his subject.

"It's a wierd process. The rector names the individual being considered; the faculty look in their folders; then they go around the table, in order of seniority, of course, and anyone who wants to say anything can do so. Anything at all, positive or negative." The group's attention remained fully focused. Nobody asked how Frank could know the details of this highly confidential procedure.

"I heard that a guy in the third year class came up for consideration. They went round the table and nobody had anything bad to say. Then one of the faculty said, "He passed me during long rec and didn't speak to me." They went round the table and everybody voted "no" for ordination to major orders." Miller paused for dramatic effect. It worked.

"You've heard of Spy Wedneday, haven't you? The day before Holy Thursday, when Judas was spying on Jesus?" We nodded. "That's why it's the Sulpecians' favorite feast day." The liturgical irreverence made his point another way.

"I heard that Peterson has been clipped all the way through," someone else volunteered. "They'll have to do all of his orders at one time." Obviously, this would be a private ceremony. Others in the group confirmed. Peterson again. Our man from Rockford. How had he lasted?

Rec ended and I made my appointment to see Father Dukehart, armed with my new information, but discounting it a bit. How bad could it be? He would assume that I had chosen him. Or would he have heard from the Rector about my cluelessness. Nothing for it but to find out.

Father Dukehart

Father Dukehart welcomed me to his office, a large study lined with laden bookshelves, wood furniture, very neat, everything in its place. He greeted me in a friendly but not effusive fashion, sat me down in front of his desk, placed his hand flat on the top and looked me over.

"Well, Mr. O'Brien, I see that you are new to seminary life. You must find it a big adjustment from Notre Dame. How is it going, so far?"

Something told me that this was not a conversational question. Clearly Dukehart had studied my folder and anticipated problems. I decided to proceed carefully myself, sticking to the obvious and avoiding the personal and the problematic.

It occurs to me now that this caution must have struck a false note with Dukehart, as it should have, but he could never say this to me, and never did.

Dukehart was a small, quiet, precise, supremely careful man who listened attentively, spoke carefully, and bore his responsibilities with a terrible seriousness. In the four years that I knew him, I never detected the least trace of humor in him—an essential quality in anyone who was going to get to know me.

What We Have Here is a Failure to Communicate

With all good intentions on both sides, Father Dukehart and I had a serious communication problem. I'm sure Dukehart disapproved of the decision to let a student innocent of seminary life directly into the lofty realms of the theology house. And I'm sure he knew of the oddball reputation of the students from Rockford, to which I was quickly, though unconsciously, contributing. In addition, our ideologies stood worlds apart.

Dukehart's views were absolutely conservative—in theology, in liturgy, in ethics, in every imaginable way. Mine, tho shallow, ill-formed and still evolving, embraced every sign of change I could detect.

Finally, "Dukes" as he was known, found himself absolutely incapable of a direct statement, so with all good will and impenetrable cheerfulness, I agreed with his observations without ever seeing them as applying to me.

"Jim," he said, at one of our early meetings, "many of the faculty are concerned that some of the students are involved in too many activies not directly related to their subjects"

"I think you're right, Father," I agreed enthusiastically, "I had friends at Notre Dame who flunked out because of that." Clearly, that didn't apply to me.

But Dukehart wasn't making conversation. He was trying to say and with some justice, was that I, James O'Brien, was involved in too many activities. But he couldn't bring himself to say it that directly, and so I couldn't hear it. I was involved in everything I could get into and continued that way during my four seminary years.

My ignorance and my innocence had led me to make a bad choice, for me personally, that is. But by pure luck and the force of the regulations, I had silenced a member of the faculty who certainly disapproved of me and might have blocked my path to ordination. The Duke could never again speak of me in a council meeting.

The Heart of the Matter.

I began my seminary life under the illusion that we were all on the same side, so to speak. The faculty: all priests. The seminarians: all guys who wanted to be priests. Why sides?

The faculty had a responsibility that I didn't think about, at least not right away. As Frank Miller had made clear, they were *watching* us. They would *weed out* the unfit. We had to discover whether we were weeds or, well..., grass, I guess.

For most of my seminary life, I assumed that my fitness depended on me—a personal, interior, spiritual process. Did I pray well? (Not nearly well enough.) Did I believe? (A question almost meaningless in this totally religious atmosphere. A fish doesn't question the water.) Did I measure up? (To what? I didn't know, so I didn't worry about it much. I did worry about my 'worthiness' but the standard answer to that popped right back—*nobody* is worthy, so forget about it.)

Actually, the winnowing process might have been the primary purpose of the seminary system. The teaching of theology; the spiritual formation; the pastoral training (such as it was)—all far secondary to the key question: would this candidate make a good priest?

I don't mean an ethically good priest, nor a skilled priest, nor an exemplary priest—"all things to all men" as we used to say. Obedience marked the man. Obedience could be observed, measured, described, assessed. Obedience was essential for the system. The good soldier would follow the rules, do what he was told, express no objections to the system.

Years later, I attended a week-long personal growth "experience" in which we were invited to conceal anything we wished about our identity. I simply left my priesthood off my resume'. An air force colonel who had been friendly at our initial meeting and had confided his rank, then rigorously avoided me for the rest of the week. At the party ending the week, he learned that I was a Catholic priest.

"You bastard," he observed in a friendly way. "I could tell by the way you talked that you were in the military, and when you didn't tell me your rank and service, I decided the hell with you."

The military. The Church. Not that different, I guess. No saluting, but obedience marked the man. Amen.

Wrapping it up.

By the end of my first week, I knew I could get along with the rigorous seminary schedule. My innocence, my ignorance, my pious good will formed an impenetrable shield against any negatives which might well have threatened a more perceptive seminarian. But how would I do with classes?

2

Classes Begin

A Catholic theological seminary of the late fifties (pre-Vatican II, that is) had a triple mission, the elements not entirely compatible. First, the daily schedule had a quasi-monastic structure—built around a life of community worship and prayer, and intended for the spiritual formation and growth of the members of that community. Second, the seminary served as a kind of graduate school for theological studies, where academic performance was important, honored, and demanded. Third, the staff trained the fledgling clergy for pastoral practice, where seminarians learned to perform their priestly functions and to exercise ministerial service to the people in the local parishes.

The theological seminary capped three levels of training, which included minor seminary (high school and two years of college), philosophy, (two years of philosophy and other study to the Bachelor's degree,) and theology, (four years of theological and other study, sometimes leading to a degree in theology, and normally, to ordination to the priesthood

The Daily Routine

I accustomed myself to the basic routine of the seminary, sometimes simply by following the crowd. We rose at 6, attended to bodily functions in the jakes, vested ourselves—cassock and surplice—and arrived at the prayer hall by 6:30. The faculty took serious note of lateness. Mass followed at seven in the main chapel and breakfast at eight with conversation.

A short rec and off to our rooms to prepare for class at 9:30. Prayer Hall at 12:30, followed by lunch, normally in silence apart from the accompaniment of students practicing sermons. Class at two, long rec from three to four, class from four to six, Rosary; Spiritual Reading; dinner and evening rec till 7:45, Compline at 9 and study (in The Grand Silence) until lights out at ten-thirty.

At the beginning of each semester, we received a packet containing The Rule, a document spelling out requirements and restrictions on our lives. Many of each. In addition, the packet contained various schedules of services, and my favorite thing—a printed sheet which divided each day into half-hour segments from 6:30 a.m., the beginning of meditation, to 10:30 at night, when lights were to go out. At the top, it was labelled simply "Schedule" and at the bottom, a dictum of St. Benedict, the founder of the monastic system: "He lives for God, who lives by Rule."

I am, and was, the least organized of people, but I loved this handout. I dutifully filled out the dozens of little squares, starting with my class schedule and the many already-scheduled devotional activities.

By the time all the classes and routine activies got listed, most slots had been filled up.

Then came our valued recreation periods. Short rec after breakfast; short rec after lunch. Long rec from two to four p.m. Evening rec after supper. Someone told me that skipping rec periods for study sent a bad message to the faculty and I followed *that* advice carefully!

Let's see. A few slots left. Those were easy—study. I filled out the sheet in pencil, to persuade myself that I had a little flexibility. I held it out and stared at the final product. Six a.m. to ten-thirty and night. Every moment filled. I felt accomplishment, as if I had actually done something.

Getting My Life in Order

Filling out the schedule gave me the illusion of control over my life. I hoped that I would become organized and follow a strict, productive and fulfilling schedule. It never happened, but my hope was renewed each semester. The whole system around me was highly structured, how could I fail?

I did not suspect at the time that this neat and total structure provided one of my basic motivations for entering the seminary—to escape from the chaos of my life "in the world."

In my years at Notre Dame, I was never taken aback by the heavy schedule: classes Monday through Saturday, ending at 12:30 on Saturday, (so we could get to the football games!), nor the strict check-in requirements at the dorms, nor the fact that they turned off the room lights at 10:30 in freshman dorms, 11:00 p.m in upperclass dorms. When I got to the seminary, I realized that ND followed a seminary schedule rather than a university style schedule.

At St. Mary's, the class schedule ran from Monday through Saturday at 2:00 p.m., with Wednesday afternoon "free" for walks. The so-called walks consisted of trips (via bus—no walking involved) to various institutions around Baltimore to give us some pastoral experience. We had little practical guidance in this process; only a multi-page list of suggestions and recommendations. We merely showed up in our black suits and Roman collars and prayed that the Holy Spirit would give us some kind of clue. Sometimes it happened. But more on this later.

On a daily basis, the period after breakfast seemed tailor-made for the many smokers in our midst. (It took me most of the period to get my pipe going satisfactorily, then almost immediately, I had to put it out.) Then upstairs in silence for quick ablutions, assembling of books and notes, and down to classes at 9:30, 10:30, 11:30, 1 and 4 p.m. If you count up, the total comes to about 24 hours of class time a week, a schedule that would appall a normal college student today (excepting engineers.)

I felt excited about the beginning of classes, though deeply fearful of my impending encounter with Latin. I had spent a little time peering at Tanquery's *Theologia Dogmatica*. I found I could kind of crawl through the basic ideas with repeated dippings into the Latin dictionary. I had been a pretty good student at Notre Dame, although where there was a crack I slid through it. Maybe I could get away with it at St. Mary's, too.

Classes

Kehoe and I didn't talk much in the few minutes before class. We didn't have time. Brushed our teeth, packed up our stuff and headed off to class.

I stuffed my briefcase with the texts for the three morning classes, plus note paper, pens, etc., and hurried down to the first year classroom where I would have all my classes for the next nine months. I still found it weird that three hundred and fifty guys could be hurrying off to classes at the same time in total silence, apart from the scuffing of shoes on the terrazzo floors. By this time, I had figured out that observing the silence was important, not for spiritual reasons but because talking made you stand out in the eyes of the watching faculty.

We found the study load in the seminary to be substantial. The major areas of study, Scripture (Old and New Testaments), Dogmatic Theology (called Systematic Theology in Protestant seminaries), and Moral Theology each met four hours a week in the mornings. Other studies were scattered throughout the afternoon: Canon Law, Church History, Music, Liturgy, Preaching, Ancient Languages (Hebrew and Greek) and Modern Languages (Spanish and Italian). The later in the day, the less important the subject seemed, both to the faculty and to the students.

By the way, 'dogmatic' has come to mean 'rigid, fixed, arbitrary, superior, unyielding'—a style of communication which many people find unpleasant, for some reason. In Catholic theology, dogma represents the official teachings of the Church, based on the Scriptures—the revealed truth of God's interaction with man. The Church perceives this truth, or body of truths, as non-negotiable. People from another perspective perceive this stance as, well, 'rigid, fixed, arbitrary, superior and unyielding.'

We didn't have any problem with calling theology 'dogmatic.' That's what we expected it to be. As to the *content* of that theology, another issue entirely.

Dogmatic Theology: Father Frank Norris

In the usual silence, we filed into the large room, locating ourselves in alphabetic order in wooden student chairs, themselves bolted to a long plank which ran under the seat. Six across on each side; twelve rows front to back; 144 seats.

The bolted-down seats came as no surprise to anyone familiar with Catholic education, at least at that time. In the public mind, Catholic schools stood for "order," maintaining the maximum possible control over the students. In my years at St. Mary's and St. Edward, I never sat in a "loose" chair or desk in school till I went off to college. This clearly formed a central principle in the system of Catholic education—thou shalt keep the students in order, bolted down if necessary. Why would I be surprised?

Well, in my case, it WAS necessary! A mover and jiggler from birth, I only held still when reading. As a child, my mother punished me by putting me in a chair and commanding: "Sit STILL!" Catholic school seemed to me to be an extention of this punishment for a full 12 years. In those innocent days before Ritalin and school counsellors, I presented myself to a series of nuns as a jangle of nervous energy waiting to rush off in all directions, unless something held my interest. Father Norris would fill the bill.

A wooden dais in front ran the length of the three-panel blackboard and a standard wooden desk. A portable lectern stood on the desk, and a standing lectern beside the desk. Everything wood, except the long blackboard which had seen many years of service.

Tall casement windows lined the outside wall, so tall that they could only be opened from the top using a long pole with a brass hook on the end. Tall windows also lined the hall side, so the room was well lit. A few pictures hung in the back—portraits of old Sulpecians as I dimly recall. An old-fashioned classroom, high ceilinged and spacious, designed to be dominated by the teacher.

I nodded to the guys on either side; Ted Obaza on my right; the inevitable O'Conner on my left. They seemed friendly but focused.

We set out our books and waited expectantly for our first class in theology. The older students had filled us in on Norris, one of the theological stars of the Sulpecians, and the subject of intense admiration by students of a certain theological bent. Norris represented the cutting edge of a new, bible-based reanalysis of age-old Catholic theology.

De Ecclesia (Regarding The Church.)

At precisely 9 a.m., we rose to our feet as Norris entered, bounded up on the dais, piled his books and notes on the desk and plunged into the morning prayer, *Veni Sancti Spiritus*, as if we had not a moment to waste. And so he would enter for every class day for the year.

Norris, a smallish, dark-haired, bespectacled man, taught Dogmatic Theology or rather, he proclaimed Dogmatic Theology. One of the younger faculty members, incredibly intense, a brilliant and passionate teacher, Norris, the *bete noir* of the older and more conservative members of the faculty (that is to say, most of them) intimidated them (and us) with his intellect, his mastery of his field and his total willingness to engage in dispute at any length. His lectures seemed almost like empassioned sermons, with lightning-fast ironic asides and vast references to the work of contemporary theologians, mostly European, of whom we had never heard.

Norris didn't improvise his lecture style. We learned later that Norris practiced his lectures aloud in his room, word for word. This seemed to me somehow unfair, even showy, but at the time we found him incredibly effective.

Norris' subject, *De Ecclesia*, (regarding the Church) took its foundation from a phrase in the writings of Paul: "You (the faithful) are the body of Christ." Norris argued that from this assertion, the entire nature and mission of the Church could be understood. In fact, he built the entire year marshalling arguments from the old and new testaments in support of his contention.

We had all been told, from time to time, that we all, clergy and laity, were the Church, but the assertion didn't carry much weight. The lay people of the Church had no liturgical function and nothing to say about how things went. But now Norris seemed to suggest that all the community of the baptized had exalted status. By implication, the clergy had only a modest, funtional role in relationship to the whole body of the Church. Tradition-minded clergy found this implication profoundly dangerous.

Many of us found this exciting, as Norris passionately built his case. If we would follow out all the implications of the idea, the Church, the heirarchy, and Christian life itself might be transformed, and transformative.

None of us had heard anything like it before. I, for one, felt dumbfounded. After sixteen years of Catholic education, including the Honors religion sequence at Notre Dame, I knew nothing of what Norris so confidently asserted.

Not So Honorable Honors

I should admit a couple of things here. Truth to tell, I got into the Honors religion sequence not through merit but because I simply went to the registration desk and asked for the admission card. The student clerk gave it to me without question and no one ever challenged it.

And I chose the Honors religion sequence not out of piety nor intellectual curiosity, but because the honors sequence demanded one less credit than the normal religion requirement.

I may have missed a couple of doctrinal points along the way. Priests taught my high school religion classes at St. Ed's in Elgin. Or sort-of taught. Father Shanahan, a shy man, never showed up for Freshman religion. Father Boland, a jock, spend sophomore religion reading aloud from Catholic novels for young people. *Brass Knuckles* leaps to mind. As comedian George Carlin summarized the plots of this genre, "Danny was a Catholic, and Buddy………was NOT!" We loved the reading, but we didn't learn much. Only in our senior year did the priest assigned to the class, Father McNamee, actually try to teach the course material.

I Ask a Theological Question

In a history course at Notre Dame, I asked the professor some question about the papacy.

"Are you a Catholic?" Professor De Santis inquired.

"Yes."

"Did you go to Catholic schools?"

"Grade school and high school." I answered.

"Then how could you ask a question like that?" De Santis offered, incredulously.

I shrugged it off. I can't remember the actual question. It must have been something like "Does the Pope's wife have to be a Cardinal?" But I don't remember.

A Church of Doctrine.

The Catholic Church in America puts a lot of weight on education. The Catholic faith concerns itself with content rather than experience; with truth rather than with commitment; assent to the faith means accepting the Church as the authority on the meaning of God's revelation. Since most Catholics become so at Baptism in infancy, they grow into the faith in the context of Catholic institutions, the family, the parish church, the Catholic school.

Catholics typically speak of "the" faith rather than "my" faith. They belong to the faith by Baptism; they learn the content of the faith from many sources, many of them ill-informed. Every individual member of the Church has to pick a personal way through the vast material of the Church's two thousand year history, a way based on opportunity, interest, intelligence and chance.

I had had the whole nine yards of Catholic Education, brought to my learning more than average interest and intelligence, or so I always thought. And yet, how little I knew! And how confident I felt about what I knew.

My studies at St. Mary's would poke holes in that confidence, and open my mind to further learning. That's uncomfortable, unsettling, and exciting, too.

The class divides.

If you bought into Norris' teaching, you found yourself slipping into one side of the liberal/conservative split that seemed to be rapidly developing in the class. Norris was the darling of the liberals—not merely teaching progressive doctrine, but doing so aggressively. His followers saw his vision of the Church as a cause to which we might devote our ministry. World, look out!

To this point in my life, I had no idea that church doctrine had room for more than one interpretation. We had all been raised to think of the Church as ONE, meaning one Pope, one Bishop, one Pastor, one ritual (the Latin Mass) and one Doctrine, what everyone believed. Although, at Notre Dame, some priests invited active participation in the Mass, they were not well regarded, and labeled as "litur jickles" for their preoccupation with the liturgy. Indeed, the word 'liturgy', rarely used in normal Catholic speech, became a buzzword of the time. A perfectly neutral technical term meaning "an official act of worship' became a marker for which 'side' you supported.

Now that I think of it, our growing divisions were preparing us for the sixties, before they became 'The Sixties.'

I took notes in Norris' class furiously and illegibly. Norris made everything sound important. I had had good teachers before, at Notre Dame and elsewhere, but I had never encountered such intensity. Norris taught as if he were an attorney at a murder trial, summing up before a jury—us.

The ten minute break between classes found most of us sucking up nicotine and getting to know where the other guys stood on the issues thrust before us. I didn't offer a lot of deep talk about class matter as yet. In fact, lots of us were well out of our depth, theologically speaking. Most of the guys already knew each other; they had attended Paca Street, the philosophy level of St. Mary's, for two years. The rest of us had come from other seminaries, or, in my case, from "the world."

Most of the guys came from dioceses in the Northeast corridor, although the term had not yet been invented. Then there were a sprinkling of southerners and a handful from Illinois and Wisconsin, genuine curiosities to the easterners. Tom Dempsey, a Chicagoan, had done minor seminary at Quigley Preparatory in Chicago, then opted for the rural wonders of the Rockford diocese. At that time, the Chicago archdiocese had so many priests that many would never become pastors.

Dempsey was my only classmate studying for Rockford, or so I thought, but he had gone to Paca street for philosophy and so had connections with most of our classmates. I sought out Dempsey, who was open and friendly, but rather more interested in talking to his Paca street classmates than this unknown stranger from his diocese of choice.

"Oh, well," I thought, "I'll give it time." I puffed on my pipe and listened in on the chatter. A bell rang; silence fell. I snuffed my pipe on the heel of my hand and slid back into the classroom, pumped and intimidated at the same time.

Sacred Scripture: Larry Dannemiller

Bible studies! Like most Catholics of the time, I had little clue. The Bible served as a sacred object—a talisman—more than as a source of knowledge about Christianity, let alone Judaism. We heard short readings from the Gospels and Epistles at every Sunday mass, but with little or no context. For Catholics, Bible-reading seemed a Protestant thing, leading inevitably to the doctrinal sinkhole of "private interpretation." I'm not exactly sure how we came to feel this, but we had a general sense that Bible-reading could be dangerous.

The curriculum made clear the importance of scripture study. Three years; six semesters; four class hours a week. We better learn something.

"Gentlemen." Father Dannemiller began after leading us in prayer and then carefully, even fussily arranging his books and papers on the table before him. "The word "Bible" comes from the Greek word *"biblia"* which means "books"—plural. As I'm sure you know, there are many books in the Old Testament, many more in the new. And the key to understanding each book is to understand what *kind* of book each one is.

Larry Dannemiller, young (relatively), slim, precise, came formidably prepared in studies of ancient near-eastern languages to say nothing of Latin and Greek. Despite his California golden locks he hailed, I think, from Michigan. The early word on Dannemiller: positive. Though firmly liberal in his thinking and background, he made a considerable effort to present his material in a balanced rather than confrontational way. And his background meant that he could easily handle the more contentious of the students in the class of '61, though he faced a daunting task in that regard.

Most of us could be called fundamentalists, although we didn't know it. We believed that the Bible was the Word of God; that it meant what it said; the meaning should be obvious. If there appeared to be contradictions, either with other parts of the Bible or with modern science or history or anything else, the contradictions meant that we didn't understand the text correctly, or that it was a "mystery"—a classic Catholic school explanation for any difficulty in the complex fabric of the faith.

I also knew that there was some exciting stuff in the Bible, and some hot stuff, too. I had discovered the Song of Solomon during a high school retreat. Of course, I could never tell anyone about this. Surely it was some kind of sin to find the Word of God sexual, although the sex is unmistakable, as Cecil B. DeMille has made so clear.

"I'm sure all of you have read the book of Genesis," Dannemiller continued confidently, "But perhaps you have run into some confusions. For example, in Chapter one, there is the famous account of the creation of the universe, but in Chapter two, the sacred author seems to start again from a different point. What's going on?" We didn't know. We waited.

Literary Form

"You've got to know what kind of a book you are reading before you can understand it." Dannemiller insisted.

"For example," he continued. "If I say 'Have you heard the latest one about the pope?' you know that a joke is coming and you understand the story in that way. If I say, 'Once upon a time....' you know that a fairy story is coming. If animals are talking, you understand that the story is a fable. Jesus often answered questions with parables, such as the famous story of the good Samaritan. The truth of the story is in the MEANING of the parable, rather than in the historicity of the details."

Well, hey! Looking for "meaning" in the Bible might be a dangerous process. We all knew the *sound* of the Bible, particularly the King James version, which was translated with a specific ear to how it would sound aloud. We all were stirred by the Christmas gospel, "In that time, there went forth from Caesar Augustus that all men were to be enrolled...." Opening the presents couldn't be far behind.

We all knew about Adam and Eve and the apple and the serpent, and the nakedness and the fig leaf. (Well, the fig leaf can't actually be found in Genesis, but we would have bet on it.) But we had stuff to learn. Dannemiller began to open our minds, or many of our minds.

"Genesis is a book of proto-history, attempting to explain to its hearers how things got to be the way they are. If you are trying to read Genesis as if it were a contemporary history, you'll end up in confusion."

Well, we did and we had. We read the Bible as the history of the world, starting 'in the beginning." History meant facts, and Bible history—the word of God—meant true facts, as we sometimes said. If the book of Genesis said God created the world in six days, that must have been it. Some religion teacher once suggested that they could have been "very long days."

Someone suggested this "out" to Dannemiller.

"No, no," he insisted firmly, "the sacred writer meant 'days,' but he didn't mean a twenty-four hour period, determined by the rotation of the earth. He cared nothing about astronomy in the modern sense." Whew. But what, then?

"You must ask yourselves 'What does the writer intend to communicate?' and you must look at long passages together, and see them as the writers saw them, as the people heard them." Dannemiller spoke with confidence and conviction. He seemed well aware of our problems and willing to address them without evasion.

"The first chapter presents God as creating order out of chaos. It's not what the theologians call 'making something from nothing—*creatio ex nihilo*—it's bringing order out of chaos. If you line up the first three days of creation with the second three days, they make a perfect parallel."

This all seemed crystal clear to me, and I was swiftly if superficially converted to a contemporary understanding of how to approach the often difficult and ambiguous writing, particularly of the Old Testament. And I became a Dannemiller fan, and an active participant in the class—too active, as it turned out.

I get zapped!

I had always been one of those "hand-in-the-air" kind of student that most students hate. The behavior went with my hyperactivity and my need for attention. At Notre Dame, active class participation had been encouraged. I found myself ill-prepared for involvement in the seminary pedagogy, where the large classes and the authoritarian teaching model made questions an annoying interruption. Particularly true when the question is only partly formed, as I quickly found out.

My hand shot up. "Father, do you mean that Genesis is, as it were, a kind of….." I got no further.

"Why do you say 'as it were'?" Father Dannemiller barked, quite unexpectedly. He looked infuriated. "'As it were' doesn't mean anything. It doesn't mean anything at all. Why would you say it?" He seemed to be screaming, although that was probably because he had always spoken quietly.

I was totally taken aback. I fumbled around and backed down with a feeble "I don't know." It would be a long time before I ventured another question in Scripture class.

A class divided against itself....

Scripture class became the primary source of division between liberals and conservatives in our class. It confronted us with questions we had never considered. We believed that the Bible was "inspired by God," but how did inspiration work; if the work existed in spoken language before it was transcribed, was the oral form inspired or the written form.? Or both? And, if both, were the copyists also inspired, or at least divinely protected from error? And how about translations? Was an earlier, less scholarly translation, *more* inspired because of its antiquity, or was the scholarly translation, well....better?

You can probably see the pit of issues being uncovered. Could we only truly understand the scriptures if we knew ancient languages? And ancient history? And the history of all the texts and translations? Was there any end to it? Some part of me wanted to plunge into those exotic studies. And hey, I was starting Hebrew that very afternoon!

If you wanted to "get something" from the Bible, the alternatives to demanding and life-long study seemed to be two: you could believe that a sincere and pious person, seeking to know the revealed truth, would not be misled by the sacred text, whatever version. Private interpretation, in a phrase. One way of expressing the division between Martin Luther and the Roman Church of the time—a serious issue. And hence, an RC no-no.

Or, you could simply believe in the interpretation set forth by the priest, minister, parent, evangelist, authority of the moment. An essentially passive position—go with the professional. Maybe how most of us go when confronted with issues beyond us. Maybe I had better follow that approach in Scripture class, at least for a while.

Dannemiller presented as a highly methodical man, from his careful arrangement of his papers and books on the table before us, to the marshalled arguments that he articulated in his quiet, somewhat high voice. Well aware of the undercurrent of resistance to his teaching, he addressed the material confidently, competently, and persuasively, anticipating problems but refusing to be sidetracked. Maybe that's why I got shot down.

Or maybe I just interrupted him. Anyway, I shut up, scribbled away and made it to the end of class.

Where do we stand?

Responses to Dannemiller during the smoke break between classes tended to be admiring or dismissive, without a lot of substance to our discussions. Humor papered over the divisions. We typically siezed on memorable-sounding phrases and repeated them pointlessly.

Larry Spiece, a bright and antic classmade, took to repeating "*Peshitta*" (The Syriac version of the Old Testament, as I remember) and "*Bar Kohkba*," a famous second century Jewish rebel. This became Bar Coke Bar, to the obfuscation of the original intention. Spiece's mocking illustrated our sense that a lot of this stuff seemed very exotic, to say the least.

One time, trying to persuade us that everything in Scripture need not be taken literally, Dannemiller cited (without actually singing) the song from *Porgy and Bess*, "It Ain't Necessarily So." Spiece immediately took it up as an anthem. The literalists probably found this near blasphemous, but it was hard to resist.

Where Do We Stand?

We found ourselves gradually separating into two ideological camps. Some of us found enlightenment, vision, depth, in the new vision laid before us. Some of us, simple faith threatened by the complexity of the issues, clung to the Old Time Religion, which was and would remain "good enough for them." And for all their parishoners down to their fiftieth jubilee.

Some of the division had to do with style. The liberals preferred sweeping Roman vestments as opposed to the old "squareback" Gothic vestments; generous (not to say theatrical) gestures in liturgy; cursive writing as opposed to the old "nun-style" Palmer Method penmanship; Jubilee Magazine for aesthetic guidance; The National Catholic Reporter for the real dope. And, dream upon dream: English in the liturgy.

I found a lot of these concerns trivial, despite being liberal markers, but I did buy myself one of those cursive pens and filled several pages with great black scrawls. Looked impressive, but equally illegible as my Palmer Method scratchings.

I found a fair amount of posturing about this stuff, too. One day, as we were pouring into the chapel, one of the seminarians dipped his hand in the holy water font, then extended his hand to me to take some holy water. Never happened to me before. I took the pass, and found the gesture pleasingly fraternal.

On my way out, I dipped my hand and passed the water to a deacon leaving next to me. "*Numquam in exitu.*" he replied haughtily, and refused the pass. I blessed myself and figured out that we weren't supposed to take holy water on the way out, for some obscure liturgical reason.

But we had been taught that blessing yourself with holy water carried an indulgence of three hundred days, going in or coming out or just standing there. But didn't Luther have some serious problem with indulgences? And didn't we have some serious problem with Luther. I resolved not to think about it any more.

Much to my surprise, I found myself becoming a liberal. I never thought about it before. In college, I rooted for Adlai Stephenson because he, too, was an "intellectual." And for Hubert Humphrey because he seemed young, a fresh face. However, I disliked attempts by some hall rectors to involve us in the liturgy by "participating," that is, saying aloud the responses at Mass.

Seminary liberals favored the new vision of scripture, expressiveness in ritual, congregational participation in liturgy, vernacular in the language of worship (this was the time of Latin and only Latin in the liturgy, not counting Greek and Hungarian and the other orthodox liturgies, of course.) We opted for meaning over form; scholarship over tradition; the new over the old. We would be, of course, the utter bane of our pastors and bishops.

The Times, They Were A-changin'…

We didn't know it, but we had gathered on the brink of a world-wide cultural revolution, generally referred to now as "The Sixties" although this was only 1957. But Elvis had happened, Rock and Roll was happening, the Baby Boomers were hitting adolescence, *Blackboard Jungle* portrayed a bleak future for inner city schools. Rosa Parks sat in the front of the bus and started the civil rights movement. *Rebel Without a Cause* seemed to my generation like a documentary about young lives and feelings. And "The Pill" had happened, and Women's Lib would not be far behind.

The Catholic Church also teetered on the brink of a revolution, driven by advances in theology, scripture scholarship, and pastoral practice. In the U.S., the post-war church became more and more middle-class, with an educated laity far less willing to accept as gospel whatever the pastor or bishop (or pope, for that matter) would proclaim.

Despite my sixteen years of Catholic education, or maybe because of it, I didn't even know there were conservatives and liberals in the Church. At Notre Dame, we heard about the Catholic Worker movement, but that came from France, and was tainted with socialist tendencies—dangerous stuff in the fifties.

But hey, time for me to get back to class!

Another quick shot of nicotine from my now rather rancid pipe and we returned again for our third class of the morning. Our next professor was new to the faculty and we had no advance word to help us generate attitude. Scary!

Moral Theology: Father Falcone.

Father John Falcone climbed up onto the dais, plopped down his books and began by introducing himself. Unheard of! He actually wanted a relationship with the class. Falcone presented himself as open, candid, often funny, not always intentionally. Though clearly on top of his subject, Falcone seemed to be no intellectual, nor as belonging to any one school of theological opinion. He never talked down to us. He was teaching the subject and that was his job.

Falcone didn't look like an intellectual, either. Young, swarthy, more than plump, very Italianate and proud of it, he seemed to think of himself as an ordinary guy and ourselves as guys like him. We duly appreciated this, exhausted by the intensity of the previous two classes. Falcone served as the clown of the faculty, though unintentionally. He just had a clown persona. Once, he reported a bit ruefully that he had called one of the senior members of the faculty, Father Brennan, who responded, "Oh, Father Falcone, I was just laughing about you."

Fresh from his summer working in a parish in one of the Massachusetts dioceses, he regaled us with stories from the field. In the parish where he was assigned, the pastor, a monsignor who had served there for many years, saw himself as a pillar of the community. One evening, the priests in the rectory decided to go to a movie and invited the Monsignor along.

"I can't be seen at the movies," the Monsignor protested, "What would my parishioners think?"

"Hey, Monsignor," Falcone chimed in, "We're going to a drive-in. Nobody will know you're there. Just sit in the back."

Assured that the group would attract no attention, the Monsignor was persuaded and rode along, reciting the Divine Office from his thick black Breviary by flashlight to the mystification of the ticket-seller, who asked, "What's wid him?"

After they parked, Falcone headed to the popcorn stand to pick up the eats. Getting about six cars away, he suddenly realized that he hadn't checked with the Monsignor. He turned and bellowed, "Hey, Monsignor, do you want some popcorn?" Half the cars in the drive-in must have heard him. So much for not attracting attention.

I turned to Dan O'Connor on my left and murmured, "This guy is pretty cool." O'Connor smiled and nodded, but didn't speak, thus not violating the rule. I took it as a very slight rebuke, but he was right.

Dan O'Connor

In the curious and rigid seminary system of heirarchy, Dan O'Connor seemed fated to follow in my footsteps, almost literally. In class, we were seated alphabetically. O'Brien. O'Connor. O'So-on. Our position in prayer hall and chapel followed from our rank in orders. I was the senior (oldest) non-cleric; O'Connor was the next in seniority and sat next to me—in class, in prayer hall, in chapel, but somehow never in dining hall. Go figure.

O'Connor came to St. Mary's without prior seminary experience, like myself. He had graduated from Catholic University, gone on for a Masters in Education and then made his decision to enter the seminary. As we learned later, the faculty constantly compared the two of us as examples of those who had come directly "from the world."

O'Connor was a quiet, orderly, obedient, careful, systematic, thoughtful, studious, modest fellow, who played a good game of tennis and took the seminary rule very seriously. I was pretty much the opposite, particularly on the tennis court.

Of course, the faculty assumed that someone who had never been in a seminary would take some time to "adjust" to the monastic regime. And, in my case, they had it right. I never DID adjust, nor even really figured out what was going on. O'Connor never HAD to adjust since he fit in perfectly already. So the faculty was "concerned" about him. He was "too quiet," "too reserved," "We don't really know him." and so on. He was called in on more than one occasion by the Rector to have the faculty's concerns addressed, although how he was to change was never made clear. Whereas I, a loose cannon, was never "clipped (denied orders) or "tailed" (called in for a reprimand) because I fit the faculty's expectations.

O'Connor had sandy red hair, freckles, and looked as he was, a total Irishman. He had a good sense of humor and was well-liked by his classmates, but his quiet ways invited targeting by the jokers in the class, myself included.

Hazing O'Connor

One glorious late spring day a big group of our classmates, perhaps fifteen or twenty, had seated ourselves in a big circle out on the front lawn during long rec, talking and bantering about nothing. O'Connor, who had come out late, walked toward the group in his deliberate fashion. Someone in the group—I fear it was myself—said, "When O'Connor gets close, let's all run and sit somewhere else, as if we were avoiding him."

The plot worked magically. When Dan was about 20 yards away, we sprang up and dashed off at a 45 degree angle, to another spot about a hundred feet away, then flopped down in our circle. The odd manoever drew the attention of the rest of the seminarians scattered around the lawn.

Grinning but determined, O'Connor altered course but did not increase his pace. Once again, as he approached the group, we sprang up and dashed away, then once again falling to the ground, by now laughing like fools. O'Connor, his face now bright red, kept coming doggedly, and finally came up to the group, now weak with laughter.

"All right, you guys," he demanded, "What's going on?" We had no answer for him, of course, and he reluctantly joined in the helpless laughter. We were easily amused, it appears, but then, we didn't have television.

Another time, we had gathered in the jakes for an after-lights-out chat. (This was against the Rule, of course, but rarely interrupted by the faculty, who had toilets in their own apartments.)

At any rate, O'Connor, who never willingly broke the Rule, came padding in, wearing slippers and bathrobe, for a late night pee. He nodded at us, but did not speak, and slipped into one of the toilet stalls. (We did not have urinals, because of the potential immodesty involved.)

As O'Connor prepared to do his business, someone said, "Shhhh." and we all fell silent, listening. O'Connor, suddenly self-conscious, found himself unable to go, and the problem intensified as the listening period lengthened. Finally, somewhat sheepishly, he tied up his robe, and red-faced and frustrated, made his way out of the stall, and to the door, presumably to seek another jake. As he opened the door, he turned and broke the Rule.

"You bastards." he said, simply, and vanished into the hall. He was right, I guess.

Lunch

As Moral Theology ended, we hastened out in silence, and headed for our rooms to dump our books. I wasn't absolutely sure where to go next, but I knew it would be somewhere and soon.

Ed Kehoe had made it to the room ahead of me, and I said, "Now what?"

"Noon prayer," he responded. "Prayer Hall," he added, noting my uncertainty. Well, I knew where that was.

The Prayer Hall filled quickly. I found my spot and, following the lead of the others, knelt on the worn wooden kneeler in front of my seat. The seats were old wooden theatre seats with folding plywood bottoms and arms. Not a lot of space for the big guys, but plenty adequate for my spare 125 lbs. Father Laubacher took his place at the dais, placed down a black loose-leaf notebook, opened it, pulled the standing microphone toward him and began the noon prayers, in Latin.

He spoke slowly and reverently, enunciating the words, which was good for me, since I needed all the Latin practice I could get. As he came to the word "*Eloquia*," he turned the page which crackled slightly. Always fascinated by the sound of turning pages, I forgot to pay attention to the words.

It also amazed me that, despite the fact that the Rector had said these words hundreds and hundreds of times, he still used the book. Perhaps he was setting an example for us. Perhaps he feared to draw a blank in front of us. Perhaps he had never thought about it.

As I think about it now, we weren't really praying; we were listening to the Rector pray. Or, even more precisely, listening to him read prayers. But not my place to question what was going on, and I never did.

After about ten minutes, we filed out, in silence, and made our way to our places in the Dining Hall.

I had already come to realize that places held high importance in the seminary process. 'Place' is the spatial expression of heirarchy. You were expected to be in the right place at the right time. That expectation was so powerful that it was very rarely violated, and the violation might become an issue. I was NEVER in the wrong place.

(Well, maybe a couple of times.)

I found my table, surrounded by strangers, and took my place in the continuing and, to me, awkward silence. The Rector and a few faculty members took their place at the head table, a brief Latin grace followed, ending in the phrase "*tu autem, Domine, miserere nobis.*" (You, however, Lord, have mercy on us.") Spoken aloud, the "*tu autem...*" meant that we could talk during lunch, and talk we did, guys introducing themselves around the table, and eagerly passing around the provided food.

Food Issues

Traditionally, students hate and complain about institutional food. I never had a problem with it. From my earliest years urged with enormous parental pressures to "finish my plate," I had most reluctantly learned to do so, and could now eat pretty much anything put before me. The dining hall food at Notre Dame was rigidly routine, generic, and always generously covered with salty brown gravy, whatever the entree. I listened with bemusement as my classmates bitterly railed against the offerings, but I ate mine up quite eagerly.

At the seminary, I found the food pretty good. The invisible nuns in the kitchen had to prepare 400 meals to be served at one time (the faculty ate with us, and pretty much the same fare, saving special diets and the occasional round of steak.) We took turns serving food, two tables, a week at a time, all quite democratic.

But no choices,no seconds, never leftovers, and the big eaters suffered more than a little. Springs to mind the tragic story of Jack Atkinson and the ice cream, but later. First to Pat McCarthy.

Pat, a notable member of our class, at least for a short time, had quite a different background. An Aussie in his late fifties, older than many of the faculty, Pat had been a religious brother all his adult life, had always wanted to become a priest, but his religious superior consistently refused. But persistence won out, and he found himself sent round the world to St.

Mary's for a quick update in theology prior to ordination. He was a quiet man with a wonderful sense of humor (fortunately for him) and he had a great tolerance for the post-adolescent wags who surrounded him.

The one adjustment Pat found most difficult—the curious Yank custom of eating only three times a day. Accustomed to the usual meals, plus high tea, low tea, bush tea, and a bite whenever he felt peckish, which was frequently, Pat found himself wracked daily with hunger pangs. He appealed to the Rector, a man of his own age, and was given a special dispensation to slip down to the kitchen and make himself a bite when he needed one.

The rest of us had to make do with our non-mealtime hunger. With virtually no way to store food in the bare, cell-like rooms, we had little recourse. And besides, food and drink in the rooms was Against the Rule. Of course, some took this rule more seriously than others. But the faculty took the rule very seriously. If "contraband" was brought in, it was done with great caution.

Take the case of Fat Jack Atkinson.

One Saturday afternoon, Atkinson, a seminarian from Tennesee, found the seminary's provisions quite inadequate and decided to supplement them. He walked a good mile down Charles street to a nearby shopping center and acquired a quart of ice cream. As the gods of bad timing would have it, he arrived back at the the front steps just as the Rector opened the front door and started down toward him.

Though his package suggested nothing untoward, Atkinson panicked, whirled around and thrust it into the nearest hiding place, which happened to be the U.S. Post Office mail box. In an instant, he had passed from seminary rule-breaker to federal criminal. (We all knew that destruction of federal property was a serious crime, more serious even than putting pennies on the railroad track for the train to flatten.) Regretably, we were deprived of the drama of an invasion of G-Men when Atkinson, surely trembling in his boots, confessed his crime to Father Meyers, who simply called the post office and had the package removed.

Afternoon Classes

After lunch we had time to brush teeth, grab a smoke, chat, gather our books and make our way to the one o'clock class. The mood of high seriousness which generally attended the morning classes faded to a mood of high sleepiness. The afternoon subjects, taught once or twice a week in various semesters, had lower status academically. As a result, those professors were often perceived as lesser members of the faculty. Also, for whatever reason, the "afternoon professors" tended to be well up the eccentricity scale, although Willie O'Shea didn't think so.

You have already heard a bit about Father James Laubacher, S.S., the rector (Numero Uno!), and something of the dean, Father Edward Cerny, S.S., of whom many further stories will be told. Taken as a whole, the faculty seemed rather an odd lot, and living in the confines of the seminary for ten months of the year certainly didn't help them to become less odd. They served as our teachers, our keepers, our watchers, our nemesis. They also served as our primary source of entertainment (as we were theirs, come to think of it) and for that reason, we didn't want them a bit less odd.

Father William O'Shea

For example, Father William O'Shea, S.S., a nationally known liturgy scholar, may have been the most nervous man I ever met. If you pointed at him suddenly, he would scream. The least little anomaly in his classroom threw him completely. I can remember him rushing to the window one glorious spring day, and screaming at a bird in his high, piercing voice, "Go away. Go AWAY!" and vainly flapping his arms. We hadn't even noticed the bird till Willie began his campaign.

Another time, one of the workmen washing windows well down the hall, caught Willy's eye. He went to the door and called, "James, James," but the workman either didn't hear him or didn't choose to have his work interrupted.

Willie came back into the room, shrugged his shoulders in defeat and opined, "I guess his name isn't James."

Father O'Shea, a man of no more than middle age, acted (and looked) rather like a fussy old matron. Red-faced, on the plump side, he pulled up the sash of his cassock over his pot belly with the effect of emphasizing rather than hiding it. He carried his hands tucked up, rabbit-like, and wore steel rimmed spectacles well down on his nose like a character from Dickens.

The faculty were our defined antagonists, though most of us liked most of them, and respected most of the rest. Only a few did we dare to mess with and, bad luck for him, Father O'Shea became one. I think he had the intelligence to see this as a sort of backhanded sign of affection.

We knew Willie could be got at, and get at him we did. A couple of our more enterprising spirits used a few moments before class to tip the pictures hanging on the back wall. Willie noticed them immediately, managed to suppress his reaction for some period of time, but finally, in the middle of the lecture, he screamed out in exasperation, "Ok, enough. Straighten those pictures," startling many of the students who hadn't even noticed.

In an exceptional burst of creativity and imagination, several students procured a half dozen live chicks from somewhere in Baltimore, sneaked into Willy's faculty apartment in his absence, and proceeded to hide the chicks everywhere: in desk drawers, behind shelves of books, in the closets, and so on.

The long hall, without "James."

When Willy returned to his room, he was surrounded by high pitched cheeping, coming from everywhere. We wept with laughter imagining the scene, since there were no witnesses. On a somewhat later occasion, Father O'Shea mentioned that "someone" had hidden the baby chicks in his room.

"What did you do with them?" asked one of us, perhaps an innocent bystander.

"Oh, I found them all, I hope." piped Willie, in his high voice. "And I flushed them down the john," he added, ending the prank on a macabre note.

One of the deacons told us about Willie, attending a national liturgical conference. He was something of a celebrity since the publication of his book *Worship*, an ecclesiastical hot seller of the time, and was holding forth to a group of priests and seminarians from all over the country. Someone asked him if the Sulpecians were not noted for having a good number of eccentrics among their ranks.

"Oh, NO!" he cried, waving his hands about for emphasis. "All the ECCENTRIC Sulpecians are DEAD!" His very response belied his assertion. He may have had a point, but he was far from right.

Explaining about the Sulpecians

This will not be easy. Sulpecians are not religious. Well, I mean, some of them *are* religious but they don't belong to a religious *order*, like Jesuits, Dominicans, Franciscans, Teutonic Knights, and hundreds of others. Sulpecians belong to an association, a Society, although not like the Society of Jesus, a religious order. Are you following so far?

Sulpecians are diocesan priests. They belong to a diocese, which is a territory presided over by a bishop. The bishop releases them, more or less voluntarily, to the Society of Saint Sulpice, for the sole purpose of teaching priests in Catholic seminaries.

Plenty of people feel confused about these matters, and these are only the people that CARE.

In my priesting days, people would ask me, "Father, what order do you belong to?"

I would answer, "To no order. I'm a DISorder priest." People took it as a joke, but a lot of truth underlay the one-liner.

Adventures with Bull Noonan.

One o'clock, and time for Church History and our first contact with Bull Noonan.

Father "Bull" Noonan, first name unknown to me then, did not appear unusual, at first glance. But Bull Noonan stories abounded. A tall, hefty, quiet man, referred to only as "Bull." We didn't know why. Apparently a nickname attached to him in his long-ago seminary years had stuck, and he didn't seem to mind. We didn't mean it insultingly, and he didn't take offense.

Bull taught Church History to the first year students and American Church History to the second year men. At first encounter, he seemed not that much different from my college history professors, so I was looking forward to the class, despite the hour.

Bull, a master of his field, lectured largely without recourse to his notes—a good strategy for engaging the class, but not always best for accuracy.

One time, speaking about the torturous (sometimes literally) politics of the papacy during pre-renaissence times, Bull spent a good ten minutes explaining the difference between the Guelphs and the Ghibbelines, two powerful political families of the period. He paused, asked, "Any questions?" We sat silent, overwhelmed with information we didn't want.

The Bull continued his lecture and immediately confused the two families! "The Guelphs began to, uh...., that is, the Ghibbelines....well."

Bull shrugged said, "Perhaps it really doesn't make that much difference." On that we all agreed. Nonetheless his lectures came steeped in the minutiae which can make history come alive, and I looked forward to the class.

Bull had greater difficulty in making himself come alive, however. Somewhere along the line, he had gotten out of phase with the world and now found himself unable to sleep at night and unable to stay awake in the morning. It is rumored that he took pep pills in the morning to wake himself up, and sleeping pills at night, with the result that he was perpetually in a kind of twilight haze.

The sacristans had a standing bet that Bull's server, who led him out to say Mass in one of the side chapels every morning, could lead him down one aisle, across the back of the chapel, and up the other aisle, unvest him, and he would never remember not having said Mass. I don't know that it was ever tried, but we freely speculated on the possibility.

I do remember that he came into class one afternoon—afternoons being the worst for him—plopped down his books on the desk, and began what he thought was the class prayer: *Veni, Sancti Spiritus* (Come, Holy Spirit.) What he actually said was, *Adjutorium nostrum in nomine Domini,* (Our help is in the name of the Lord.) the beginning of the prayers at the foot of the altar, perfectly well known to every altar boy in the world. Indeed, some of my classmates instinctively responded, "*Qui facit caelum et terram.*" (who made heaven and earth). A moment of confusion followed while Bull reoriented himself to his surroundings, then began again, grumpily, "*Veni, Sancti Spiritus…*"

Another time, during the tense final exam week, Bull marched into the Deacon class, and began handing out History Finals to the startled Deacons, who were expecting Father Brennan for Moral Theology. No one bothered to interrupt him until Father Brennan himself marched in, assessed the situation at a glance and kindly (of course) persuaded Bull Noonan that he had the wrong class.

Bull Noonan Gives a Grade.

As first year students, deacons advised us that Bull gave huge, horrendous exams, but only read the first set of exams he gave each term. The grade for that exam became your grade in history for the next two years, for all papers, quizzes and finals. The catch? No one dared to take a chance that this was true. It was proposed that someone write one page of a paper, and then fill the rest with random selections from a newspaper, but no one did.

For our midterm in Church History, Bull eased into the room at his slow pace, enunciated the prayer, turned to the board and wrote the numeral 800 on the board in large letters. We stared at it for a minute.

"For your essay," Bull announced, "Explain why this date makes a good dividing point for Western Church History. We stared at the numeral for several moments. What if this year were 1600 a.d? No, that wasn't it.

What? Wait! I had it. The coronation of Charlemagne! Or was it the birth of Charlemagne? Let's go with the coronation. Wait. Bull wants a four word essay? Why is the coronation the midpoint?

After a little thought, I realized that the question meant: write the history of western civilization. Would Bull really read all this stuff? Did I dare to take a chance? No. I wrote my arm off.

As it happened, I received an 87 on that first midterm from Bull, and 87s on all succeeding work.

Long Rec

Or recess for big kids. We had almost two whole unprogrammed hours. Time for sports; games; long walks and conversations; the pressure of the schedule somehow suspended. I tended to hang a bit with Kehoe, since he was about the only person I knew. Some guys had put on sports clothing and chucked footballs and baseballs around. But it was still Baltimore hot, and most guys simply headed for the abundant shady spots on the lawn. The building was not air conditioned, of course, although a few of the faculty apartments sported portable units.

As yet, sports had not been organized, although that time would come soon enough. I noticed a rugged, supremely hairy Italian guy sweating copiously and heaving a football to anyone who would receive. He didn't match my image of the typical seminarian. He turned out to be Evasio DeMarcellis, an euphonious appellation, as W. C. Fields used to say. My next glimpse of Vas, as he was called, came in the music room that night. A Beethoven symphony on the box and Vas following the music in the score. That didn't fit the jock stereotype, either. Vas—a man unto himself.

I didn't heave any footballs, but I sweated beneath the unbreathing black rayon cassock, and I headed up early to catch a shower before my 4 p.m. class. There I would face another new professor whose distinctive style of speaking was frequently parodied by the upper classmen.

Father Miles McAndrews

Father Miles McAndrews, S.S., taught Hebrew and some other class that I can't quite think of. An old man, tall, bent, ruddy, with a shock of white hair rather like the poet Robert Frost, he had been shipped off to St. Mary's from the West Coast, where a minor scandal had occurred. The theological students in the seminary there were also, *de facto*, residents and voters in the small community where the seminary was located. As a prank, the seminarians went to vote in the local elections, and by pre-agreement, wrote in Father McAndrew's name as Dogcatcher. He won in a landslide.

Duly elected and delighted, Miles fully intended to take up the post. Wiser heads prevailed, Father McAndrew was persuaded to withdraw his "candidacy" and to ensure his removal from local celebrity, the Sulpecians transferred him to St. Mary's on the other coast.

Miles enter the seminary in the ninth grade and, to my mind, presented a classic case of arrested development. Although well into his seventies, he had gotten stuck stuck emotionally at about age twelve, as his bizarre teaching style and his grade school sense of humor were to reveal.

Miles marched into Hebrew class, recited the opening prayer and launched into his opening lecture. I can remember the sound of that class as if it had been recorded.

"Gentlemen!" he trumpeted, in an odd, artificial, clipped delivery, without identifiable accent. "Gentlemen, the secret of success in the acquisition of a language is constant and thorough review. Open your books to page one." The twenty or so students who were taking beginning Hebrew, languidly opened their books.

"Gentlemen," Miles continued, as if he were addressing a military parade, "The first letter of the Hebrew alphabet is Aleph. Aaaa-LEPH!" he shouted triumphantly. "Repeat it after me. Aaa-LEPH!"

"Aleph," the class repeated dutifully. Miles traced the Hebrew character on the board a foot high, then stepped back to contemplace it.

"Aleph!" he echoed, with great satisfaction. "Turn your books to page TWO!" We dutifully turned the page.

"But first, gentlemen, I'm going to tell you a JOKE!" His face turned bright red, possibly at his daring in interrupting the "lecture" or in contemplation of the hilarity to follow.

Blessedly, I can't remember any of the details of the jokes, which he told on a regular basis, but they tended to involve the words "ass" and/or "fart" and they absolutely killed Miles. He would blare out the punch line, then collapse against the desk, snuffling out a silent, helpless laugh. When the response had died down, (and we always gave him a big, encouraging response) he would repeat the punch line, as "How am I supposed to play this piano, with my ASS?" and then collapse again in helpless mirth. The big response was a bit harder to come by the second time.

He would then collect himself, pick up the book and announce, "The second letter of the Hebrew alphabet is......BET! BET! Pronounce it after me." We would respond, he would write it on the board, we would copy it down, he would go off on a tangent, and somehow the 50 minute period was gone after covering two or three letters.

A week later, Miles would begin the class by announcing, "Gentlemen, the secret of success in the acquisition of a language is constant and thorough review. Open your books to page one." And we would go through the whole process again, perhaps gaining one or two letters a week. Clearly, learning the entire 23 character Hebrew alphabet was going to consume most of the semester, to say nothing of the vowel points.

Pope Archibald the First

Father McAndrews had an endless fascination with the papacy and the ceremonials surrounding the pope. Indeed, he fantasized about being named pope, and had even chosen his papal name: Archibald the First. He confided these immodest yearnings to the class on many occasions, and finally, in desperation for liberation from the relentless plod through the Hebrew alphabet, some members of the class decided to stage a papal coronation right in the classroom.

The ambitious insiders found an old ceremonial chair, which they rigged with an overcurtain in white and gold, devised a white papal mitre (tall, pointed hat) and a long white robe to be draped round the shoulders.

An elaborately lettered and solemnly phrased proclamation was inscribed on a scroll. The whole business was set up in place of the usual wooden desk and chair on the front dais of the classroom.

When Miles walked in, he fell for the whole rigamarole with total delight, his face reddening with pleasure as he cried out, "What's this? What's this?"

Someone cued up celebratory trumpet music, and the class reader, Bill Newell, proclaimed in stentorian tones: "*Annuncio vobis gaudium magnum. Habeamus Papam! Miles Cardinale McAndrews. Archibaldo Primus.*" We cheered and clapped. Miles mounted the "papal throne," donned the white mitre, sat down and began to shower papal blessings right and left. Photographs were taken.

Eventually, the whole charade began to trail off, the trappings were dismantled, Miles reluctantly gave up his "papal vestments" and resumed teaching for what little time remained. I learned later that the rector called in certain "ringleaders" for a talking-to, but couldn't make much headway since Father McAndrew had been such a willing participant. He also called in Father Miles for what must have been an unpleasant and embarrassing interview. In subsequent weeks, Father Miles was chastened and withdrawn, offered no jokes or stories in class, and generally appeared daunted in spirit.

Hebrew, another of the afternoon classes, was only taken by those of us who aspired to degrees in theology. My bishop had specifically advised me to take Spanish, rather than Hebrew, but I in my wisdom decided to do both. Could he really object if I knocked off a theology degree as well? It never became an issue, because I decided that at the pace we were learning, I would never acquire any useful knowledge of Hebrew by the time of ordination. But I still remember my Aleph/Bets.

Father Ben Selner

I looked forward to the afternoon class in Gregorian Chant. 'Musically inclined,' as the saying went, I had a good ear if a very ordinary 'shower soloist' voice. I had seen Gregorian chant in the pages of art books with the elaborate illustrations. I just didn't know how to read it.

Strangely enough, most of us hadn't reckoned on all the singing. Now, I'm not just talking about Gregorian chant in chorus or singing hymns at Mass. We aspired to be soloists, although we hadn't thought about it that way. Every one of us would have to stand up in solemn ceremonies and intone the Latin prayers, as best we could. Some of my classmates had fine voices, most of us were average—guys who could carry a tune, more or less—and then there was Joe Schneider.

Father Ben Selner, S.S., an organist, hymn-writer and conductor of some reputation, served as the primary teacher of church music. An older man, of sentimental but volatile character, he was soon to discover that the class of '61 had what today would be called an attitude problem. He taught the class in sacred music once a week. We were not only to learn the principles of reading and singing Gregorian chant with its unusual modalities and unique notation, but we were supposed to be learning some standards of appropriate aesthetics regarding church music in general.

Selner fancied himself a brilliant and innovative teacher. Among his unusual notions was the denial of the concept of tone deafness. "I can teach anyone to sing a scale," He asserted confidently, on the first day of class. "Is there anyone here who thinks he's tone deaf?"

Joe Schneider raised his hand. A student from the Baltimore diocese, Joe is distinguished in my memory primarily by the fact that he was balding in his mid-twenties, and a fierce baseball player. In any case, he had the guts to admit to tone deafness.

"Nonsense," said Father Selner, with great confidence. "I'll teach you to sing a scale in five minutes. Now, give me a note." Schneider, abashed and mystified, opened his mouth, but nothing came out. "Just any note at all," Selner insisted, "If you can talk, you can sing. You can talk, can't you?" he added sarcastically. Schneider nodded. "OK, then, say something and just hold the tone."

After a bit more hesitation, Schneider issued some sort of note, very quietly. "Louder," Selner shouted.

"Uhhhhhhh," moaned Schneider, sounding a bit like a fog horn, but at least holding the note on pitch.

"Good!" Selner enthused. "Now, think of that note as number one, on a scale of eight. For two, add just a little energy. For three, add just a little more, and so on, up the scale to eight."

Schneider looked dubious. "Do it," Selner insisted, his face darkening a bit.

Schneider, hesitated, drew breath and then began, obediently to "sing" his scale. "Uhhhhh, uhhhhhh, uhhhhhh…" Each "Uhhhhh" was slightly louder than the previous one, and each one was exactly the same pitch. The effect was hilarious, and the class burst out laughing. Father Selner's face turned a deep red, and he slammed down his *Liber Usualis* on the desk, stunning us to silence.

He glared at Schneider, who clearly had no idea what he had done, other than follow directions. Father Selner struggled with his temper, clearly a lifetime occupation. He knew that Schneider was not putting him on, but wanted someone to blame for the failure of his experiment. "Fine, fine, you want to make a joke of it. It's fine with me." It was unclear whether he meant the innocent Schneider or the class as a whole.

Gregorian Chant in the seminary.

I don't really want to get into a lot of technical stuff about Gregorian chant here, mainly because I don't know a lot; indeed, hardly anything. Let me just say for my purposes now that there are three kinds of chant: plain chant; fancy chant; and something in between. If you are trying to do something impressive, you go for the fancy chant, with a lot of notes on all the vowel sounds. Highly melismatic. Whoo! It sounds amazing, but quick it is not. One simple prayer can take a full ten minutes. The medieval monks had nothing but time.

Not so in a modern city parish, trying to squeeze in six Masses of a Sunday morning. And even in the seminary, if you're trying to get through a lot of Latin psalms, you do *recto tono*, or plain chant, with a lot of words on one note and a little bit of inflection at the end. I'm humming an example here, if you can make it out.

The *Liber Usualis* (Book for Use) became our constant companion in the chapel. A genuine tome, this eighteen-hundred-plus page volume held all the chants which might be used in the course of a year's liturgy, together with many pages of closely-printed technical stuff about chant, the notation and its meaning. You've probably seen medieval manuscripts with Gregorian chant painted in black fancy lettering with enormous red and gold capitals taking up half the first page. Well, none of that stuff in the *Liber,* as we called it. Just business-like printing of the chants, which looks a little but not very much like modern musical notation.

An antagonistic relationship

Father Ben Selner, a competent, even gifted musician and teacher, remained very much a man of the old school and quite a prima donna as well. As our class became more and more marked for its preference for the new, the progressive, the experimental, the rift with Selner became more and more obvious. He approached our Chant class balancing that chip on his shoulder, and intently aware of the multiple chips on ours. Little hope here for things to go smoothly.

One day in the fall, Father Ben climbed onto the dais, dropped into the chair behind his desk, and began to organize his music, gathering himself in anticipation of our real or perceived resistance. He noticed a draft from the open window at the front of the classroom to his left. "That's great," he commented, bitterly. "Why don't you open all the windows?"

Warren Willis, a quiet, diminutive student who sat in the front row by the windows, impervious to sarcasm, rose obediently, picked up the long wooden window pole (the enormous casement windows in the old building reached almost to the ceiling) and methodically began to open the windows from the top, working his way from the front toward the back of the room.

As Father Selner watched in mounting frustration, the brisk October breeze began to blast through the room, scattering sheets of music and chilling the atmosphere. Oblivious to Selner's fury, the mounting breeze, and the class's amusement, Willis continued to open the windows to the very back of the room, as he was directed.

Selner blew up! "Damn it to hell," he shouted, startling the class (and the innocent Willis) considerably. "What the damn hell are you trying to do." He was a man in a fury, but unaccustomed to public swearing. Willis returned meekly to his seat. The October breezes continued to blow vigorously through the room. The class assumed a blank anonymity, but Selner had lost it. "Damn, damn, damn, damn, HELL!" he shouted, unimaginatively. He snatched up his books, stuffed them into his old leather case, and, still swearing under his breath, stalked to the door, wrenched it open, stormed out and down the hall.

The class sat uncertainly, entertaining mixed feelings of vague guilt and anti-authoritarian delight. In the quiet and regular rhythm of the seminary, moments of high drama were few and far between, and we savored the moment—not to be the last in music class.

Selner's Christmas Stories

During the last week before Christmas, Ben Selner would set aside time in his chant class to read us a Christmas story. From the older men, we learned that these stories had the same essential plot. Some hard-hearted and skeptical individual would run across a bum or a little boy or a poor family. Against his every inclination, he would share his dinner or his toys and of course, the bum or the little boy would turn out to be the Christ child.

Selner felt these stories deeply. An excellent, if overdramatic reader, he would choke and even tear up as, lowering his voice to a dramatic whisper, he would reach the revelation: "And that little boy was the Baby Jesus."

We felt choked up, too, but with suppressed laughter. The stories might test the credulity of a third grader, to say nothing of a classroom full of male graduate students, however filled with faith and piety. At the end of the reading, an audible snicker cut through the silence, and Selner blew again.

"You guys think you're so..........superior," he raged. "Wait till you get out into the parishes. I pity the people who have to put up with you. You'll mock their simple faith; you'll destroy their trust; you'll........oh, what's the use?"

In disgust, he slammed his books together and strode from the room. A feeling of uneasy triumph pervaded the class, but maybe Selner had some points, too. Some of us neo-sophisticates heard some truth beneath the rage.

But hey, we got out of class early. T'was the season to be jolly.

Selner, letting the chant go down.

The Chapel gleamed in the afternoon sunlight slanting down through stained glass windows; reflecting off marble floors and columns and the highly polished oak choir stalls stretching the length of the high-vaulted room. Darker side corridors were lined with tiny chapels where the faculty said their private Masses every morning. The floor scrubbed and waxed, gleamed softly, the air redolent with candles and incense The memory returns vividly.

A distinguished visitor avails himself of the chapel. John Paul II, undated.

As the faculty musician, Selner conducted Chant practice every Saturday afternoon in preparation for the Solemn High Mass celebrated every Sunday. Many guys hated this incursion into our free afternoon, but I didn't mind so much. I liked to sing and the practice seemed OK, even though reading the chant did not come easily to me.

Chanting the Divine Office creates a powerful impression: three hundred plus young men sitting in two choirs facing one another and chanting antiphonally the ancient verses of the Psalms in Latin. The sound of Gregorian Chant communicates a sense of timelessness and for good reason; some of the chants dated to the ninth century, a.d.

Holy Week, from Palm Sunday to Easter, represents the peak of the liturgical year, and also brings the most complex and a-typical liturgies. Critical eyes are sharpened, expectations are heightened, blunders are magnified.

Leo Kelty, the band's clarinetist, had a fine high tenor voice, and got tabbed as the Lead chanter for the Holy Thursday service. Well aware of the intensified scrutiny, Leo felt plenty nervous as the time for his unaccompanied solo exercise approached.

Leo stepped to the lectern, opened the music, and received a pitch from the organist. He nodded, cleared his throat and, just then, someone slid a chair, creating another, much higher pitch. Rattled, Leo cleared his throat again, and began his chant on the much higher note. He could barely reach it, and few in the choir could get up there to respond, though we tried. I forget how it became resolved. There's no "starting again" in the liturgy.

Particularly on Good Friday, there's a whole lotta chanting going on, most of it *recto tono*, in respect of the tone of the day, and the length of the service. And we had no accompaniment. From the end of the service on Holy Thursday until the first Mass on Easter, no organ or bell could be sounded, though a single pitch note on the organ was permitted.

As we plowed through page after page of sad and gloomy Latin, our voices tired and our pitch sank, lower and lower. This drove Father Ben Selner mad with frustration.

As we sagged and sagged, Selner played the pitch note again and again, his insistency revealing his irritation. Finally, in a rage, he simply let the chanting go down and down without playing the pitch tone. We chanted on, lower and lower, till even the basses in the group could sing no lower.

As we went lower, we went slower, till there was nothing but a grumbling rumble coming from the 350 chanters. It was absurd, guys began to laugh—a most inappropriate response for Good Friday—and the Rector, in a rage of his own, sent a message up to the choir loft that Selner was to get us back on pitch.

This he did with extremely ill grace. We stole glances at Father Laubacher at his stall in the rear of the chapel, saw his set jaw and darkened complexion and suspected that strained relations with Selner would be continued.

Winding Down the Day

On that first day, as with so many others, Kehoe and I climbed the stairs to our room, schlepping our copies of the huge *Liber Usualis* and very limited notes from the Chant class. We had a few minutes to get organized before the next exercise, recitation of the rosary.

As a scheduled devotion, the private recitation of the rosary was unique. The familiar and highly repetitious prayer series, directed to the Blessed Mother, formed a staple of Catholic non-liturgical public prayer for many years. The rosary could be recited at any Catholic pious function, could be led by anyone, could be followed by anyone who knew the Lord's Prayer (always called the 'Our Father' by Catholics) and the Hail Mary. More sophisticated reciters could meditate on the Scriptural events commemorated in the Fifteen Mysteries.

At St. Mary's, we recited the rosary privately in common, if you can follow that. Most spent the fifteen minutes allotted to the devotion walking around, outside if the weather permitted, or inside. It would have seemed a curious sight to an outsider—hundreds of black-cassocked young men wandering silently around the halls, beads dangling from their hands, seemingly unconscious of one another.

I had a tough time with meditation in the morning, but this wandering (and relatively short) meditative form worked pretty well for me. My favorite spot, if not outside, became the library reading room, book-lined between the tall windows and cork floors, heavily waxed and polished. Shoes produced an odd, muffled click on the floors which fascinated me.

I don't remember any religious or other insights from my Rosary meditations, but it became a good quiet time for me, a fundamentally unquiet person.

A bell ended the quiet and summoned us to Spiritual Reading. There, the Rector began a survey of the Rule, with explanations, a topic that would consume several weeks. Obedience to the Rule meant obedience to God, a monastic principle for sure. That this dictum gave the Rule equivalent status to Holy Scripture didn't seem obvious to me at the time. Certainly, I never for a moment thought that Father Laubacher was kidding. I paid attention.

At the bell, we moved in silence to dinner. Once again, a *tu autem*. We could talk; I could get to know a few people a bit.

Short rec. Study at eight. The Great Silence at nine. Lights out at 10:30 p.m. I have little recollection of any of this from that first day. I felt drained. I opened up one of my Latin texts and stared at it, trying to extract meaning. Even when I managed a kind of translation, I didn't find much meaning. An experience to be repeated often.

Curiously, lights out operated on the honor system. At Notre Dame, the hall rectors turned out room lights at the main switch. A difference in philosophy? Too tired to think. I hit the rack and fell asleep.

Wrapping it up.

I found classes exciting, stimulating, challenging, especially theology and scripture studies. At this point, my deficits in Latin did not cause me a serious problem, although my daily exposure to prayer Latin did not help at all with theological Latin.

The great discovery—the division of the class into conservatives and liberals provided an unexpected sense of underlying tension to all the issues we faced. This drama turned classes into an ideological battlefield, though a quiet, interior one. The conflict, to be played out across the whole culture in the sixties, provided a sense of intensity and mission to my studies which I had never experienced in my college work.

For better and for worse, I was becoming a liberal, or maybe discovering that I had always been one. Never a part of my plan, but never a moment of doubt where I stood.

3

A Busy Place

Founded in 1791, St. Mary's Seminary & University in Baltimore is the first Catholic seminary established in the United States. The original St. Mary's was established in Baltimore on Paca Street. In 1805, St. Mary's was chartered as a civil university in Maryland, and in 1822, Pope Pius VII established the seminary as the country's first ecclesiastical (pontifical) faculty with the right to grant degrees in the name of the Holy See. The seminary continues to offer the pontifical STB and STL degrees for all qualified students.

In 1929, St. Mary's Seminary moved the four years of theology studies to its present location at Roland Park in Baltimore. Designed by Maginnis and Walsh of Boston, the seminary's classic entrance and massive facade are a recognized landmark in the city. Inside the main doors stands the marble statue of Mary known as the Sedes Sapientiae, Our Lady Seat of Wisdom, *patroness of the seminary. Further on is the Main Chapel, designed in marble and oak, with its Cassavant pipe organ and stained glass windows from Paris.*

The Building Itself.

St. Mary's Theological Seminary located itself on a huge tract of land—I'm guessing several many acres—in the then-fashionable northern Baltimore section of Roland Park. Since one of its main purposes was to separate young men from the world, the Sulpecian Fathers felt that the more land they had, the better. (This didn't always work as well as they had hoped.)

A Busy Place 77

St. Mary's Seminary and University, Roland Park, Baltimore, Maryland, undated.

St Mary's Seminary actually comprised three institutions in my time: St. Charles Seminary, serving high school and two years of college; Paca Street, the two-year philosophy house, founded in 1791 (featuring the original faculty, as I used to say), and Roland Park, the theology house. (By 1977, the decline in religious vocations had shrunk the institution to one building at Roland Park.) Amazingly, a number of my classmates had gone through all three institutions and most of them professed to be heartily sick of seminary life!

The single huge building, shaped like an enormous E, stood on a slight rise in the center of the property, and faced northeast (for no particular theological reason) toward the corner of Roland Avenue and Belvidere Road. There was a large, well-trimmed but not impenetrable hedge along the two front sides, a vast front lawn where we walked, sat, played games of considerable violence, and generally recreated ourselves.

One lovely fall afternoon I found myself staring up at the building, at its grey and bulky best, trying to make some architectural assessment of its style. It seemed to have no identifiable stylistic pattern.

Charlie Porier, one of the deacons came by, followed my gaze, guessed my purpose and nailed it on the first try. "Neo-national Bank." he offered without inflection. (*Pace* Maginnis and Walsh!) I laughed at the irreverence and the accuracy of his identification.

Oliver Twist

I had a tiny history with Charlie, a Deacon seminarian from the Maine diocese, then presently seated at my table in the refectory (although he probably thought of it as HIS table!). Charlie had something of a waspish tongue and referred to me as "Oliver" because I reminded him of the waifish Oliver Twist in Dickens. Others were amused, and it didn't bother me.

Another time, during a *tu autem*, Charlie was going on at length about a new and rather expensive cassock he had purchased from a noted local tailor. The semi-Jesuit style featured sweeping skirts, a sleek front with no buttons and a wrap-around sash with a fringed hanging-down thing.

I found it all a bit much, and jumped in. "My cassock's pretty new, too. It's a roman style, of black rayon, from Hanson's." I had named the cheapest and most generic cassock to be had. My only one and I was wearing it.

Charlie shut up like a clam and after lunch, he took me by the arm and urged me to a quiet corner.

"Jim," he said, seriously, "I have to apologize to you for talking about the cassock. I had no wish to offend you. It was thoughtless and uncaring and I'm ashamed of myself."

I was stunned. I hadn't been the least offended, only slightly bored. My little parody now felt meaner than his original comments. I was too embarrassed to say anything.

Charlie went on. "I'm sorry, too, for calling you Oliver. It's a stupid joke and I won't do it again." He looked crestfallen and humbled, unaccustomed to apologizing for anything.

"Charlie," I tried to reassure him, "I wasn't bothered by it a bit. I thought it was kind of funny." I wondered if we were going to get past it, or if the awkwardness would continue through the whole time we were at table togther. A smart-mouth myself, that kind of stuff didn't bother me, but clearly Charlie had a crisis of conscience. I felt much relieved, at the evening meal, when he seemed returned to form.

Al Lingus makes his mark

Though Bill Peterson's escapades no doubt contributed to the odd reputation of the Rockford seminarians, migrants from the vague and distant Middle West, the main and major contributor must have been Geneva-born Al Lingus. One class ahead of me, with longish, straight blond hair and a kind of rawboned look, Lingus seemed straight off the farm. No impression could have been farther from the truth.

Lingus had appeared at the seminary on starting day a year before, wearing sandals, torn jeans, a tee shirt and carrying a kind of duffel bag filled largely with books, many in French. He affected a kind of holy simplicity, saying in effect, "Here I am, Lord, do with me what thou wilt."

The rector, Father Laubacher, was mystified. Was he dealing with some kind of beatnik, or a nut? If Lingus had been from New York or San Francisco, the image might have made some sense. Or maybe he represented some new incarnation of Francis of Assisi, embracing poverty and the simple life. Lingus offered no assistance. He had no clerical garb whatsoever.

The rector made a few calls, and rounded up a stray cassock and collar from one of the faculty, presented Al with a copy of the rules, and sent him off into the system, still thoroughly mystified.

As was Father Meyers, a few days later, making a routine room check. Lingus had stripped the room of its minimal furnishings. The desk and chair—gone; bedstead gone; the mattress lay on the floor. Lingus' books had been lined up on the floor against the wall. He had removed the statue of our Lady from the sconce on the wall and constructed a kind of floor-level shrine underneath the wash stand. The closet was empty, save for the duffle back hanging on a hook. The shrine probably saved him. Otherwise, I'm sure that Lingus would have been hitting the road later in the day, but then….well, what *about* the shrine? So Lingus stayed.

As it turned out, Lingus was neither beatnic, mystic, or nut, but merely a genius, both genuinely pious and totally cynical, a spectrum of attitude that perhaps only a genius could compass. He was also quite sophisticated, both socially and theologically, and was not the least embarrassed to reveal this.

He could read Latin like a native, and French and German. While he never missed class, he sat uninvolved and read French novels, most of them on the *Index Librorum Prohibitum* (when it still existed. The Index featured a list of forbidden books, including plenty from the standard Great Books list. Books not explicitly listed by title had a coverall prohibition, good old Canon 1099.)

The professors waited for midterms to bring him to his senses, but his grades were among the top in the class, and his written Latin far and away the best. He admitted to "glancing over the texts" the day before the exam. By the second semester of his first year, in order to keep mentally busy, he enrolled for a Master's in Education from DePaul University in Chicago by correspondence.

Meeting Lingus

When I heard the Lingus stories, I began to understand a bit more about the Rector's concern about my lack of clericals and my Rockford origins. I couldn't wait to meet this brilliant eccentric from my own diocese, who might be a fellow priest with me for many years, if either of us made it.

One day, walking around during long rec, one of my companions pointed out Lingus in another group, and, filled with a sense of our mutual brotherhood, I determined to meet him. Atypically, I strode up to the group, put a hand on his shoulder and announced, "Al Lingus? I'm Jim O'Brien from the Rockford Diocese.

The accosted Lingus turned, looked at me coolly and drawled, "Say something brilliant so I'll remember you." His group laughed.

"What bullshit," I thought to myself, turned my back and walked away. The hell with Lingus. Not a particularly Christian wish, but mine at the moment.

Media-deprived

As part of the monastic character of the seminary, we found ourselves media-deprived. No 'secular' newspapers, no radios, no television, no newsweeklys, no secular periodicals in the library. The small gap in the system occurred when sections (and even mere pages) of the New York Times might be found in the jakes, probably left by some compassionate faculty member. We snatched them up with delight.

As a result of this protective shield, if I may call it that, we missed the announcement that Searle, a small pharmaceutical company, had begun marketing a birth-control drug called Enovid—a pill packed with a high dose of progesterone and a dollop of estrogen, a proven if toxic preventer of pregnancy. I can scarcely think of another technological innovation which would have greater effect on the Catholic Church during the next decades.

The canny developers of "The Pill" as it came to be known, realized that opposition would come from the Catholic heirarchy, so they later recruited Dr. John Rock of Boston, a leading physician in gynecology and a noted and deeply committed Roman Catholic, to front the marketing campaign.

Despite growing evidence of The Pill's toxicity, demand proved intense and ambiguity over how The Pill actually worked permitted both priests and conscientious Catholics wiggle room. But we learned little about the issue, which seemed distant from our concerns.

In retrospect, The Pill and its progeny (so to speak) contributed to the sexual freedoms associated with the fast-approaching "Sixties" and the "Women's Movement," of which we remained totally unaware.

Insight in the music room

In the absence of radio or TV, I made my way now and then to the Music room in the basement. I perceived it as a study room such as would be found in the basement of any college dorm. A large "Hi-Fi" set, a 'record album' collection, beat-up easy chairs; a few card tables; ash trays. Just like the study rooms at ND. It never particularly struck me that the music room, crowded during evening rec, seemed empty after Evening Prayer!

Some weeks after my abortive encounter with Lingus, I was sitting in the music room during the evening study period, smoking my pipe and listening to some jazz—these activities were so strictly forbidden that no one ever checked—when Lingus came in, sat down beside me, said, "O'Brien, right? Listen, I'm sorry I blew you off like that. I understand that you're pretty cool."

With a compliment like that, I found it pretty hard to hold on to my irritation. Why Lingus thought me cool is a mystery I never solved. Probably he saw my flagrant disregard of the rules about the music room as a rebellion or protest though this had never occurred to me

In any case, Lingus proceeded to analyze the faculty as teachers, going systematically through all the first year teachers, giving advice about tests, warnings about particular obsessions, recommendations for stuff to ignore. In retrospect, it was a keenly observed and frighteningly accurate picture of the academic dimensions of my forthcoming seminary year.

Getting a Handle on Norris

I had faced our first quiz from Norris with confidence. I had good notes, studied with concentration and felt on top of the information. But when Father Dukehart told my my grade, the results were indifferent, like a B.

I couldn't understand it. I strove to be concise. Norris insisted on it.

"No bullshit!" he emphasized repeatedly before the exam. Answer the questions; tell me what you know. Short. Condensed. Precise. No bullshit!" We heard him loud and clear.

I asked Lingus about my difficulties with Norris' class.

"What's the story on Norris? I just got my grades and I didn't do that well." I must have sounded whiney. I hate that.

"Did Norris tell you to be concise? Short answers? No B.S?"

"Absolutely," I confirmed. "And I followed the directions. Short and to-the-point."

"Well, forget that." Lingus said confidently. "He says it and he means it, but the more you write, the more he thinks you know."

"OK," I thought. "Next time I'll write my fingers off."

I did and it worked. My grades improved dramatically. Thanks again, Al.

I don't recall another conversation or even encounter with the brilliant and storied Lingus. He left in the middle of the year, and Charley MacKay later reported having seen Lingus wandering around Europe with a parrot on his shoulder. (I could not make this up!)

Lingus actually appeared again on the seminar radar screen a year later, though I didn't get to meet him. Around about November, he drove up one afternoon in an ancient and battered Dodge, filled with his duffel bag and a rather bedraggled blond, who he ensconced in the library work room while he went to see the rector there. My turf! I went to check it out.

Sure enough, I found her there, smoking and staring indifferently at the piles of theology books. "I'm waiting for Al." she offered.

"OK, fine with me." I responded, and got the hell out. I certainly didn't want to be found alone with some girl whose presence I could neither understand or explain. We didn't run into a lot of unattached young women in the seminary, nor any other kind for that matter.

I learned later that Lingus had asked the rector for shelter for the night with the girl, and, when refused, announced that he would sleep in the car with the girl. So the rector found him a room, and the girl got to sleep in the car, alone. The fact that they had been sleeping together in the car for the previous month or so didn't seem to be a consideration. By the time of morning rec after breakfast, Lingus was gone from the sem and forever from my life, leaving only his story behind.

Domestic responsibilities

Coming in from long rec one day, I opened the room door and found a chair sitting in the middle of the floor, a note lying on it.

"Clean this room! Father Meyers." I looked up to see Kehoe grinning behind his desk.

I looked around with suddenly opened eyes. The floor lay coated thickly with dust. Clear paths marked the way to our desks, our closets, our beds and the sink. Elsewhere the dust was untouched. We had no cleaning implements, nor the will to buy them. I guess I had *seen* the dust, but that didn't move me to do anything about it. Nor Kehoe, for that matter. We had maids at Notre Dame; the administration had little faith in the cleaning impulses of adolescent boys.

"We better borrow a broom and stuff," I offered to Kehoe.

"Yeah, right." he agreed. I did and we set about our housekeeping chores in a silence tinged with mild embarrassment, plus the awareness that we had been watched, and caught!

Burning the String at Both Ends

Father Meyer's clandestine visit made us pay a bit more attention to the room, as did a later rush of deacons. Understand that entering another student's room constituted a very grave violation of the Rule. Nonetheless, Kehoe and I, dutifully hitting the books one afternoon, heard the cry 'Fire!'

Our door burst open and three deacons rushed into the room and stared around.

The cause of the alarm quickly became apparent. I had received a 'care' package from my grandmother earlier that day. Between Kehoe and me, we found nothing at hand to cut through the string-bound box. Without thinking, I pulled out the ever-present matches of the pipe-smoker, struck one and burned through the string.

"Smells good," offered Kehoe.

"Yeah," I responded, "And look, it keeps burning. Like punk." I pulled off the strings, still smoldering, and hung them over the supports for the lampshade. A pretty column of smoke moved straight up toward the ceiling. We settled back to study, only to be burst in upon by the deacons, who stood staring at the lamp. The column of smoke still rose, moved directly across the ceiling and out the open transom.

"Oh, uh......" I offered lamely. "I was just burning some.....string." I pulled the string off the lamp, wet my fingers and pinched out the still-smoldering tips. The deacons stared at me, wordless. I dropped the string into the wastebasket. The deacons came to themselves, turned and walked out of the room. Without even looking, I could feel Kehoe grinning at his desk. He did that a lot.

Behind the Bushes

I've already mentioned our preoccupation with food.

One glorious late spring day, an enterprising Good Humor man and his truck happened to be stopped at the corner of Belvedere and Roland Avenue during the very time of long rec. A group of seminarians strolling along the hedge and hidden from view of the seminary by a grove of lilacs, called the man over, and bought several Good Humors. They also pointed out to the driver that they had recreation the same time every day, and they also told a few of their friends.

The next day, there were twice as many seminarians, and three times the sales. By the end of the week, at least 50 seminarians were in on the rendezvous, and the word was spreading fast. That night in Spiritual Reading, the rector, who was presiding, finished the opening prayer and then sat in silence, looking over the throng with more than his usual displeasure. He touched the steel-grey hair over his temple in a familiar gesture which I now recognize as mild embarrassment and began, quietly but firmly, "Well, gentlemen, we know what you're doing out there behind the bushes."

A moment of stunned silence, then the entire student body broke into roars of laughter.

The rector's head snapped up in surprise, and his face reddened in anger and embarrassment. He slammed his fist down on the table next to the microphone, and shouted, "Silence!" Three hundred laughs were cut off in their prime. We waited, choking, while the Rector mastered his fury.

Realizing that the double-entendre was his own fault, and suddenly seeing the matter in a better proportion, he began more softly, explaining the rule against food in the rooms, urging us to a sense of self-denial, then providing an out for the desperately hungry.

"If anyone has difficulty with this rule, he may come and see me personally, and we can make some arrangement." he concluded, gently. ("As if…" the kids would say today.) He paused, feeling that something further should be said. After a moment, he added, oddly, "We give milk, you know." There was a murmur of suppressed chuckles, but no outbreak. Later on, at dinner, the line had become a catch-phrase of psuedo-concern—a pitying look followed by the words, "We give milk, you know."

Invaders

A winding blacktop driveway moved across the property from Roland Avenue, widening in front of the front steps, then proceeding down a fairly decent hill to Northern Parkway. Next to the street stood four pretty good tennis courts, which were occasionally invaded by the neighbors, since we only used them during long rec.

One time Father Cerny, the dean, walking along the drive saying his office during morning class hours, came upon two young women playing tennis. Scandalized, he rushed to the rector's office, announcing in his breathy voice, "Father, come quickly. There are two women on the tennis courts. They're wearing nothing but breast-plates and panties." The rector moved quickly to his window, but was relieved to note that the invaders were wearing shorts and halter tops. Nonetheless, a messenger was sent and our visitors firmly invited to depart.

Near the tennis courts stood a row of one-wall concrete handball courts, and below them, a wood with a stream running through it. One winter, an enterprising group of seminarians received permission to construct a dam and fashioned a small skating rink which received a couple of years of enthusiastic use.

Despite our heavy schedule of classes and religious services, we had a mandated three hours of recreation a day, as well as Saturday and Sunday afternoons. For the most part, we couldn't "go" anywhere. Leaving the seminary was permitted only with, well..., permission, and the practice was frowned upon. But we were determined to recreate ourselves and we did.

Of course, our prime source of entertainment was the faculty, watching them, gossiping about them, speculating about them, categorizing them and so on. They must have been doing the same with us, but it never occurred to me until this moment that this was other than their responsibility.

Walks: Baltimore General

There was one important exception to our voluntary imprisonment. Every Wednesday afternoon, all classes but the Deacons went on "walks." Not much walking involved, however. As a gesture toward pastoral training, we found ourselves transported to institutions large and small around Baltimore where we might come into contact with the general public. Or at least, that part of the general public which would welcome or accept visits from the RC clergy. No actual training involved. We got on busses, were transported to the institution of our choice, went in and talked to people. The walk leaders told us *not* to proselytize. Hey, I couldn't even spell it.

I had no idea how to pick a Walk. I ended up with a group that went to Baltimore General Hospital, a vast, grey, bottom-rung social institution for the sick poor. In many cases, the sick poor had no place to go where they would receive any follow-up care, and so they just stayed. For years.

We were required to wear black suit and roman collar (rather than a shirt and black tie) and we looked like priests (or, in some cases, priestlets) and were taken for such in our settings. The people we saw rarely had any choice of the people they saw and at least we weren't going to hurt them.

"What do we say to them?" I asked the second year man riding in the bus seat next to me. I was terrified. A naturally shy person, I didn't feel protected by the uniform; it just added another layer of pretense to be explained away. And I didn't like hospitals. And I never approached strangers. Baltimore Hospital was a typically brilliant choice.

The third year man in charge parceled out the new guys to various wards. I was sent to 3-A, for long term patients. Feeling totally inadequate, I moved hesitatingly into the huge wardroom. Maybe fifty patients were more or less screened off from each other by hanging white curtains.

An elderly man was lying in the bed, staring up at me.

"Hi, there." I said, with completely false cheerfulness. "How you doing?"

"OK." The patient offered.

"Well, uh......" Where to go from here? "How long you been here?"

"Twenty-six years." The old man croaked.

I stared down at him. I was twenty-three. This man had been in this hospital since before I was born. I was struck virtually dumb. It didn't occur to me for many days that the information might be incorrect. I never learned the facts.

"Well, that's a long time." I muttered helplessly. The patient stared up at me, digesting this piece of wisdom.

"Well, I guess I better get on down the line." And I slid on to the next cubicle.

The man lying in the bed had a cut throat; not a careful job, either. For some reason, it was not bandaged.

"Wow." I offered, trying to keep from fainting. I couldn't handle cut throats even in the movies. "Can you talk with that?" I gestured unwillingly toward the wound. The man moved his head in a very careful "no."

"OK, well, take it easy." Out of there.

I must have seen other patients that afternoon, but my memory has been wiped clean. We were there about an hour, all told, but I was emotionally drained by the time I crawled onto the bus for the long return to Roland Park. I didn't even want to talk about it.

Walks Look Up

It was on-the-job training with a vengeance, but some guidance would have been helpful. Clearly the faculty felt that the clerical suit and our good intentions would compensate for our various ignorances and ineptitudes. I don't think they did.

Amazingly enough, as the next Wednesday rolled around, I again chose to go to General Hospital. I decided that if I couldn't face this challenge, I didn't belong in the seminary anyway. And I was probably right.

As luck would have it, I was assigned to a totally different ward, a tuberculosis ward for adolescent girls. They were mostly black, they were desperately bored, they were VERY casual in their attire, and they were delighted to see me. Particularly when they realized my embarrassment at their revealing hospital gowns. I concealed my response to them by turning bright red, probably the best moment by far in their week.

I was such a hit that they requested me by name, I returned to the ward, got to know the girls, got used to the glimpses of lovely black legs and breasts without turning red, and maybe did a little bit of good, at least in terms of lightening their burden of boredom.

George Nesbit

"You guys want to come to the music room and try something? I've got some music here." George Nesbit, one of the "older" guys in our class —he was in his early thirties—came up to us as we were standing around on the front steps. On this brilliant October afternoon, we found ourselves reluctant to mount the stairs and hit the books.

"Whoa, not me," said Kehoe. "I can't sing a note." I could confirm that from memory. He headed up the steps.

"Sure, why not?" I offered, my usual answer to any invitation. "I should tell you I'm not much of a music reader." That too, I could prove. I learned stuff by ear, singing or playing. Those funny marks on the page just distracted me.

"Let's go," George Baldino added, and Larry Spiece nodded and followed along.

In the music room, Nesbit pulled out a four part arrangement of *Lo, How a Rose Ere Blooming*, and handed them out.

"Any tenors here?" he said, hopefully.

"I'll try." Larry Spiece said modestly. He actually had a fine tenor voice.

Baldino got the bass part, I took the baritone, and George picked up the second tenor. Under his direction, we plowed through the lovely piece, George offering corrections in a cheerful but authoritative way. Right near the end, there's a 'suspension,' where the tenors maintain their note and the baritone and bass move. But I didn't move.

"Let's try it again," George said cheerfully. Again I didn't move.

"This time slowly, and I'll sing your part with you." George's tone was still cheerful, but much firmer. With George's big voice in my ear, I managed the move.

"I think I've got it." And indeed I did. George knew what he was doing. *Lo, How a Rose* sounded better and better, echoing in the big empty room in a satisfactory way.

I remained and fell into conversation with George Baldino, a black-haired and passionate partisan for all things Italian. George's family hailed from Ischia, a small fishing village in southern Italy.

"*Testa dura* (hard head! But, as you see, I have a Roman nose," George proclaimed. No way to deny that. As one thing led to another, he began extolling the virtues of the tenor Carlo Buti.

"The greatest Italian tenor of the twentieth century." *Pace* Caruso!

I expressed some doubts about this opinion. George held forth with great vigor, citing the fact that he and his family listened every Friday night to a radio broadcast featuring Buti, which held the rapt attention of Italian families all across the Northeast. That left me out.

George Baldino with the head of Dan O'Connor

Baldino went on to extol the virtues of ASL (American Sign Language) and ended up persuading me to engage in some studies of the art. I eventually got a little farther than in Hebrew, but that story comes much later.

A Glee Club is born!

Finally, Nesbit collected the music and we went off to our rooms, pleased with ourselves and the experience. We had no idea that George had determined to start a glee club. The next week after walks, a larger group of us were invited, slotted into voice groups, and handed *Lo, How a Rose*. Voila!, a glee club. And I already knew the baritone part! We agreed to meet regularly during evening Rec for glee club practice.

I hunted down George Nesbit one evening rec to find out how he had managed this.

"You've done this sort of thing before," I accused mockingly.

He smiled. "I've been directing the choir at our home church in Pittsfield for seven years." Aha!

Turns out that George had done lots of things, including a stint in the navy, acting as a travelling accompaniest on the piano, teaching school, and a couple of years at Notre Dame on the G.I. bill. He felt himself to be very old among the twenty-somethings that surrounded him. He used to warn me about going out without a hat. "Just wait till you get to be my age." He cautioned, seriously.

Despite his great age, ten years older than I, and a strong tendency to the conservative in theology, we became good friends, sharing memories of professors at Notre Dame, bemoaning our weakness in Latin, stuff like that.

"What did you teach in high school?" I asked once.

"English," he answered. "And I was strict."

"Would you mind reading a paper I'm writing for history? See if you pick up any errors?"

"I won't cut you any slack." George warned, looking at me professorially. Actually, I was very proud of the paper, a piece on feudalism in which I had done some real research. And I was proud of my writing too, for that matter. Confidently, I handed over the pages.

Later that night, I heard the paper slide under my door. I picked it up, looking for complimentary comments. What I saw was a mass of red marks, every page studded with them. I felt offended. I slid a stiff note back under George's door, requesting a face to face session.

We met the next evening; we argued every single mark; he won every argument. I was humbled. I went back and re-wrote the paper, even though word was that Bull Noonan didn't read them anyway.

I received my usual 87 for a grade.

Insiders and outsiders

Like every society, seminarians formed subgroups, real or perceived. The Paca Street grads, who had done the first two years of major seminary in Baltimore, represented about three quarters or more of our class. They knew the sulpecians; knew the system; had shared experiences of the Paca Street faculty and the odd, 160 year old building.

The rest of us shared our outsiderness. A group from the South; a group from the Midwest; a small handful who didn't fit any category. Naturally, I felt most comfortable with the midwesterners, particularly the three guys from the La Crosse, Wisconsin diocese, a mere hundred miles north of Illinois. Jack Melloh, Mike Braun and Mike McKenna talked right, acted friendly, knew of Rockford, knew nothing of Paca Street.

I saw Melloh a lot. He shared my love of singing and show business in particular; joining the Glee Club; trying out for the plays; helping to harass O'Connor.

The smart guys formed a sort of understood group, although we didn't always know who they were. Grades were posted only in the faculty council room, and you learned your marks from your Spiritual Director. Lest you became vain.

But somehow, the word got out. Ernie Kallenbach, a quiet and somewhat distant Paca street grad, had the rep of being the top grade getter.

"No wonder," someone commented bitterly, "He's a Sulp candidate."

"What's a Sulp candidate," I asked, although I could kind of guess.

"They sign on to join the Society; the bishop releases them up front; and they don't have to pay tuition." Clearly my informant knew of what he spoke.

"They're usually the top students; get the best grades, and no wonder." The speaker held the natural suspicion that the Sulp candidates got breaks that we didn't know about. Not that it would make sense for the Sulpecians to underchallenge their candidates. Of course, they knew about the suspicion and dealt with it as best they could.

Charlie MacKay led the Sulp pack. Smart, sardonic, direct, more than a little cynical about the system he was joining, MacKay could be counted on for candor and insight.

Bob Friday didn't seem a likely candidate. From the Pittsburg diocese, he was friendly, a great jock, didn't engage in theological dispute. But he would later become Rector of St. Mary's. Ed Allemand, a tenor in the Glee Club and a brilliant student, hailed from Sterling, Illinois. Technically a Rockford seminarian, he didn't seem to identify himself as such, hanging out with some Paca street friends.

My buddy, Jack Melloh, joined the Sulps during his second year, but quit before ordination. I don't remember him saying much about it. So who can tell? I never had the inclination.

Bull Noonan on the job

I never learned who selected the books for Spiritual Reading, which ranged from contemporary novels with Catholic themes to critical writing with a theological bent. When no announcements or issues required addressing by the Rector, we turned to the book at hand.

One evening, during an exceptional example of Spiritless Reading, one of my classmates was droning on from a novel set in the iron ore mining region of northern Michigan. We learned far more about the technology of ore extraction that we really needed to know.

Bull, as Assistant Rector subbing for Father Laubacher, sat stolidly at the desk as the reader, seated facing the student body, plowed ahead with the reading. Fatally, Bull began shutting his eyes, which stayed shut for longer and longer periods, until they were fast closed. His head began, slowly, slowly, to tip forward. His body followed until his chest rested against the front of the desk and his head hung forward, suspended about an inch above the surface of the desk. There it remained.

We stared at the top of Bull's head, transfixed. A low murmer ran through the room as more and more people recognised that Bull had fallen asleep. The reader, oblivious, came to the end of a chapter, then stopped, waiting for instructions to go ahead. Silence reigned, punctuated by chuckles and murmers. After about five minutes, the absence of sound penetrated Bull's consciousness. He woke up and, trying to cover up, raised his head very slowly and stared straight ahead. His face was suffused with red, and his daze was evident. We all waited.

Bull paused, knowing that something was supposed to be happening, but unable to remember what. He glanced over at the reader, who waited obediently, then blustered out, "Well?..." A solid laugh broke out, Bull grinned ruefully, then raised his hand to silence the audience. He turned again to the reader and said, "Continue," but the bell for dinner froze the moment.

That moment became one of the high points in Spiritual Reading, better than the time one of the readers mispronounced a word, referring to the "hot coals in a flaming brassiere." The Rector corrected him calmly before the laugh could take hold.

My own turn at Spiritual Reading would become, accidently, another of the high points, but that came much later.

Lend me a Tenor

Joseph Laderoute, a man of middle age, resplendent in tie and tails but very nervous, bowed at our applause, shifted around, rubbed his hands, cleared his throat repeatedly, finally nodded to his accompaniest and began. A Handel aria from the Messiah, *Comfort Ye My People*. His voice soared over the crowded prayer hall. We sat transfixed by the sound. At the conclusion, a moment of silence and then thunderous applause.

The tenor, clearly relieved and delighted, bowed repeatedly, then held up his hands for silence.

"Thank you; thank you," he said with feeling, "I was pretty nervous there." A little laughter.

"I've got a terrible cold; I didn't think I could sing at all." A little more laughter. He nodded to the piano player and began another aria. Brilliant!

Again the applause. Again the thanks. Again the hands. "I'm Joseph Laderoute," he announced, a bit shyly. From Canada." More applause.

"I used to be a seminarian." Big applause. "I have ten children." Huge applause. His timing, perfect. He had won the house completely. It's not clear to me exactly what we were applauding there.

Guests in the seminary turned out to be extremely rare. In fact, in my four years, Laderoute was the only performer. For the most part, we did our own thing.

Performances

Of course, we HAD to do our own thing. We didn't go out to the movies, or plays, or concerts, or anything. The alternative—do it ourselves. And the faculty encouraged this activity, again rationalizing that many of us might have to direct such activities in the parish.

Do-it-yourself didn't pose such a huge problem, either. Actually, the student body boasted considerable talent, both musical and dramatic. We found ourselves capable of of tremendous energy and great resourcefulness if provided the opportunity. In retrospect, I guess we had a lot of steam, physical and psychic, to let off.

The glee club developed an elaborate series of concerts, and even left the campus to perform on a couple of occasions.

The jazz band gave the occasional concert, but only in-house. Most notably, the drama club produced current Broadway-hits, despite the fact that we had only one sex available for casting. Imagination and considerable re-writing made up for our limitations.

For example, during my first year, the ambitious dramaturges of the third year class decided to present Jean Anouil's *The Lark*, a dramatic examination of the trial of Joan of Arc, this shortly after the triumphant Broadway production starring Julie Harris. The advantage: a large male cast, many of whom were priests and monks. We ought to be able to handle that.

The disadvantage, however, seemed extreme. The central character—inescapably a woman; admittedly, a woman dressed in armor during the whole first act. On the other hand, a large plot point in the play consisted of the monk's attempt to get Jeanne to abandon her armor and dress as a woman, which she does in the second act.

I Audition for a Part

I had an immediate connection to the production. Bert Fay, the Head Reader, was sittting at my table during the current rotation. Funny, engaging, snidely critical of the seminary system, he nonetheless intimidated as a high aesthete, who had seen everything, assessed everything and found most things wanting. As director of *The Lark*, he invited his tablemates to try out for parts.

Stagestruck as always, though unburdened by talent or experience, I showed up, game but nervous.

"Hello, uh…Jim, was it? Bert's mellifluous voice greeted me, a bit vaguely. "Did you want to read for something?" Clearly, much of the casting had already been accomplished.

He handed me the script; announcing, "Act II; Scene three. Read the part of Friar Albert."

I fumbled through the script, found the part, glanced through the scene. A Dominican monk, Friar Albert, attempts to comfort the emprisoned warrior in a transitional scene. Myself a member of the Third Order of St. Dominic, with a bit of facility in French, the part was made to order for me.

As the actors read the scene, I entered and spoke my opening line, "Jeanne!" which I pronounced "Gene."

"It's "Zhawng," Bert corrected. Of course.

I entered again. "Gene!"

Finally, Burt suggested, as gently as possible, that I find some other way to contribute to the production. I ended up writing some lyrics for a song the producers added as a transition.

The role of Jeanne was played, rather well, by a young Irish seminarian I remember only as Kevin. By the third act, the trial has ground to a halt, stymied in the face of Joan's innocence and deep faith. The interrogators find themselves at a loss. The Grand Inquisitor, presiding over the trial, elaborately robed and deferred to, startles the audience.

"I have not till now spoken." Up to this point merely set dressing, the Inquisitor resets the issues of the trial, and we realize that Joan is doomed. In my experience, one of the great theatrical moments, even after all these years.

The audience received the production thunderously. As I recall, every production got the same response, perhaps because no other source of entertainment existed within the walls.

Father Laubacher attended the performance and, by custom found a way to comment on the moral of the play and to praise every contributer individually. I found this a bit silly, but was inordinately pleased when the rector got to my name and said, "I see we have added a poet to the student body." This appellation produced a certain amount of jeering among my friends, but I lived it down.

Father Laubacher's best comment came following the next production, an incredibly long and taxing version of *Long Day's Journey Into Night*, Eugene O'Neill's unrelenting examination of the collapse and destruction of his own family.

As the audience waited, silent and exhausted, the Rector rose, paused and then said, "Well, I guess the moral of this play is 'God bless our happy home.'" Hit the bullseye on that one. We all dragged off to bed.

A Seminary Holiday

Like all schoolboys (I mean, we were all in our twenties or older, but schoolboys we were), we seminarians lived for holidays. Rare they were. Thanksgiving. Christmas. Major feasts. Founder's day.

On one memorable occasion, the Apostolic Delegate came to visit us. The AD represents the Pope in the country of his appointment. The main man! By the rules governing seminaries, He had the power to grant us a free day at his whim—a princely power and doubtless the origin of the privilege.

The delegate, whose mellifluous Italian name (Amaletto Cicognani, I believe) became a byword among us, rose at his farewell banquet, and cried in ringing and heavily accented tones, "I geeve you wan free day!" Enormous cheers. As the hall quieted, he added, "I geeve you TWO free days." Even more enormous cheers. The Delegate, obviously caught up in the spirit of the thing, cried out, "I geeve you T'REE free days."

Pandamonium ensued. Even the reciting of grace after meals served only to somewhat mute the buzz, which broke forth anew at the *Tu Autem*, the end of the grace. Speculation rampaged regarding the possibility of having the three days in a row.

"They'll never give us the three days," Frank Miller, the embittered one offered.

"They've GOT to." Charlie MacKay insisted, prepared to argue the case legally, if not Jesuitically. "The Delegate gave the days; the Faculty can't take them back."

At Spiritual Reading the next day, the Rector announced that, after a discussion with the faculty, the free days would be distributed over the next three years. We muttered and grumbled, but knew in our hearts that the Delegate had gotten carried away and that we should be satisfied with the one extra day. The rector announced the date of the free day so that we could make plans, and we settled down to that.

Our Nation's Capital: Art

As a new guy in town, so to speak, I had no idea of where to go or who to go with, but Bill Boyle, a sax player in the seminary band, came up to me shyly and asked if I might want to go to the National Gallery in Washington, an hour-long bus ride from Roland Park. I took him up on it.

Boyle, one of a small contingent from the (way) upstate NY Ogdensburg diocese, qualified as a strange bird. Pathologically shy, with a compulsive giggle when he was nervous, he was also a witty and keen observer of what was going on, and a brilliant, hard-swinging jazz sax player. I didn't belong on the same bandstand with him, jazz-wise. I think he focussed all his quirks and anxieties and intensities into his playing and it blew the mind, in the terminology of the time.

In any case, we got along ok, took the bus to DC—an hour away—and headed for the National Gallery. The hot exhibit at the time featured a retrospective of the works of Salvador Dali, climaxing with a full-room display of Dali's "Last Supper," a compendium of Dali's Spanish sensibility, humor, exquisite draftsmanship and irreverence. The piece was about 8' by 10' and confronted by an arc of about 20 people staring reverently at the work. This struck my funnybone immediately, and I told Boyle, "Follow me and play along." He nodded.

In those days of casual security and sporting the authority of our Roman collars, we strode confidently right up to the left-hand corner of the painting, where the brilliant, creased white tablecloth hung down to a well-stitched point. I pointed to the cloth, gesturing in a painterly way, and said, "See what I mean?"

Boyle nodded sagely and we turned and walked from the room without even glancing at the rest of the painting.

As we left the gallery, we turned and looked back through the arch. Sure enough, the whole group of viewers had bunched around the painted tablecloth and were peering intently at the place I had indicated.

I love art.

Thanksgiving with the Lieblers.

By rooming with Ed Kehoe, I became friends with Mark Liebler, another Ogdensburg seminarian and a passionate lover of music and art Mark, a genuine aesthete, had a sharp critical tongue and a pointed sense of humor. When I first met him, he introduced himself, a bit oddly, as MarKKK….. Liebler.

"Yeah," I said, a bit quizzically. "I've got it. "Mark Liebler."

He picked right up on it. "I hate it when people call me Kleibler," he explained.

"That happen a lot?" I asked, a bit snidely. I was not all that careful about people's names. Still amn't.

"Well, it does," Mark confirmed.

Not more than a week later, I was sitting in the Music room after dinner with Liebler and John Murdoch, a tall, intelligent, somewhat withdrawn type. Liebler, an enthusiastic talker, was describing in lengthy detail, a cartoon he had seen in the *New Yorker*. Murdoch and I were listening politely but a little impatiently, perhaps waiting to jump in.

And Murdoch did jump in. He launched into the description of a cartoon HE had seen. As he went on, it became clear that he was describing the same cartoon. Liebler took this as an elaborate form of mockery and said, bitterly, "Well, John, you could just have stopped me." He was clearly offended, rose and strode out of the room.

Murdoch was mystified. "What did I say?" he asked me.

"Well, John, you just described the same cartoon Mark was telling us about. He thinks you were mocking him."

"Oh, God," Murdoch, a great avoider of controversy, admitted that he couldn't hear Liebler well, picked up just the gist of what he was saying, and pretended to be listening.

"Well, you'll have to make it up to him." I said, neatly avoiding involvement in the task.

A Family Thanksgiving

But Liebler and I remained friends and, come Thanksgiving, Mark invited Kehoe and me to come with him to Washington, D.C., to have dinner with his brother and sister-in-law. Great deal for both of us. Kehoe lived too far away to go home and I didn't want to hustle dinner with my grandfather in DC. Connie Lynde had spent time and much money trying to make me into a young Republican attorney and was disappointed with my choice of seminary for graduate school. "Why rub it in," I thought.

Paul Liebler functioned as an assistant producer for a Washington television station—a glamorous if underpaid position—and his young wife, Mary Rose, had some other job. They welcomed the three of us into their small but friendly D.C. apartment.

In a burst of inspiration, I spotted a florist when we got off the bus, went in and bought a single long-stemmed red rose, for Mary Rose, you know. This obvious, even corny gesture made a huge hit with the young wife, and I made myself welcome at the Liebler's many times over the years.

The warmth and friendliness of our meal made me realize something of our isolation from this kind of emotional environment, but nothing I could do about it. That's the way it was.

We ate, we drank a bit, we listened to *The Piano Artistry of Jonathan Edwards*, a hilarious musical parody perpetrated by Paul Weston and Jo Stafford. Then we boarded the bus and wound our way back to the seminary.

Seminary Jazz

"We'd like the band to play for the Gaudeamus," said Father Laubacher, somewhat uncomfortably. The rector disliked any element that might not be fully under his control. "But no jazz!" he added, emphatically. We agreed enthusiastically, confident that the rector would not know jazz if he heard it.

The fifties witnessed the revival of Dixieland and the birth of "cool jazz" in response to the challenge of bebop. The 'beatnik' movement had immortalized the concept of 'cool' as an informed but unengaged (and implicitly superior) attitude. Ordinary folk were "square" or "straight." They didn't "dig." Of course, I wanted desperately to be cool, but never achieved it.

Straights feared jazz music, and maybe with some justification. "Jungle music," the crudest characterization, carried racial and sexual overtones. Jazz would strip off the constraints of civilized decorum and anarchy (and orgies) awaited. I regretfully report that this never happened at any of MY gigs. Clearly, it was something like this that Father Laubacher feared.

A Gaudeamus gig

Gaudeamus involved a celebratory meal on the occasion of the Feast of San Sulpice, the patron of the Order. Better food; fancier desserts; and we could talk. The only additional element would be the band. Essentially, a welcome break in the routine of silence and sermons.

One thing the rector seemed not to understand; we WERE a jazz band, fundamentally: in the tunes we chose; in the approach we took; in the way we played (for the most part.) If the rector wanted us, he was going to get jazz, even if he didn't think so. Or so we rationalized. Jazz for us had already become a 'cause.' We agreed to start with slow, quiet numbers, and work slowly up to more hard-driving stuff.

I got the word about the jazz band and knew that a Deacon named Fitzpatrick led the aggregation. I also knew that his major player, my friend and classmate, Bill Boyle, had left the seminary after one year, possibly due to the nervous giggle which he brought with him to interviews with the rector.

I approached Fitz during an evening rec period, my confidence exceeding my talent. I knew he needed a tenor sax player, even tho I was not in the same league with Boyle.

"What do you play," Fitz asked me, naturally. He struck me as a kind of fussy, schoolmarmish guy, far from my image of a jazzman.

"Tenor." I offered brazenly.

"Can you read?" Ouch.

"Well, kind of. I'm more used to reading clarinet music."

"It's the same key. It's the same music." Fitz said, looking at me oddly. Surely I must know that.

Although basically a clarinet player, I had acquired a shiny new tenor saxophone which I brought with me to the seminary my second year. On tenor, I was a barely marginal player, but I loved the big sound of the horn and I trusted my feel for jazz. I had a good ear and could get through pretty much any of the standards. I also knew that the jazz talents of the band members varied considerably.

Fitz's alto man, Cornelio Parado, played pretty well but had no jazz feel whatever. A sentimental Filipino with a Spanish heritage, his taste ran to the syrupy sweet love songs of the islands, and his solos oozed from his horn and turned every tune into a caramel.

Lean Leo Kelty played clarinet. A superior musician in every way, he made me grateful that I hadn't brought my own clarinet. I couldn't touch him. If we had a trumpet player, he doesn't spring to mind. Woodwind players don't like brass players, anyway. Too much power.

James "Fitz" Fitzpatrick was the leader; maybe HE was the trumpet player. I seem to remember him conducting the group with a baton. A jazz band? Not any jazz band I knew of.

Fitz sat us all down in the music room and handed out copies of Woody Herman's *Woodchopper's Ball*, a somewhat challenging 40's piece that I didn't know at all. I faked my way through it, gradually picking up on the tune and ignoring the funny looks that Fitz threw my way.

Finally, at the end of the practice, he said wanly, "Well, ok, O'Brien. I guess it will do. But work on it." I nodded, but I knew he had no place to go for another tenor man. I was in!

If Fitz' manner seemed fussy to me, it may well have gone a long way toward reassuring the rector that we wouldn't be playing "jungle music" and arousing inappropriate passions at the fete.

Gaudeamus swings!

Our plan for the Gaudeamus worked perfectly. We started with a familiar, mellow piece and received generous applause, both from the students and the faculty. Let's face it, any novelty was welcome in the normally serious and silent refectory. The music got faster, louder, and swung harder and we finished with a driving version of *Woodchopper's Ball*. Tumultuous applause and cheers. We had put one over on the Rector, and if he accused us of playing jazz, he could not withdraw the unanimous response of the audience.

The Nameless Five: Paul Santyr—drums; Neil Parado—alto; Jim O'Brien—tenor; Leo Kelty—clarinet; John Davis—piano

But the rector had it right in a deeper sense. Jazz is not "jungle music" but it is rebel music—spontaneous, improvisational, challenging of rules, difficult to codify, fundamentally anti-organizational. If was always *my* music, long before I understood its nature. I was never a very good musician, by lack of discipline or lack of practice, or lack of talent, I don't want to know. But I was always a jazz man, and will always be, for better and for worse.

Seminary Sports

Whatever the rationale, and I'm sure there was one, a lotta sports were played at St. Mary's. *Mens sana in corpore sano.* (Sound mind in a sound body.) Hey, anything in Latin should be ok. Buncha guys with excess energy; competitive spirit; working off testosterone. (Actually, we didn't do a lot of talk about testosterone in the fifties, come to think of it.) Maybe we were just engaged in the sublimation of sexual desire. (There was no talk of that at all!)

Seminary games followed the seasons in sports. Football dominated the front lawn in fall, then segued into basketball on our court. We had major leagues; minor leagues; and scrubs (touch football). That's where I belonged.

What our sports leagues lacked and dearly needed—a referee. In a highly regimented masculine society, shot through with civility and Christian civility at that, where could we go with our aggressions? The arena! Even the scrub league touch football got rough.

I Take My Shot

I lined up across from Leon Kasprzak, a huge, serious, friendly, clumsy Pole, noted for his ability to memorize large hunks of theology texts in Latin, which gave him a big edge in Father Dukehart's classes.

As the ball was snapped, I slammed into Leon, bouncing off without effect, then whirled, ran past him and waved my arms for the ball. Leon stumbled after me, waving his long arms which he smashed down on me as I muffed the pass. I crashed to the ground, pride and body equally bruised.

"Sorry." said Leon, sincerely.

"It's supposed to be TOUCH football, Leon." I protested bitterly.

"I was just touching you." Leon explained.

"Right." I muttered. "It's OK." I resolved to keep my distance from Leon.

I didn't get the one-wall handball courts familiar to the neighborhoods of New York and other major cities. I had played with enthusiasm if not skill at Notre Dame, in tank courts. St. Mary's courts had one concrete wall and a kind of angle corner at each end. A game for muscle rather than finesse. I stayed the heck away, for the most part.

Tennis? Another matter. Despite an indifferent and erratic game, I loved the sport and substituted hard running and enthusiasm for my inability to make shots. All about exercise anyway, right, and getting out those ya yas.

Once, I enviegled Dan O'Connor into a game, possibly in the context of some tournament. O'Connor, a serious player, hit all the strokes well and found himself embarrassed by my shambling, scrambling game. Although he beat me easily, my erratic play brought down the quality of his game 'til we ended at the bell.

"Last time I'll play you, O'Brien," O'Connor muttered at the net, while properly shaking my hand. "You're ruining my game."

"That's good enough for me, Dan." I offered in response.

Later in the fall, basketball started, another game for which I possessed enthusiasm but no ability. Tom Dempsey, lean, athletic, and quickly acknowledged as a top player, encouraged me to come out. One game taught me all I needed to know. Short, slow and timid, I had no intention of venturing into the thicket of flying elbows and knees which marked the path to the basket.

"Drive, OB!" Dempsey shouted, "Take it to the hoop."

No way. I passed off or fired from the outside and decided to find less risky recreation.

Why did the faculty permit, even encourage all these incredibly unsupervised and often risky games? The obvious rationale—some of us would find ourselves unwitting coaches for grade school teams when the pastor found himself unwilling to pay for a layman coach.

A deeper and unspoken reason: priests should learn to recreate with one another and avoid involvement with the laity.

Wrapping it up.

I had found a safe place! I could handle the religious life; the rigid schedule; the classes; the Latin, even. I had friends; I had activities; I had a sense of accomplishment and purpose, if vague. We used to joke at Notre Dame, "I found a home under the dome!" Something like that had happened at St. Mary's, too.

And I had terrific learnings. Norris' class gave me a new, deep, scripture-based understanding of the Church and its function in the world that my previous sixteen years of Catholic education and practice had not afforded me. Dannemiller's scripture class taught me that this ancient, complex, 'holy-history' which we called The Bible could be made sense of. No more relying on "well, it's a mystery."

In a word, I had acquired a vision. A rich, holistic, multi-dimensional vision of a vast community, stretching across the world and across time. I felt a sense of coming-together which gave my studies a sense of purpose. Clearly I had much to learn, but I felt the learning happening.

4

A Summer in Sterling

Leading the Congregation

I took my place at the commentator's microphone, clutching a copy of the new hymnbook and wishing to God (so to speak) that I could get out of this. The congregation, about a hundred people, almost filled the small church, Sacred Heart in Sterling, Illinois, but not because I was there. They had come for Sunday Mass, as they had done all their lives, and they expected it to be the same as it had been for all their lives.

I must have presented a piteous sight. Small, skinny, topped by a shock of unruly brown hair, and looking maybe sixteen, robed in cassock and surplice like an eighth grade altar server, I was about as far from a confident congregation leader as could be imagined.

"Good morning," I offered lamely. No response. "I'm the seminarian who, uh.......well, Father Bonnike (shift the blame, quick) asked me to teach you a hymn from the new hymnal." I could feel my voice shaking.

"Turn to page 41. *Praise ye the Lord.*" Silent but obedient, the people, many of them members for generations, took up the new books, and turned to the proper page.

"I'll sing it through once, then we'll all sing it through together." (I desperately hoped.) I liked to sing, but not as soloist or songleader. But I could hardly complain. I had done this to myself.

Seminary Summers

Diocesan seminarians followed a typical college schedule: Christmas vacation; semester break; summers off. At this period, Bishops rarely required anything of their almost-employees. Having, in effect, no home in Elgin, I had no connections for living or setting up a summer job.

To my rescue came Father Frank Bonnike, a friend and former neighbor of mine, now a young priest and a diocesan hotshot, always out front on every issue, experienced and educated beyond most of his contemporaries, and deeply committed to pastoral work rather than the career ladder of the chancery office.

Offered the chance to act as the bishop's personal secretary—a fast track to promotion for a young priest—Bonnike refused, opting for any alternative. The bishop was not pleased, but determined to make good use of Bonnike's competence and 'can do' spirit.

Frank had been appointed pastor of a very small German national parish in Sterling, Illinois, and also superintendant of a not-yet-built central Catholic high school. The "central Catholic high school movement" if it can be called such, involved building an area school to serve a number of neighboring parishes.

The 'central school' concept had a number of advantages from the point of view of the heirarchy. It focused church energy on a broader level than the local parishes, forcing the pastors to yield some of their autonomy. It provided a goal for fund-raising, and a chance to break through the minimalist donation patterns of the previous Depression-scarred generation. Finally, the central high school might provide a source of vocations to the priesthood and religious life.

The movement also fit in with Bishop Loras Lane's plans to rise in the heirarchy of the American Church. At one time, the second youngest bishop in the U.S. (after John Cardinal Wright of Pittsburg), Lane's ambitions were not to be realized for whatever reason or for no particular reason. He would die, still a young man, as bishop of Rockford.

Anyway, I responded positively to Bonnike's invite and arrived in Sterling, a small city in northwestern Illinois, filled with untested pastoral notions and no ministerial skills. In 1958, the RC church stirred uneasily beneath the Church's business-as-usual operation. The need for change was stirring in the wind, to coin a phrase. The laity, no longer working-class immigrants with little education, were beginning, here and there, to challenge the previously unquestioned authority of their clergy.

A Time of Change

Beyond the Church, young people across the world chafed against the restrictions of parents and custom. Rock and roll happened. *Blackboard Jungle* (1955); and *Rebel Without a Cause* (1955) offered vivid images of rebellion. Elvis (1955) happened. Jack Kerouak's *On the Road* (1957) became the bible of the disaffected. The stirring civil rights movement, and the vivid songs of the folkies spoke tellingly of injustice and, by implication, of the failure of the adult generation.

Bored with the cold war, and the communist paranoia of the fifties, frustrated by the complacency of the suburbs and fueled by the affluence of the nations, a kind of cultural revolution was breaking out across the Western World among the younger generation, later spreading to the USSR, China, and Japan. In the U.S., the so-called baby-boom generation was just hitting adolescence.

We seminarians, born in the pre-war thirties, nevertheless found ourselves caught up in this spirit, if somewhat unconsciously. Well, some of us! Lots of guys opposed significant change, opting to belong to the 'good soldier' authoritarian model of the clergy most of them had grown up with.

But not I! Things couldn't change fast enough. Right now was already too late.

I can't say that I found small-town Sterling exactly eager for the new things. These social movements seemed to occur first on the coasts and in the big cities, and spread slowly slowly across the nation. But something was going on, and I wanted to be a part of it.

Active Participation

In the pre-Vatican II Church, "active participation" served as the shorthand buzzphrase marking the "with-it" young clergyman. In practice, this meant encouraging (or forcing, from another point of view) churchgoers to involve themselves in the liturgy by answering responses and singing hymns during Mass. It's hard to imagine how silent our churchs had been other than at Christmas and Easter, and the crowning of Mary services in May. Liturgy was the clergy's job; the people's job was to BE there.

Catholics that I knew didn't like active participation for the most part, but we young activists knew we were right, and we used our presumed authority of the pulpit (and amplifying system) to push our opinions on our passive congregations. The fact that we disapproved of that autocratic style didn't seem to bother us that much. No voting in the Catholic Church!

So I arrived in the tiny parish—about 90 families, as I recall—preaching the word of 'active participation' to Father Bonnike, though I don't recall his asking. Probably amused at my enthusiasm and always up for something new, Bonnike replied cheerfully, "Let's do it! You can start teaching the congregations the new hymns on Sunday."

Singing in Church

My blood quickly ran cold, my enthusiasms drained away, cautions emerged unbidden. "No, no," I insisted, "You have to prepare the congregations first; explain what's happening; show them the background in scripture and history. At least ten weeks of sermons; there are outlines available."

"I don't need any outlines," Bonnike replied coolly. "I've been involved with the liturgical movement for years." I had no reply to this. "Tell you what I'll do," he continued firmly. "I'll preach about participation for three weeks and then you'll start." The bargaining had ended.

The very fact that I, a green first-year theologian, could argue with the pastor showed what an a-typical situation I had. Assistant pastors dared raise little objection to the pronouncements of a pastor, and could offer suggestions about parish operations in only the most tentative way. Of course, Bonnike felt no threat from me.

The next Sunday, as promised, Frank began to introduce the idea of participation. Starting with a vast historical overview, stretching back to the apostles, he described the evolution of the liturgy during the first few centuries of the Church, and parish life in the dark ages. I could plainly see that the series would never get to the present.

Suddenly, it was my turn. Frank informed me that next Sunday, I would march out before this silent and (presumably) stubborn congregation of elderly folk of Germanic extraction, who barely knew me and probably cared less, and teach them to sing hymns they had never heard. My perception anyway.

Now, here I was!

As I made my trembling way through the hymn, the congregation joined in, indeed with some vigor. I'm sure they felt pity, or possibly they feared that I would simply die right before their eyes. In any case, something worked! By the end of the Mass, the congregation was responding with conviction and I had overcome the worst case of liturgical jitters in modern history.

By the time of the late Mass that morning, I felt confident, even looking forward to performing. Because, though I had always been desperately shy and lacking in self-confidence, at the same time I was a natural show-off who loved attention. However contradictory this may sound, it's really quite common, as you may find by reading the biographies of professional actors and performers. I must also add that I didn't know this about myself until many years later.

The Rectory Household.

In addition to the pastor, Sacred Heart Rectory boarded a housekeeper, Agnes Mierzwa, an elderly refugee from WWII who taught me all the German I know—at least twenty words. Agnes had a room off the kitchen, maybe a small apartment for all I know. I had the guest room at the head of the stairs. Father Bonnike and I shared the bathroom in the hall.

Housekeepers! A parish could barely function without one. The rectory, tyically a residence for the priests of the parish, an instruction center and an office, required a sense of order and continuity. Also cooking, cleaning and dusting.

As female co-workers of the celibate clergy, housekeepers normally were expected to have reached a certain age, and to present themselves as pious, quiet, receding individuals who would cause no talk. Ideally, they were widowed, thus experienced in dealing with the male psyche. Housekeepers served variously as cooks, cleaners, butlers. Also surrogate mothers, surrogate wives and mistresses, surrogate siblings, and ears to the parish. I doubt that any of these latter functions had been, or could be explained to them.

Some housekeepers violated these requirements and DID cause talk, but not Agnes. A woman of keen intelligence and good humor, she performed ideally, handling both the Bonnike ego and the O'Brien post-adolescence without damaging our frail sensibilities.

"*Zerstreuter Professor,*" (scattered professor) she called me, referring both to my penchant for knowing everything or acting as if I did, combined with my highly disorganized mind and life.

"*Das Menchens ville ist seine Himmelright.*" she would say, without correcting my spelling. "A man's will is his heaven." A succinct grasp of the male ego, key for dealing with the clergy. Why fight Mother Nature?

And Agnes got along with Leona, another key to the smooth operation of the rectory.

During the day, Leona Regan Jenkins, the parish secretary, presided over the small office off the front hall. Leona had an older brother who was a priest in the diocese and she retained a healthy disrespect for the clergy, whom she regarded with considerable justification as overgrown boys pretending to be men. Bright, competent, and borderline sarcastic, Leona wouldn't let us get away with any pomposities, or other ego trips, from the bishop on down.

The four of us formed the Sacred Heart "team." There must have been someone doing the janitor work, but I have no memory of that person. Maybe Agnes did it, but I don't think so.

Front Man

"You're going to visit the Evangelical Baptist Church tonight." Frank announced cheerfully one morning.

"Me?" I answered, my years of education and experience deserting me in an instant. Though I was 24 years old, I had been in a Protestant church perhaps twice in my life, both times on the occasion of funerals. I had perceived the experience as exciting and dangerous, although I had no idea what the threat might be. A sudden conversion, perhaps?

"The Evangelicals are putting on a weekend revival meeting, and I want you to be there. Their main speaker is a man who claims to be a fallen-away Catholic priest. A lot of these guys are phonies, and I want you to see if he's the real thing."

Appalled, I had visions of myself standing up in the midst of a hostile congregation, pointing a quivering finger at the imposter and accusing him of........well, what? Imposturing?

"What am I supposed to do?" I stalled, already knowing that Frank wouldn't back off. He was nothing if not a confronter.

"Don't do anything," Frank said, easing my mind just a tiny bit. "Just check him out and see if he's a fake. It'll be real obvious. Then let me know, and I'll go and expose him. The evangelicals have a speaker's bureau of these guys, and they go around bashing the Church and stirring up anti-Catholic feeling. There's enough of that around Sterling without a rally."

A Spy in the House of God

I felt only the tiniest bit relieved that I would not have to make a scene, but I felt sneaky and fake, not unfamiliar feelings, but I couldn't see a way out. I resigned myself to the mission.

That evening, "disguised" in slacks and a checked shirt, I showed up at the small, neat church, entered, smiling vaguely and obliquely and avoiding anyone's gaze, lest I be drawn into conversation. My disguise was quite pointless, it soon became clear. I'm sure the entire audience belonged to the congregation. If I had been wearing a neon propeller beanie, I couldn't have been more conspicuous.

We sang a hymn. I fumbled through the unfamiliar hymnbook, fearing that I might incur an automatic excommunication for "participating in Protestant worship," a post-Tridentine (Council of Trent: 1545-1563) prescription of the *Code of Canon Law*. Perhaps mumbling the words or leaving some out or the high purpose of my mission would protect me from the sanction. I knew just enough about Canon Law to be mindlessly fearful.

The pastor offered a prayer, then introduced the speaker, claiming him to be a former Benedictine priest, and jumbling up some of his supposed credentials. I waited, eagerly I'm afraid, to find out if he was a fake.

But no, it was quickly clear to me that his story was real, personal, painful, having largely to do with the difficulty of accepting the rule of celibacy. In a word, he had fallen in love.

The lack of anti-Catholic rhetoric clearly troubled both the pastor and the congregation. Clearly the former priest felt proud of his ancient order of St. Benedict and his priestly ministry. He missed many aspects of the priesthood, and said so. Not what the congregation had come to hear.

The pastor went and murmured in the former priest's ear. He nodded, turned over some pages and embarked on some standard Catholic-bashing material, the corruption of the papacy (drawn from the Renaissance, the Medici popes and that whole crowd), the sexual orgies in the convents (how did I miss out on that?), the sale of relics and indulgences. For a contemporary audience the material was almost patently absurd, given the famous asceticism of Pius XII and the generally Calvinistic tone of American Catholicism in the mid-twentieth century. The speaker was clearly uncomfortable with this canned material, and the congregation disappointed.

After another hymn, the pastor took over the pulpit to make his appeal for conversion. Since I was the only non-member present. the appeal, while general in terms, was clearly aimed directly at me. I squirmed and looked down and prayed for the pitch to come to an end, as it finally did. As the service ended, I was surrounded by welcoming faces who wanted to seduce me with cookies and decaf coffee. Smiling and nodding, I slid through the crowd and, almost running, made it to my car and the hell out of there.

I reported to Father Bonnike that the man was clearly a former priest. Frank seemed disappointed. He obviously wanted to confront the man and expose him in front of the congregation, as he had done on some previous occasion. But no such drama would happen. Bonnike asked me if I had confronted the man myself, but didn't hold me to his own standards.

I felt both relieved from the situation and disappointed in my own performance. So it goes.

A Certain Level of Sophistication

I did have a seminary classmate in Sterling, but I scarcely knew Ed Allemand, nor he I. A Sulpecian candidate, we Rockford seminarians didn't think of him as one of "us." Quiet, reserved, intelligent and gifted, he moved with a different group at St. Mary's. During his time at Paca Street, he had been released to study keyboard at the Prestigious Peabody Institute in Baltimore. He played classical piano and church organ with a competence beyond my imagining.

Despite our differences, in the cultural isolation of Sterling we had our seminarian status in common, and we began to share some free time.

I Try to Buy a Bus

"I want you to drive down to St. Louis and buy a bus." Father Frank intended to startle me, and I was determined not to react.

"OK," I answered, "Today?"

"I think tomorrow will be OK," Bonnike answered, just a shade disappointed. "The Air Force is having a sale on used school buses. Forty two dollars! Even if they're in pretty bad shape, for that price they're worth fixing up."

It sounded like a dubious proposition to me, but who was I to refuse a trip to St. Louis, or anywhere, for that matter. A man for the road.

"You'll take my car," Bonnike continued, "get another driver. One of you can drive the bus back, the other can drive my car back. Maybe Allemand would go down with you."

I called my classmate, with whom I had grown friendly in the isolation of Sterling, and he agreed with alacrity, finding the summer as slow-going as I was.

We departed early the next day, armed with cash and certificates from Bonnike, indicating that we represented Newman Catholic High School and were authorized to act in its name.

Got to St. Louis about 1:30 p.m., called then drove to the airforce base. A sergeant showed me a long line of busses. They looked pretty good, their khaki paint gleaming dully in the sunshine. I climbed aboard, attempted to start one. Nothing.

"They got no engines," the sergeant commented incisively. "For forty-two bucks, you don't get an engine."

I called Bonnike, he said to forget it, enjoy the evening in St. Louis, come home.

Allemand and I headed for a cheap motel. Ed intended to visit a friend at Webster College. After a morning of typical St. Louis heat and humidity, I couldn't wait to get into the pool. Alone in the small room, I suited up, leaped into the air in anticipation and smashed my head into the light fixture.

Cascades of glass showered down, followed by cascades of blood. I made my way to the bathroom, wadded roll after roll of toilet paper, finally stanched the flow, cleaned up the mess, and was sitting on the end of the bed, pale and trembly, when Allemand returned.

"You look nice and cool." he commented, assuming that I had been swimming.

"Oh, yeah," I sighed, not wanting to get into it.

We got downtown about eight p.m. and discovered that St. Louis had closed for the night. Found a meal in a hotel coffee shop and came back to the motel. After staring at the grainy black-and-white TV for a bit, Allemand challenged me to a pillow fight.

I jumped at the chance. I had plenty of experience in pillow-fighting from my boys camp days, and I was bursting with frustrated energy. We siezed our pillows and began to whale away.

Or I did. But something was wrong. Allemand's reprisals seemed more flirtatious than aggressive. The conflict trailed away in embarrassment. I didn't know what had happened, and didn't want to discuss it. The moment passed. We went to sleep and took off for Sterling the next day. Nothing more was said, but apparently, I had failed some sort of test.

The CCD First Communion Class

In my day, that is, the forties, "real" Catholics went to Catholic schools; the "others" went to public schools and got a "Sunday school" version of the Baltimore Catechism, typically on Saturday morning. "Sunday School" we understood to mean "Protestant Bible Studies."

Sacred Heart parish had no school; therefore the parish children either went to St. Mary's school or to the CCD (Confraternity of Chriistian Doctrine) classes taught by the local nuns. I got the assignment to prepare our children for First Holy Communion. This I could handle. For once, I had a congregation more intimidated of me than I of them.

Our own preparation for Communion involved many stories from the nuns which illustrated the supernatural power of the Eucharist—the Real Presence of Jesus. We were taught never to chew the wafer, which was received on the tongue. Indeed, the teeth were not even to touch the wafer. Under NO circumstances were we to handle the wafer, or take it out of the mouth. Sister Francesca, our second grade teacher, spoke vividly of the consequences.

"One little girl took the host from her mouth and wrapped it in her handkerchief to take it home," Sister whispered in an awe-filled tone. "When she unwrapped it, the host had turned to blood." Yipes! We didn't question the source of this information; nor were we encouraged to experiment.

At the end of the First Communion ceremony, we were to be "enrolled" in the Scapular, a small cloth medallion worn over the shoulders—hence the name. My seven-year-old mind siezed upon the word "enrolled" and I visualized the priest somehow rolling the entire class in some huge sacramental blanket. When, at the end of the Mass, Father Ouimet passed down the line, merely touching our shoulder with the scapular, I confess to a sense of letdown.

I don't think we did the "enrolling" ceremony at Sacred Heart and, needless to say, I did not find it necessary to beef up my instructions with magical stories of very dubious authenticity. The whole event went well, as the picture seems to prove.

The Rev. Mr. O'Brien with his First Communion flock.

Great Books!

Despite the ocasional assignment, I didn't have a lot to do in Sterling. I hardly knew anyone other than Allemand. Of course, I could always study, and I did a little of that, but Father Bonnike was an activist, always on the go, and that's what I wanted to be. But I didn't have any place TO go, and nothing to do when I got there. I found myself sitting in the church hall, trying to learn to play *Till There Was You* on the battered old piano. It had little to do with music OR ministry. But at dinner that evening, Frank offered me an exciting opportunity.

"How'd you like to co-chair a Great Books program for high school students?" The offer surprised me a bit, "but hey," I thought immodestly, "who better?" After all, I had majored in philosophy, had even read at least two or three of the Great Books. I once attended an extensive presentation about the series conducted by Mortimer Adler, a co-founder of the Great Books program.

"A Catholic group?" I asked. Some of the Great Books would present ideas a bit, shall we say, "advanced" for young RC kids.

"No, it's open to anyone," Frank replied, "but some of our kids from Newman High will be taking the class. It's being run by a student from Shimer College named Reuben Chapman. He's bright and enthusiastic, but I'm not sure about his ideas. I agreed to co-sponsor the program provided you could sit in and provide some balance."

Flattered, it didn't bother me that Frank had clearly presumed my answer. And he was right. Itching for something to do, for contact with some younger people, for a chance to flaunt my learning, I showed up enthusiastically for the first session, introduced myself around, and was determined to be open and democratic, not trying to take over the show. Good thing!

A Gateway to the Sixties!

Reuben turned out to be super-smart, well-educated, charismatic, passionate, and ultra-left. He provided my introduction to the coming Sixties and what we came to think of as a cultural revolution. Despite what I saw as my superior background, Reuben dominated the discussion and easily dismissed my unconvincing arguments for the Church's positions on, for example, the rights of censorship (which I didn't believe myself).

In my heart of hearts, I found myself in complete agreement with Reuben in his demands for justice, for reform in society, for multiple sources of truth, for listening to the voices of "the people," which obviously meant "young people"—that is, US.

The sessions quickly moved from the classroom to Reuben's pad, where he began playing the records of the folk movement, stuff you couldn't hear on the radio anywhere. Pete Seeger, Paul Robeson, Robert Johnson, The

Weavers, Odetta, some scraggy-voiced young "singer" called Dylan, the clarion voice of Joan Baez, and so on. A devotee of white-bread, middle-of-the-road radio, I had never heard of this stuff. Blown away, as we used to say, I borrowed a bunch of the records and taped them on my bulky reel-to-reel tape recorder, bought secondhand years earlier at Notre Dame. (I still have those tapes, nearly fifty years later.)

One of the class members, Susan, a pretty young Lutheran girl, the smartest in the group, seemed somewhat troubled by the cult response to Reuben. Dark, slim, terribly intense and serious, she cared deeply about the issues Reuben raised. Her passion came off as highly attractive, and I was attracted, but not too seriously. I mean, I was in no position to put on any moves, even if I had any moves.

The Lundstroms

Susan looked to me to provide some sort of alternative to all Reuben's ultra-liberalism, despite the fact that I myself was quickly moving in that direction. We didn't talk much to each other at the group sessions, but she must have mentioned me to her father, because he called the rectory and talked to Father Bonnike about my visiting them at the house.

I was dumbfounded, but pleased. I said nothing. I couldn't believe that Frank would go along with it. But he did. Perhaps he thought me impervious to female charms. Perhaps he thought I was harmless. Perhaps he didn't think about it at all.

Bob Lundstrom, Susan's father and a florist by trade, saw himself as something of a rogue intellectual, a self-taught astronomer and classicist. In me, he hoped to find both an intellectual friend for himself and, possibly, an appropriate mate for his young daughter. A religious skeptic, he nonetheless approved of young ministers and their dedication, and enjoyed a debate on religious subjects, possibly over a glass of scotch or two. Why he may have thought that a Roman Catholic seminarian, destined for the priesthood and a life of celibacy, might prove a likely partner for Susan, I'll never know.

In any case, Bob set up a couple of awkward date-like situations which Susan and I survived, despite their obvious artificiality. In fact, the setups were so odd that we managed a candid talk about them.

"I have the feeling that your father is trying to fix us up." I finally said to Susan as we walked along the dark summer streets of Sterling one night. It was a staggering burst of candor from me, made possible only by her own total sincerity and seriousness.

"I know," she said, "and I don't know what to do about it. I've told him that I'm not interested in boys......I mean, well, you're not a boy, but, well, you know what I mean."

I did and didn't. I was perfectly aware that there was no sexual chemistry between us. However, it never occurred to me that she might be a lesbian, a word and a concept so unthinkable in those days that I, well..., didn't think it. I only knew that we weren't connecting in a way that I normally connected with young women (a connection which I vigorously, even fearfully, suppressed.)

"I'm not trying to say that I don't like you," Susan went on, "Because I do like you, but not in that way." She trailed off embarrassed, but I understood that this little, odd, abortive relationship was coming to an appropriate end, to the disappointment only of Bob Lundstrom.

He didn't take it hard, though. He gave me a remarkable going-away present, a translation of a late Latin classic, *The Golden Ass of Apuleus*, printed and bound in the 19th century, and probably of some value. I carried it around with me for years, but I don't know where it is now.

At any rate, the summer over, I returned to St. Mary's, Susan went off to college, and the relationship ended, or so I thought.

Wrapping it up

My months at Sacred Heart in Sterling had given me a privileged taste of rectory living, a chance to perform before a congregation, some revealing interactions, some contacts with priests as one of them, sorta. I had also learned some uncomfortable things about myself: an incapacitating shyness; an inability to study without a specific assignment; a huge cultural lacuna in the developing movements for social justice. And a continuing attraction to and fascination with women! Would ordination magically take care of that? I had to hope so.

1958–9

"The times, they are a-changin'................"

—*Bob Dylan*

5

Second Year

Progress in the seminary, and in clerical rank, was marked by a succession of steps: Tonsure, (clipping of the hair) as a mark of entering the clerical state; Four Minor Orders: (Exorcist, Acolyte, Lector, and Porter,) which conferred certain limited powers and ceremonial functions. Lectors, for example, were empowered to bless bread; Exorcists—to drive out demons (although the actual exercise of this power was very strictly controlled by the local Bishop and never performed by minor clerics.) Most seminarians, after being observed for at least two years, were admitted to Tonsure and Minor Orders at the beginning of their theological study. Those who had been denied Orders ("clipped"), and those who entered the seminary late, had Orders conferred at the end of the first or second year.

Changing the Guard

As an outsider I was not eligible for orders until the end of second year, so that the faculty could give me a good scrutinizing. As I've mentioned, they must have taken my clueless violations of the rules as 'typical' of one coming straight from 'the world,' so I never got called in for a talk. We called that "getting tailed." I never knew why.

The faculty had changed significantly over the summer. Father Laubacher, after fourteen years of demanding and dedicated service, stepped down as Rector and his second-in-command, Father Eugene Van Antwerp, took over.

Van represented a huge change in personality and, inevitably, in tone. Friendly, approachable, open, Van had served for years as a military chaplain in the Navy. Notably, he had the bad fortune to be serving aboard the

Navy's battleship Missouri when it became stuck in the mud for three weeks offshore of Norfolk, its home harbor. A period of singular embarrassment for the Navy, it must as well have been a hard period for the chaplain aboard the stricken ship, but Van never spoke about it.

Even more notably, Van acquired a Purple Heart in Korea for a shrapnel wound which led to his nickname, Brass Ass. No one asked him about it, and he didn't volunteer any information. Rec periods often found him on the one-wall handball courts where he played a powerful game with enthusiasm.

Van announced no major changes in the Rule, no modifications in the schedule, but tiny cracks in our isolation began appearing. And the tone of high seriousness with which Laubacher conducted himself just didn't fit Van. The pressure eased, and we felt good about it.

Another change affected us even more directly. After repeated clashes with our class and with the now-departed rector, Father Ben Selner had been moved to the less-prestigious Sulpecian house at Catholic University.

In My Room

For the first time in my academic life, I had my own room. As an only child I always had my own room, but as a student, I had always chosen roommates, considering it an important part of my education. And I was right.

But now, I had a tiny kingdom all to myself. I could arrange the desk, the chair, the lamp, the bureau, the bookcase and the single bed any way I wanted, constrained only by the long narrow room. No problem with the TV, the radio, the stereo, the refrigerator, the wet bar, the multiple furnishings of the contemporary college dorm room. I didn't have those and neither did anyone else.

After careful thought, I left every piece of furniture exactly where I found it. Looked good to me. I actually liked the spartan simplicity of the room.

Feeling More Confident

As I surveyed my kingdom, I experienced the to me unfamiliar feeling that I belonged. My summer in Sterling, despite a very uneven performance, had given me a sense that I was on the right track, and farther down that track than lots of my classmates. I felt that I should share these "insights" with my bishop, and headed for my portable Smith Corona, almost a knee-jerk reaction for me.

In addition to recommending a similar experience for all Rockford seminarians, I took occasion to invite Bishop Lane to direct my future studies on a higher path. I had managed to achieve good grades (though not top grades) the first year and saw the possibility of studying for an advanced degree in theology.

"I could add Hebrew or Greek to my class schedule this spring," I pointed out to the Bishop, "which would make me eligible to receive the STB (Bachelorate in Sacred Theology) at the end of my third year." I clearly implied my capacity to handle the additional load successfully, and I didn't mention Miles' class in Hebrew.

"Or I could add Spanish to my schedule, which would be useful in a pastoral ministry." I chatted on about my observations about the growing hispanic population in Sterling, fully aware that Bishop Lane had begun his clerical career teaching Spanish at Loras College in Dubuque. My openness to direction, my concern with my future ministry, my flexibilty, my potential. What a guy!

I received a reply from Monsignor Louis Franey, the Vicar General (*Numero Dos*) of the diocese, expressing Bishop Lane's wish that I study Spanish. Disappointed not to be directed to the theology degree, and disappointed that I had not heard directly from the bishop, I figured, "Hey, I can do them both. Why not?" I signed up for Hebrew for the spring term, figuring that I'd just stick in the Spanish later, closer to ordination. As it turned out, my reach exceeded my grasp, particularly my grasp of Hebrew!

Getting a Pet, Quite Briefly.

As I said, I liked my single room, but it began to feel lonely. My own company grew too familiar, evening after evening. A solution presented itself. A pet.

We're not talking your dog, your cat, your bird, even. These possibilities were too unthinkable even to be mentioned in the Rule. But one day, walking by the tennis courts, I spotted a huge praying mantis, a full five inches in length—motionless, waiting for prey.

I found a paper bag in the bushes, popped it over the mantis and scurried back to the room. I dumped it out onto my desk blotter, where the mantis righted itself, raised up and surveyed the scene. I couldn't tell if it regarded my presence or not.

The mantis began to crawl along the desk, probably hunting for insects, and I realized that I would have to constrain it. I fashioned a kind of lasso from string and, careful of the beast's powerful jaws, slipped the string around the mantis' thorax, drew it tight, and fastened the other end to my lamp. The bell rang and I rushed off to class, feeling oddly one-up on my petless classmates.

After dinner, I fed the mantis a small piece of ham secreted from dinner. It didn't seem particularly pleased with the dead meat, doubtless preferring to pick and chose its own fare. Too bad.

For bedtime, I extended the string and placed the mantis on the floor beneath my bed. I didn't want it springing onto my head and taking a bite of live meat. I turned off the light and hopped into bed from a distance, singularly aware of my toes. As the room fell quiet, I could hear the tiny 'scratch, scratch' of the mantis' clawlike feet. I listened for about ten minutes, wondering where the mantis might be heading. I wasn't going to get any sleep like this.

A moment of realization. I sprang from the bed, snapped on the light, opened the window, cut off the string and offered the mantis to the night. No more pets for me. And I hadn't even named it.

Father Dukehart

Back in the classroom, I faced the usual lineup of subjects, but quite a different set of professors.

Dogmatic Theology gave me some concern. Word had it that Dukehart would teach in Latin. I hadn't made great improvement in reading theological Latin, despite my daily exposure to the language at Mass and in prayers. But Dukehart would provide a respite from Norris' intensity as well as a relief for the conservatives.

Father Dukehart, a quiet, orderly, shy man, deeply conservative and firmly convinced of his views, taught from the text, Adolph Tanquery's pedestrian rehash of Aquinas' magisterial *Summa Theologica*. Tanquery provided a printy jumble of Aquinas, more recent (up to the 20th century, but not including it) theological and papal opinions, with each newer opinion printed in smaller and smaller type, probably representing Tanquery's judgment of the worth of the opinion. I'm sure the planners of the seminary's curriculum thought of Dukehart as a way of offsetting Norris' radical ideas with which we were indoctrinated in our first year.

In addition to the party line theology, Dukehart tried valiantly to uphold the Vatican's decree that the major courses in the theological seminary be taught in Latin. With great relief, I discovered that most of my classmates had little more fluency in the ancient tongue than I, and Dukehart gradually yielded to the wall of incomprehension that greeted his attempts to lecture in Latin.

The Latin problem received a classic illustration in a confrontation between Father Dukehart and one of my classmates, but you'll have to meet him and some of the others first.

Ariyasu

As I remember, our class was very "white-bread." We had no blacks and, as I remember, no Hispanics. (This seems amazing to me, in retrospect. Could I be wrong? Yes! I had forgotten the flamenco-playing Fernando Gamelero, possibly a native of Panama. It shows how exotic Francis Soji Ariyasu seemed as he took his place among us.

The circumstances of his coming were unusual—almost mythical. We were told nothing, of course. But, toward the end of September, in the front lobby by the seminary office, there appeared a number of carefully crafted wooden crates, labeled in Japanese and English, addressed to Mr. Francis Soji Ariyasu. They appeared and they sat. For weeks. We wondered and wondered, and then forgot about it. No explanation was offered nor asked for.

Then, suddenly, toward the end of September, Francis Soji arrived. He was dark, tall for a Japanese, smiling and nodding, and saying very little. His English accent was almost impenetrable. We learned later that he had learned English from French-Canadian Sulpecians in his minor seminary in Japan. It didn't help much.

Frank carried with him a rice-paper Japanese/English dictionary of many many pages, and he would whip back and forth in the book with lightning movements of his long, brown fingers. Finding the appropriate word, he would brighten, say "Ah, yes," repeat the word a couple of times under his breath, and bow slightly. This process made conversations tedious, but his quickness and good humor helped bridge the communications gap.

Ariyasu Speaks!

The first day he spoke in class caused a minor sensation. Dukehart did not encourage questions, often ignored raised hands, or waved dismissively, rather than get into it. He knew that the majority of our class favored a more liberal theology, and determined to plow ahead without dealing with issues.

But one day, our little-known and mysterious new member raised his hand in the middle of Dukehart's lecture. Unwilling to squelch the hitherto silent new student, Father Dukehart paused, and said, "Yes, Mr. Ariyasu?" An anticipatory hush, and a sudden focusing of attention.

There followed from Ariyasu a volley of Latin! Heavily accented, and sounding like Japanese, but unmistakeably Latin. If we were surprised, Father Dukehart was stunned. Though he taught in Latin, he found himself unused to hearing the language, particularly with a Japanese accent.

Ariyasu was clearly very nervous, both from speaking in class and from being the focus of attention. He began to speak faster and louder. His accent intensified. We, and perhaps Dukehart, could make out the occasional word, no more. Sweat broke out on Ariyasu's forehead. He concluded, in a near shout, and fell back into his chair.

The class hung suspended, trapped between laughter, applause and suspense. What would Dukehart do? He was respected for his sincerity, but not well-liked by our class. His soft-spoken, mild-mannered style concealed an intense disapproval of our class, particularly of the liberal views espoused by many.

"Uh, uh, well....*nulle, nulle*, Mr. Ariyasu," Dukehart floundered, groping his way back toward the simple Latin of the text. "*Ego contendo haec*........ Ariyasu bent over his notes, scribbling furiously, his face brick red with embarrassment and possibly triumph.

"Does that answer your objection?" Dukehart concluded, somewhat lamely, in English. Ariyasu nodded rapidly, without looking up, and Dukehart, obviously relieved, proceeded to the next thesis as the class lapsed back into its usual torpor. But the intervention had raised our Asian colleague's status in our minds. Frank found himself less isolated than before.

Ju Jitzu

During one break between classes, a third year man named, unforgettably, Evasio DeMarcellis, slipped up to Frank, introduced himself, told Frank he was a wrestler and asked if Frank knew ju jitzu.

"Oh, yesss, Mistah DeMarcellis." said Frank, enthusiastically. His social sense conveyed a "mister" even upon his classmates, much to our amusement.

"Can you show me some moves?" DeMarcellis went on, unwisely.

"Yesss. You take wrestling hold and I show you." A group of us had gathered, watching closely. The powerful DeMarcellis, who outweighed Frank by more than fifty pounds, went behind the Japanese, took a half-Nelson grip and locked Frank's other arm.

"You ready?" asked Frank calmly. "Yes." replied DeMarcellis, setting himself.

All I saw was Ariyasu bend over and straighten up, but DeMarcellis flew through the air and crashed on his back in front of the smiling Asian, who seemed scarcely to have exerted himself. DeMarcellis got up, clearly impressed, thanked Frank and shook his hand.

As we made our way to our next class, I said to Frank, "Can you teach me some ju jitzu?"

"Oh, yes, Mistah O'Brien, he replied, bowing slightly as he always did. "But you may be killed in the practice." I took the hint and did not pursue the matter. There was clearly more to Frank than met the eye.

Ping Pong.

Our modestly equipped rec room had a couple of battered ping pong tables, that were usually monopolized by the heavy hitters among us. One day, Francis appeared and took his place among the spectators. I took it upon myself to explain the principles of the game, which I assumed that he had never seen. He listened intently and nodded his head, without comment.

Noting his interest, the deacon who had won the last game and thereby controlled the table, turned to Frank and said, "Would you like to try it?"

Frank nodded, stepped to the table without removing his long cassock, and picked up the paddle, holding it awkwardly, with the handle sticking up between his middle and ring finger.

"No, no, Frank. Like this." The deacon showed him the Western or "handshake" grip, placing the paddle in his hand the way we all held it. Ariyasu bowed repeatedly, but switched his grip back to the odd, clumsy-looking grip.

The deacon shrugged, said "Ready?" and served the ball—a high-bouncing, child-like serve. Ariyasu hit it back, the same way. Gradually, the opponent began to strike the ball more firmly, but Ariyasu returned everything, making the process look easy. Within minutes, the deacon was hitting the ball as hard as possible, and Ariyasu was hitting it back with the same pace, still gripping the paddle in the 'wrong' way.

We gathered that the Japanese knew more about ping-pong that we suspected. This occurred, of course, many years before "ping-pong diplomacy" revealed the Asian mastery of this once-Western game.

Ariyasu and the Opposite Sex

Meditation, the first spiritual exercise of the day, occured at 6:30 in the morning. The Rule expected and required us to be in our assigned places, vested in cassock and surplice by the time the bell rang to begin the exercise. After a set of prayers from a member of the faculty, we rose from the hard kneelers and settled back into wooden theatre seats, all 300 of us.

As always, I sat between Francis Soji Ariyasu, the lowest-ranked cleric, and Dan O'Connor, essentially next to me for alphabetic reasons. For most of us, the meditation period constituted a desperate struggle to stay awake. Yet most of us also recognised that meditation ought to form a crucial element of our spiritual life, so we tried desperately to do it. Most of us had a book of meditation exercises or readings—books of our own choosing—and we turned to them when the meditative process ceased, as it frequently did.

After the prayers which began the exercise, Francis Soji Ariyasu slid back heavily into the wooden theatre seat next to mine. Frank was as little inclined to wake up as I was.

On this particular morning, however, I was quite awake. I had been forewarned that Ariyasu's meditation book had been "supplemented" although I did not know how. But I waited with an unusual degree of anticipation.

Ariyasu sat slumped for some minutes, then gave a kind of small dog-like shake and reached for his spiritual reading, a text in Japanese which might have been anything at all, as far as I was concerned. As the book fell open in his hands, he saw a folded piece of newspaper. Opening it, Frank discovered the picture of a pretty Japanese pinup, nothing sexy, but definitely female. He stared for a moment, uncomprehending, then slammed the book shut on the picture, and bent forward in a posture of profound embarrassment. His brown face turned a deep brick red, particularly when he noticed that I saw the whole episode.

Francis Soji Ariyasu in a moment of study.

Visiting George

Knowing Frank's sensitivity to the subject of sex, I was sadistically delighted to learn of one of his summertime adventures which occurred the following year. Since Frank couldn't afford to return to Japan for the summer, he lived on at St. Mary's, occasionally visiting George, a classmate of his at Catholic University in Washington, D.C. Frank knew the layout at CU and the location of his friend's dorm and room. He didn't know that rooms and dorms had been shifted to accommodate summer school students from all over the country.

Among other changes, his friend's dorm had become, for the summer session, a cloistered dormitory for nuns. Of course the door had been well-marked with a large sign: Cloister—No Males Allowed. However, since the dorm was not air conditioned and the Washington summer heat was oppressive, someone had tied the doors open. The sign was hidden.

Frank marched into the dorm, climbed to the third floor, meeting no one, since it was mid-afternoon, found his friend's room, and decided to give him a little surprise. He burst through the door shouting "GEORGE" and discovered a young nun, topless, taking a sponge bath. He froze, uncomprehending, then turned and fled from the dorm, totally shaken. I am unable to report the reaction of the young nun, but I confidently believe that she remembers the incident vividly to this very day.

Now comes the sadistic part. I learned of Frank's adventure from one of the faculty who stayed at the seminary during the summer. I prepared a little inquisition for Frank, and not a holy one. As we gathered in groups after dinner early in the fall, I joined Frank's group and began chatting with him about his summer in Baltimore. The rest of the group quickly picked up on the fact that my questions had a point.

"Don't you have a friend in D.C., Frank?" I asked innocently.

"Oh, yes, my friend, George." he replied, "He's going to CU."

"Did you get down to see him at all this summer?" I went on.

"Yes, I took the bus down."

"And did you find him?" I asked, relentlessly.

Suddenly, Frank got the drift. His hands shot to his face, pressing his brow in a curious gesture of hiding and embarrassment. "Ohhhhhh, Mistah O'Brien." he moaned, throatily.

"Was he in?"

"Ohhhhhh, Mistah O'Brien." Frank's hands remained pinned to his brow, and his face was brick red.

"What's going on?" asked one of the now-fascinated group.

"Oh, I said, airily, "you'll have to ask Frank about that." and I moved on to another group. What he told them, I don't know, but I bet it wasn't much.

Confessing to Ray Brown.

After a year of non-communication with Father Dukehart as my spiritual director, I learned that it was no big deal to change directors. You just went to the Rector, asked to be changed and that was it. The relationship was considered so important that no conditions or inquiries were attached.

I decided to pick a new guy on the faculty, without any feedback from Peterson or anyone, for that matter.

Father Raymond J. Brown, S.S. is ranked as a world-renowned Scripture scholar, a specialist in the Gospel of John, his work held in high esteem far beyond the Roman Catholic tradition. In 1959, still a young man, he was already well known in scholarly circles. Most of us saw him as the leading intellectual light on our seminary faculty.

Father Ray Brown in 1959.

It was not for that reason that I chose him for my confessor, however. He seemed to me to be a reasonable guy with a sense of humor and an open quality. All of which differed diametrically from Father Dukehart, the confessor assigned to me during my first year at St. Mary's.

Though I was not a theological student of any great note, I did manage to make an impression on Father Brown.

Confession in the seminary was rather different than "in the world." Catholic churches commonly feature a confessional structure, usually with the priest sitting in the center and the two penitents kneeling facing him on either side. The confessional windows are screened, or covered with white linen cloth, to keep the matter private. The priest slides open a cover on one site, and closes the slide on the other, to promote efficiency in the days when sometimes 50 or 60 confessions would be heard in the course of one day.

At any rate, I was startled to discover that seminary confessions were pretty much face to face. The confessor sat in an ordinary chair with a prie-dieu or kneeler by his side. The penitent walked in, knelt down, and began the confessional ritual.

Now, despite the secrecy of the normal confessional, acknowledging one's sins is not a particularly comfortable process, even after many repetitions. Face to face is harder by far. So, waiting in line in the hall outside Ray Brown's office with the other penitents, I was a bit more nervous than usual. The confession actually begins with a simple formula: "Bless me, Father, for I have sinned. It has been three weeks since my last confession." Or whatever time. Then the confession is made.

When my turn came, I walked into the room, knelt down and began my confession. Unfortunately, the words which sprang to mind were not the confessional formula, but another, even more familiar formula: grace before meals.

"Bless us, O Lord," I began, "and these, thy gifts........." In horror, I became conscious of what I was saying, caught myself, then began to stifle the wave of laughter which immediately swept over me. Hand over my mouth, body heaving, I managed to choke back spasm after spasm, tears forming in my eyes, my face bright red. After some time, I managed to get control of myself, and in a quavering voice, made my confession, and waited for my penance.

I opened my eyes and looked up to see Ray Brown, both hands over his face, heaving his large body backward and forward in the chair, as completely convulsed as I was. I was set off again myself. After another good time, Brown managed to assign me some penance, recite the ritual of absolution and bid me go in peace. He followed this with a roar of laughter, which I joined as I turned and left the office.

Every eye in the waiting line followed me down the hall, adding to the hilarity as Father Brown's laugh continued to echo in the hall. What had I confessed, they surely wondered. But they would never know. It was against the Rule!

Rank and Hierarchy

Each of us had an exact place in the chapel, based on our class year and our clerical rank in that class. Those who had received Tonsure were clerics; the rest of us were not. Most people think of Tonsure (if they think of it at all) as a large shaven scalp with a circle of fringe, as in the cartoon Franciscan monks.

But we were *not* monks. Receiving tonsure did not involve shaving most of our heads—the bishop came and clipped a small chunk of hair from the side of our heads—and we became clerics, members of a group "set apart" from the laity—the great mass of the church.

In my class, I was the senior non-cleric. Most of my classmates had received Tonsure at the end of their studies in philosophy, before they came to the Theology house. Since I had come to St. Mary's Roland Park directly from "the world", I would not receive Tonsure until the end of my second year, when and if the faculty found me worthy.

Solemn Vigil

The liturgical calendar decreed December 7th to be the Vigil of the Feast of the Immaculate Conception, one of the ten major holy days in the Roman Catholic year. The following day—no classes in the seminary, a rare and welcome break in our crowded schedule. The celebration of the feast began with solemn Vespers, a ceremony we would attend fully vested in cassock, surplice and biretta and prepared to chant.

Most of our visitors found the chanting of the Divine Office to be an impressive experience. Three hundred plus young men sitting in two choirs facing one another, chanting antiphonally the ancient verses of the Psalms in Latin. The ancient sound of Gregorian Chant communicated a sense of timelessness—some of the chants were over a thousand years old.

The Chapel gleamed in the filtered light. Stained glass windows reflected off marble floors and columns and the highly polished oak choir stalls stretched the length of the high-vaulted room. Darker side corridors were lined with tiny chapels where the faculty said their private Masses every morning. The floor, scrubbed and waxed, gleamed quietly. The air breathed the memory of candles and incense.

The Vespers ceremony, which I enjoyed, proceded in its measured pace entirely in Latin through the chanting of the Psalms and prayers to the point of the Kiss of Peace, passed down from the Celebrant through the rows of seminarians to the lowest ranks—ourselves.

Now this Kiss of Peace was no friendly smooch, but a formal liturgical gesture. The Bearer of the Peace turned to his left to face the receiver, who turned right. The Bearer bowed, placed his hands on the shoulders of the receiver, leaned toward his right ear, then murmured "*Pax Tecum.*" (Peace be with you.) The Receiver murmured back, "*Et cum spiritu tuo.*" (And with your spirit,) then turned and repeated the greeting with the receiver on his right.

Wise guys sometimes replied to the "*Pax Tecum*" with "Pax Gottum." but this was lame and not very original either. I was, however, in no way prepared to receive Ariyasu's *Pax*.

He turned to me, his brown face inscrutable, bowed formally, placed his hands on my shoulder and murmured "Remembah Pahl Haba." December the Seventh! I was so dumbfounded I made no response at all, then turned helplessly to Dan O'Connor, my face red with suppressed laughter, bowed and shook my head.

One last sneak attack from the Empire of Japan had found its target.

Changes in the Unchanging Church

Catholic school children of my time learned that the Church never changed. The possessor and guardian of the Revealed Truth, what need could there be for change? Although we knew there had been many previous popes, we had experienced only Pope Pius XII, whose reign began in 1939, on the brink of WWII. Much photographed with the leaders of the world, Pius stood always to the right of center and, hands interlaced as if to avoid touching anything, gazed off into the middle distance behind and to the right of the photographer—as if he wished he were somewhere else.

One of our favorite imprecations as kids, aimed at someone acting superior was: "Who do you think you are, HolyPopePius?," the latter uttered as one word.

But, "as it must for all men" (*Citizen Kane*), death came for Eugenio Pacelli, Piux XII, after a long period of illness, and abundant speculation regarding the new pope. At St. Mary's, the in-crowd ranked the various '*papabile*' or likely candidates to succeed Pacelli. The faculty joined in the speculation with vigor and better information. Father Jack Dede informed us that the Conclave of Cardinals would probably choose an elderly "caretaker pope," someone who would not shake up the established system This would permit theologians to "assimilate" the papal teachings of Pius XII, who had written authoritatively on many subjects.

One speculation held that the Conclave would reach outside of its own select seventy-some cardinals, possibly to some archbishop behind the Iron Curtain. Many of us hoped for some dramatic choice to demonstrate that the Church's concerns extended beyond the provincial preoccupations of the Vatican bureaucracy.

"*Annuncio Vobis gaudium magnum.*" intoned the Camerlengo. "*Habemus Papam. Angelo Cardinal Roncalli............*"

Roncalli? Who the heck was Roncalli? Not a name on the lips of the guys in the know. But clearly, Father Dede had it right. Roncalli, 77, a Vatican City diplomat for most of his career, could not be expected to have much impact on the Church.

Pope Dreams

Scene: a dingy, second-floor office in a down-at-the-heels business district of an unknown city. A bare bulb hangs from the middle of the ceiling, illuminating two battered desks placed back to back. The desks are cluttered with papers, old black phones, wire baskets holding copy; dog eared, paperback almanacs, and reference books complete the litter. Front and center on each desk, a large black Underwood typewriter with worn round keys.

Two men are sitting at the desks, an older and a younger. They wear white shirts, loosened ties, vests. The younger has his sleeves rolled to mid-forearm. They wear green eyeshades; that of the older man carries the title: Editor. They are both busily typing. I am the younger man. I lean forward, pull the copy from my typewriter with a whirl of the roller, toss it into the wire basket, lean back for a minute and then speak:

"I think I'm going down for a smoke." The older man grunts assent. I rise, stretch, and head for the stairs, pulling a pack of Lucky Strikes from my shirt pocket. Oddly, I have never smoked cigarets.

As I reach the bottom of the staircase, I pull open the grimy glass door, step out into the cool spring day, lean against the iron rail of the step, and fire up my Lucky. I stare out into the street, looking at nothing. Then a long black limousine with gleaming white sidewalls turns into the block, moves slowly down and stops in front of our building. What could this mean?

Next to the uniformed chauffeur is a large, tough-looking, Italianate man. Almost invisible deep in the back seat is a tiny old man. He is dressed in the robes of a Roman Catholic Cardinal. None of the three look at me. After a long pause, the limo hangs a U-turn, impossible in our narrow street, and pulls away.

I take a long drag of my Lucky, pitch it into the gutter, and mount the stairs determinedly. I recount the encounter to the editor, who listens intently, then say: "I've been elected Pope." After a pause, I add, "You know what this means!"

The Editor rises resignedly from his seat, pulls off his green eyeshade, drops it on the desk and walks round the desk to my chair. I drop my green eyeshade on his desk, pick up his, place it on my head and seat myself in his chair. We both begin to type.

End of dream.

Seems to me that my unconscious mind had two messages: first, I had ambitions in the Church far beyond my present modest status and, second, somehow journalism would be my path to the heights. As usual, my unconscious mind knew me better than my conscious mind.

Leaving the Seminary.

Every once in a while, someone would leave. We almost never knew the specific reason, but each departure came as a shock. Very occasionally, students got booted. Such an action had to be approved by the bishop of the seminarian, and involved a sense of failure and loss on both sides. Sometimes the rector would persuade the individual to quit, based on the observations of the faculty. Sometimes grades became the problem. We almost never knew.

In the case of Frank Flemming, we could make a guess. Frank couldn't handle the early hours. A quiet, friendly kid, Frank sat two rows in front of me in chapel and a little to the right. And, unfortunately, right on the aisle.

As we knelt, waiting for the Mass to begin, Frank's head would begin to drop. He would catch himself, straighten up, balance his head carefully and drop off again. This occurred morning after morning. One morning, he got his head balanced just right, fell fully asleep and toppled over into the aisle. Deeply embarrassed, he fended off the guys trying to help him up, and resumed his place, face bright red. In a week or so, he was gone.

Did the sleeping incident do him in, or did he himself decide to leave. We didn't know.

In almost every case, the person just disappeared, and the word went round. Each departure came to most of us as a jolt. We all struggled with the various pressures—academic, personal, psychological, spiritual—of seminary life, and each departure reminded us of the possibility for ourselves.

At my current table, a well-liked deacon, Marty Hacala, seemed to be the very model of the good seminarian. An all-round guy, Marty had a good sense of humor, steered a middle course between radical and conservative, had never been clipped or tailed. One day he was gone. Departures from the deacon class occurred very rarely. These guys had been through the mill, approved for major orders, had a few short months to wait before ordination to the priesthood.

Later that semester, another tablemate, Frank Newsom surprised me one evening as the meal ended.

"Could we talk, Jim. I have some ideas I'd like to bounce off you."

"Sure, Frank," I responded, a bit flattered that a third year man would want to talk to me seriously about anything.

We headed out and Frank launched into a vast, convoluted theological speculation. I listened hard, but had a difficult time, because he never finished a sentence, just added more clauses and conjunctions. No place for me to break in at all.

Frustrated, I interrupted, rather rudely, I thought.

"Frank, you're just not stopping. Finish a sentence. Think for a minute, and tell me what you want to say."

"OK, right." He paused, looking distraught rather than irritated, then started out again. He couldn't do it. The flood of words went on, now with an anxious tone. I listened, more frustrated than ever.

As the bell rang for evening prayer, I interrupted again. "Frank, you've just got too many links there. It all becomes like a river that doesn't stop. I think you should try writing this stuff down. That would give it some structure." What did I know?

As we entered the prayer hall, Frank gripped my shoulder and said, "Thanks for listening." As I looked at him, his eyes had filled with tears. My god, what was going on.

The next morning he was gone.

The Contradictions of the System

My new confessor, Ray Brown, who got the grades from the faculty common room, told me that I had done poorly in Church History. "That's not possible, Father." I said, boldly. "Bull always gives us the same grades. I've had the same grade for two years. He doesn't read the papers."

Father Brown, a deeply engaged teacher, insisted that it was not possible that Father Noonan did not read the papers. "I'll go down and check it again," he said.

"And it will be an 87," I added smartly. Father Brown hoisted himself from the chair, left the room and returned, puffing slightly, in a few minutes.

"87," he reported, wryly, and I could see him making a mental note to have a word with Bull.

Grades carried weight, though they weren't supposed to, and we weren't supposed to care. Grade results were posed only in the faculty common room, forbidden territory for seminarians. Your Director would get your grades, although you weren't supposed to be interested. Right!

Just one of those little contradictions.

In those bygone days before Vatican II, a Roman Catholic seminary ranked as a pretty strange place. The First Vatican Council (1869-70) had laid down the pattern for all Roman Catholic seminaries. Seminaries should be run like monasteries: strict schedules based on the hours for chanting the Holy Office; solitary living; lots of silence; many spiritual exercises each day, and so on. In a word, a system designed by St. Benedict over a thousand years ago, and very effective for producing *monks.* Of course, *we* wished to be diocesan priests: in the world but not of it, as we used to say, and subject to all the variety and unexpectedness of real life.

St. Mary's Seminary and University, our official title, also acted as a graduate school providing advanced studies in theology, scripture, ancient and modern languages, church music, and pastoral practices. Academic standards ranked high, and grades considered important—high grades offered leadership opportunities during the deacon year.

Of course, many of us didn't think of ourselves as graduate students, but rather, priest-candidates, not at all interested in becoming scholars. Those who DID become scholars would find themselves frustrated by the demands of the parish ministry.

We expected to prepare for that same parish ministry among the people, from whom we were largely separated, physically as well as by our clerical garb and injunctions to celibacy. And, as parish priests, we would necessarily be public speakers and musical soloists, however poorly we might be endowed for these functions. We would also be teachers, counsellors, visitors of the sick, ministers to the dying and their families and many other ministerial roles.

By the way, we avoided the terms "minister" and "ministerial" whenever possible. They sounded Protestant. The Code of Canon Law, when forced to refer to the Protestant clergy, called them "ministelli"—little ministers—a gratuitous insult—representative of a Church attitude since the Reformation.

I think there were two reasons for the lack of attention to pastoral training. First, the priest's function in the parish was liturgical rather than ministerial. He was called to celebrate Mass and administer the sacraments—Baptism, Penance, Anointing the sick, burying the dead. He performed these functions with equal validity without regard to his own personal qualities. The people might hope for more, but they could not expect more.

Second, and more to the point, the day-to-day functions of any new priest would be determined by the wish of his pastor and the perceived needs of his diocese. The closer we approached ordination, the more we hoped for a good first appointment where we would begin our apprenticeship in priesting, though we never thought about it that way. We might be fully priests, but mostly without parochial experience, as our more or less tolerant parishoners would find out.

The seminary system, details worked out over the hundred years since the First Vatican Council, represented an uneasy compromise between these rather different goals. Different seminaries, different faculties and different students placed their emphasis in one area or another. St. Mary's, it seems to me now, leaned in the direction of the monastery. The Rule, and our response to it, measured our worthiness for the priesthood. The highest virtue was obedience, an unquestioning subservience to the constituted authority. The same system that governs the military, and produces similar results.

Sorry for the lecture, but it's what I do.

Moral Theology: Snuffy Nevins.

We called him the 'Rancid Pygmy.' You might think that referring to an elderly, long-time faculty member of the seminary by such an appellation lacked a certain respect, indeed, suggested a kind of hostility. And you would be right!

We came into Father Nevin's class filled with anticipation and foreboding, prepared by a multiplicity of stories regarding the ancient and tiny priest, at that time well into his eighties. (the retirement policy for priests in those days was death.)

A notably colorful teacher, Father John C. "Snuffy" Nevins, clearly a man who attracted nicknames, might well have earned both affection and respect from the thousands of students who passed under his tutelage at St. Mary's, but he managed to fend off such attitudes with his own consistent hostility and suspicion. Colorful he was, but loved? Not so.

Snuffy Nevins taught Moral Theology, and had achieved a kind of pedegogical notoriety for generations of priests, enlivening his classes with vivid stories and concise maxims such as, "all moral theology is about the difference between a wink and a blink." Or, "a little nurse is a dangerous thing."

For us, however, Father Nevins apparently assumed that we had heard all the stories before and therefore knew the endings. He would begin, "A young seminarian was sitting on the train, and a beautiful woman came and sat down next to him." Having now our full attention, he would continue, more vaguely, "So they began to talk, and so on and so on….." He trailed away into silence, his faded blue eyes staring out over decades of remembered seminarians. Suddenly he would come to himself, glare out at the class and snarl, "Pay attention!"

We did, to no avail.

A Vivid and Dangerous Presence

Father Nevins had lost in childhood the first two joints of his right index finger, and thus required special permission from the Vatican to be ordained. Since he gestured vigorously with his right hand to emphasize his points, the missing finger gave his imperious gesture a special intensity for some reason, as if we personally had responsibility for his missing digit.

Snuffy, as everyone called him (never to his face), remains as vivid to me now after 40 plus years as he was during my seminary time. Ancient, five feet tall, he walked hunched over (thus accentuating his shortness). His Boston accent had not faded a bit for his many years in Baltimore.

Father Nevins approached the world with the augmented aggression of the little guy combined with Irish immigrant combativeness. He seemed to regard the seminary population with contempt unmingled with pity.

"The age of reason is three in Boston," he sneered, "and goes up as you go west."

Snuffy regularly patrolled the corridors of the vast building like a bloodhound, looking for real or imagined infractions. And found them!

One time, leaving the library workroom (where smoking was permitted) I stepped out into the hall, my pipe still clamped in my teeth. As I looked up, I saw Snuffy glaring at me from some distance, and suddenly realized my infraction. I pivoted on my heel like an automaton and ducked back into the workroom. I swiftly knocked out the pipe and plunged into the stacks, feeling certain that Snuffy might be following me at the quickest pace he could manage. I never knew if he did, but my general sense of paranoia was significantly increased.

The "Railroad Conspiracy"

Snuffy was at his sharpest in class when he embarked on his pet moral argument, the right to avoid paying the fare on the railroads. His strategy was simple: when the conductor came, you went to the restroom, climbed up and stood on the seat. The conductor would push open the door, look down at the floor, see no feet and pass on. I never tried it, even though I learned it in Moral theology class. I'm not sure the conductor would have bought into Snuffy's rationale.

As Father Nevins repeated to us frequently, it was morally ok to stiff the railroads because they were part of a vast conspiracy against the American public. The conspiracy was run by the Jews and the Supreme Court and carried out by the FBI, who were unwitting dupes of the Court. How the Supreme Court controlled the railroad was not entirely clear, nor was the purpose of the conspiracy, but it was clear that no person had an obligation to pay for railroad transportation. Pay Attention!

Snuffy acted belligerently hostile to any male taller than he, that is to say, almost all of us. Particularly offended by genuinely tall students, he would walk directly into them, pushing them aside with his arms and muttering, "Get out of my way." When the students apologized, he would mutter, "Yeah, yeah, wasted material," an obscure reference to their excessive height.

The chocolate bunny incident, as it came to be known, revealed another dimension of the choloric cleric. February, mid-Lent, a dark time in the liturgical calendar and the meteorologic one as well. In a burst of enterprising *je ne sais quoi*, three seminarians who shall remain nameless (Bill Pitt, Tom Schreve and Jack Melloh) acquired a large chocolate bunny, pinned upon it the names of the faculty (a possible voodoo threat?) and placed it in the display case in the library window.

Snuffy discovered it there, rushed it to Father Van Antwerp, the rector, and recommended that Easter vacation be cancelled until the malefactors be exposed and punished. Van, more amused than offended, did nothing. As the bunny was never seen again, we may assume that the faculty consumed it non-symbolically.

Father Cerny Strikes Again

Father Edward Cerny's strange speaking style, encountered on my day of arrival, carried over into his class lectures, at length. Among our class clowns, Cerny impressions competed with Snuffy impressions, but with quite a different tone. We held both affection and respect for the ancient, wizened bohemian. In addition to his duties, Cerny acted as *Censor Librorum* for the archdiocese of Baltimore, a very sensitive position. If he approved a book later found to contain some heretical opinion, the embarrassment to the archdiocese and the Cardinal Archbishop would be immense and world-wide, at least within the Catholic theological community. But, to our knowledge, Cerny had never gotten caught.

He often spoke of his duties, which required him to read thirty to forty scripture or theology books a year, Baltimore being an important Catholic publishing center in those days. Cerny read each book submitted for approval cover to cover and, more amazingly, he remembered the contents in detail. He had a photographic memory and would quote from the books, gazing into the air as if reading them.

"Yes, yes...." he would hiss intensely, "It's right there about half-way down page two hundred ninety seven...." We would check. He would be right.

Though conservative in his own right, he often passed on rather daring works, particularly in his own field of Scripture studies.

"Yes, Yes, I passed it." Cerny would acknowledge. "I didn't AGREE with all of it, but it wasn't against faith or morals."

Crawling through Polish

Cerny loved languages. He confessed to a reading knowledge of some 23 languages, including Latin, Greek, Hebrew, Aramaic, Syriac and many modern languages.

"I'm working on Polish right now," he confided to the class one day. "I wouldn't count myself a master of Polish, but I can CRAWL through it." Embarrassed by the admission, he whirled to the blackboard to conceal his shame at bragging.

Cerny would mount the dais and plop down a large pile of books and folders containing class notes of an unknown age. But never once in class did I see him refer to any books or consult any notes.

He would begin the study of a particular book of the Old Testament by summarizing it, quite usefully, then indicating something of the context of the work in Hebrew history. Then he would talk about the text in the style and with the enthusiasm of a young boy talking about his family history, as if he had actually lived the history he was recounting. This approach led him down many an alley of minutiae.

One day he drifted off into a description of the interior of the Temple of Solomon. He turned to the blackboard and began to draw the temple and locate the furnishings. But the drawing was tiny and faint, and entirely concealed by his body. He did not bother to raise his voice and only by listening intently could I, sitting about half way back, hear him at all.

"Here behind the curtain is the....HOLY OF HOLIES. And of course, over to one side.......the altars of offering.......over here........" He murmured on, occasionally bursting forth with some word or phrase.

Giving up, I casually turned and glanced toward the rear of the room. Guys were writing, staring out the window, reading, occasionally a head down on the desk. Cerny had lost touch.

He completed his almost invisible drawing, stepped back to admire it. "There!" He exclaimed with some satisfaction. Then he siezed an eraser and obliterated the drawing before most of the class could get a glimpse of it. It seemed as if Cerny had forgotten the class.

And the lecture went on. "Of course, the FIRST temple was destroyed during the invasion of the Assyrians in……." Cerny went on, taking for granted we were all familiar with Assyrian history. This seemed faintly gratifying to us if unhelpful.

Cerny also seemed persuaded that we all read and understood Hebrew. There may have been one or two in our class of more than a hundred. He would rapidly print out some extended phrase from the scripture in Hebrew, working right to left. Then he would march back to the beginning and add the vowel points, a series of dots and accent marks making the language chantable as well as readable, though not to us.

Finishing the vowel points, he would step back and announce, "There." as if the point at issue had been clarified. (I have had Mathematics professors do the same thing with calculus problems, and with the same effect.)

Vowel Points

One day, as if he had not been using this blackboard for months, or even years, he stared at the Hebrew text with its vowel points, then said.

"Wait. There are MARKS on this board! How can you read the VOWEL POINTS with all these marks?" No one answered him. I couldn't read the vowel points anyway.

Cerny siezed an eraser, scrubbed away the text, and began pointing out the small white pockmarks which remained.

"Here's one!" He pointed to it. "Here's another one. Here's one. Here's one. Here's one." He pointed to each one in turn as if it had previously been hiding. He turned to the class, appearing to be defeated.

"I just don't see how you can read the Hebrew with all those marks." He said, resignedly. We didn't either. He went on with class.

Despite Cerny's enthusiastic welcome to me on the day of my arrival, I had never gone to chat with him about the Rockford diocese. I really didn't know what I would say, since I was not up on clerical gossip. And Cerny never made any further acknowledgement of me, despite my midwest origins.

He did influence my life, however, during one of his frequent forays from the class material into reminiscence.

A Trip to Egypt

"Have any of you seen the Nile?" he asked suddenly, apropos of something in the ancient land. A few hands went up.

"I went to Egypt when I was a young STUDENT." He burst out. "The same age as YOU." Assuming a far-away look, he drifted back on a tide of memory. Suddenly the Yoda-like old man became a young seminarian before our eyes.

"We were sailing down the Nile at night in a felluca. There were only a few fires visible on the shore. The sky was velvet black and HUGE!" His voice was filled with wonder. "You could look up into the sky and see MILLIONS of stars....." He fell silent, lost in his intense memory. We were silent, too, in the purity of that moment.

Then Cerny came to himself, looked out at the class and said, quietly. "If you ever get a chance to go to Egypt, do it." Many years later, my wife asked me if there was some one place I wanted to go. "Yes," I answered, surprised at the quickness of my response. "Egypt." And I told her the story. I did go. And I'm glad.

One of Cerny' recurrent preoccupations was the gradually diminishing size of his own ordination class.

"Father JONES died the other day." he offered, then added, "he was my seminary classmate. Let's see....." He counted on his fingers. "There are only SEVEN of us left!" He delivered this news like a headline. For some reason, we found this countdown hilarious. We were in our twenties; Cerny was of some great, incalculable age—seventy! Who would count the people left in a class, and why?

Cerny vs. Snuffy

An odd little event gave us a bit of insight into tensions among the faculty. Snuffy Nevins spent most of his time during Long Rec looking for four leaf clovers. Clearly this was an Irish rather than a trinitarian preoccupation, but Snuffy was in vocal delight whenever he found one. A day yielding two or three four-leaf clovers was exceptional. It was a testament to our general dislike for Snuffy that we found this preoccupation merely oddball, rather than endearing. One day a few of the deacons were chatting with Father Cerny, and mentioned that Snuffy had had a big day with the four-leaf clovers.

"How ridiculous," burst out Cerny, surprisingly, "for a grown man to occupy himself with such nonsense. Four-leaf clovers are all over the place. Look, there's one there." It was the blackboard dots all over again. Cerny walked over the lawn, hunched over, his wizened hand darting out again and again. His incredible eyesight working overtime, in a few minutes the ancient one had gathered a full bouquet of four leaf clovers.

"Such nonsense." Cerny affirmed, and handed over the bouquet to the mystified deacons.

It's strange. What should seem like a cute and almost touching anecdote, turns out to be faintly cruel and vengeful. And we felt a bit triumphant about it. It was the kind of guy that Snuffy was, I guess. He would have detested pity as much as he detested cuteness or, perhaps, emotion of any kind. The story went round like lightning, and Snuffy never mentioned four leaf clovers again. Come to think of it, that's pretty sad.

The Song of Solomon

As the reader may be aware, the pages of the Old Testament contain some vivid sexual material. Judith and Holofernes; David and Bathsheba (or 'Bessabee' as Cerny insisted); Susanna and the Elders. Cerny seemed embarrassed by this material, although he had taught it for years. How would he handle the erotic poetry of the *Canticle of Solomon*?

"The sacred writer describes his beLOVED," he began in his vivid way. "Her hair….her hair is like a flock of goats FRISKING…. He goes on, her teeth…..her lips like scarlet thread….her neck is like a fortress….and so on...." Would Cerny, having fully roused our interest, leave us hanging, even echoing Snuffy to do so?

"And her BREASTS," he suddenly burst out. "Her breasts are like gazelles feeding among the lilies." The class jumped and shifted. Suddenly embarrassed, Cerny whirled and began to write on the board in his thready writing.

After recovering, Cerny hastened to explain that the poem allegorically represented the relationship between Jahweh and his chosen people, as Paul would describe the relationship between Christ and the Church. But the *Song* still sounded pretty sexy to us. And to Cerny, too, I think.

Jack Dede and the Code

John Dede, S.S., Professor of Canon Law, stared out at the class with a cool, assessing gaze. After a pause, he lifted a slim volume and announced, "This book will govern the rest of your lives." Uh, oh. A distinctly ominous note.

Despite the afternoon hour, not a sleepy face could be found. The older students had warned us—Dede demanded precision and got it. Full attention, the minimum standard. Certainly the first line of the lecture got it.

I stared down at the little red, canvas-bound softback in my hand. *Codex Juris Canonicis*. A compact 918 pages of small but clearly printed Latin, organizing the two thousand years of Christian governance into five amazingly precise sections or "Books." No pictures, no illustrations, no plot lines, no relief. Not just Latin, but technical, legal Latin. Oh, boy.

As Dede began to lead us through the outline, he noted the areas which would impact us most. The second book, "Persons", included Clerics (us, or soon to be); Religious (people who take vows of poverty, chastity and obedience—*not* us) and Laity (no longer us.) We saw obligations and privileges. We expressed interest in the latter.

"Pastors of parishes have specific privileges assigned to them by the code," Father Dede assured us.

"What about Assistant Pastors?" Dempsey asked. Most of us would be Assistant Pastors for years, possibly many years.

"Assistant Pastors have the doubtful right to Christian burial." Dede answered wryly, but without qualification. We got the picture in a hurry.

"What if the Code doesn't give an answer to an issue?" A good question.

"Same as the Rule," Dede answered succinctly. "Silence gives consent. If you don't want a negative answer, don't ask." A lawyer's classic point of view. And it sounded like a great principle to me. *Silencio tacet.* Or something like that.

Another time, a classmate asked some technical question regarding which congregation of the Vatican Bureaucracy validated the authenticity of sacred relics. After answering, Dede observed that the process was not very scientific. "There are enough relics of the Holy Cross to rebuild St. Peter's," he observed wryly.

Saflarski and the *Code*

Most of us took Canon Law pretty seriously, but none more so than Frank Saflarski, who sat in the row behind me. Generally a cheerful guy, Frank approached Canon Law with a kind of obsession. I noticed him underlining 'important' words in his *Codex*.

"Why don't you just underline ALL the words?" I suggested helpfully. "In the Code, every word is important." Saflarski ignored me, as he should have.

Another time, I noticed that Saflarski had printed a passage from the Code in his "Chicago" Bible—*not* the Catholic Bible. The Code provided that Catholics who read an unsanctioned version of the Scriptures would be subject to excommunication.

"Frank. Supposed you take that Bible home for the summer and your sister picks it up and reads it and then sees this excommunication stuff. She'll think she's excommunicated." I wasn't kidding this time, but Saflarski blew it off. I never heard if his sister ever did incur that excommunication.

Proem and Points for Meditation.

At a distance of almost fifty years, I still have no idea what the word "Proem" means, but clearly it sticks in my mind.

Anyway, Saturday evenings at 9 p.m., all students except the deacons gathered in the prayer hall for Proem and Points, as we called it. The purpose of the exercise—to prepare us for a prayerful and insightful participation in the Sunday liturgy to follow. The actual result of the exercise—to give us a privileged glimpse into the personal spirituality of the various members of the faculty as they prepared a meditation on the Gospel pericope (pericope = short hunk of text) from the morrow's liturgy.

The most anticipated giver of Points for Meditation—Father Cerny, not only for the famous voice and delivery. Cerny would pick out some phrase from the gospel story, and weave a meditation out of it. And he always chose the least likely phrase. For example, in the very famous passage known as the Sermon on the Mount, Jesus begins by bidding the crowd to be seated, "for there was much grass in the place." That was the phrase Cerny picked. We were quoting it for weeks.

His most famous meditation emerged from Jesus' meeting with his followers after the Resurrection. "I am with you for a little while," says Jesus, "and then in a little while I am with you no longer, for I must go to the Father." Of course, Cerny picked "in a little while."

In his breathy, oddly-inflected style, Cerny listed the "little whiles" in our lives. "In a little while, you're born. In another little while, you grow to be a child. Then in a little while, you become crazy TEENages." He uttered this last bizarre phrase with maximum intensity, and paused for impact as the startled students suppressed chuckles. Then he continued, the ultimate message of the Points being lost, but the moment unforgettable. I'd bet anything that every single one of my classmates can remember that phrase after all these many years.

Seminary Preaching—First Run

I have mentioned that our lunch and dinner meals were usually taken in silence, but not in perfect silence. During each of the meals, two practice sermons regaled the eaters. A lot was riding on the sermon. Not preaching skill, but doctrinal correctness measured the success of the preacher. Not only the seminarians but the faculty sat listening, waiting for any hint that the speaker might stray from the Path. We negotiated a minefield of potential heresy.

Each faculty member had his area of specialty, and a particular slant on it. If you quoted the Bible, each of the Scripture teachers would listen intently to see if some principle of interpretation had been violated. If you alluded to some doctrinal point, theologians across the full range from liberal to arch-conservative, waited like vultures to pounce.

(Fortunately, they did not pounce during the sermon, but later, in the conferences, one's doctrinal shakiness would be brought forth, with the sermon as evidence.)

Of course, we didn't pick our own topics. Ben Selner had an ancient list of topics and assigned them to individuals at the end of classes each year. We had the summer to research, write, polish, purge, practice and perfect these gems. As if such an opportunity would come during the ministry.

The list offered great topics (the Beatitudes, The Sacraments, the Church); dangerous topics, (Church History; the Blessed Virgin; the Reformation), and groaners (topics so vague, general, irrelevant, that no preacher in his right might would even consider them.) I got a groaner. "Heaven and Hell."

I showed Kehoe. He shook his head. "No way to get anything out of that one." he opined.

But the nuns had gotten miles and miles out of hellfire stories in grade school. Hell was clearly more interesting than the static, vaguely golden vision of heaven. Somehow, my instinct for self-preservation suggested that the Annual Sermon was not the place to display any sense of humor, and I duly avoided that natural path to disaster.

The result—a labored and tedious essay delivered in a monotonous voice with only one tiny relieving moment. I remember using the phrase "when I was a boy....." Since I looked about 15 at the time, this produced a fairly substantial chuckle, but it also told me that people were listening. That didn't ease my anxiety.

Apart from that moment, I remember nothing whatsoever from the experience. A few friends came up during rec after the sermon and said "Nice job." but we all knew that the phrase had been emptied of meaning by the experience. "Nice job" served the equivalent of "interesting" in a conversation, and meant "not very."

An Enlarged Heart

Scripture courses balanced Old and New Testament studies in an even-handed way: Fall—Old; Spring—New. In the spring of first year, Dannemiller took us through the three synoptic Gospels—Matthew, Mark and Luke. In contrast to my Notre Dame religion class on the same topic, Dannemiller emphasized the differences between the Gospels, arguing that each had been written for a specific audience, with a specific theological point in mind, by a writer with a specific background and influence. This approach illuminated the Gospels in a new way and enriched my understanding of them

Fall of second year brought us the Old Testament historical and wisdom books in Cerny's inimitable style. In Spring we turned to the Gospel of John, still with Cerny. Some in the class asked, "Why Cerny?" We had a world-class Johannine scholar on the faculty with Ray Brown; yet we had to make our way through another four months of Cerny's almost impenetrable style.

Scripture class had only gone on a few weeks when Cerny's health began to fail. He appeared late for class, almost unheard-of for any of our professors. One day in the middle of class, he suddenly rose and left the room. One of us ran to report to the rector.

The next day, Cerny appeared in class, clearly miffed.

"Somebody ran off to the RECTOR!" he hissed accusingly. "There was no PROBLEM! I had a cup of coffee before class, and it was PRESSING!" Clearly the elderly priest didn't want anyone fussing around with him. Infirmary insiders spread the word that Cerny was taking diuretics for a heart condition.

About a week later, Van Antwerp appeared in class in place of Cerny, informed us that he was ill.

"Go to your rooms and study." the rector told us. "You will be informed when Father Cerny will return."

He never did. Later in the week, the Rector informed the student body at lunch that Cerny had passed away early that morning. A solemn funeral would be celebrated at the seminary in two days.

Most of us felt stunned more than saddened. The passing had come suddenly; death was largely incomprehensible to most of us.

After the solemn funeral, as we stood about on the front steps, one wag observed wryly, "Cerny was the only Sulpecian who ever died of an enlarged heart." No one laughed.

Tonsure

At the end of the year, I received Tonsure and the four Minor Orders without any negative intervention from the faculty. Although the Auxiliary Bishop of Baltimore came to administer the conferral on a group of us, I have no memory of the ceremony, an anticlimax to the announcement, I guess.

Wrapping it up.

My call to the clergy confirmed my sense of belonging. Like the proverbial sophomore (wise fool), I felt on top of things. I recognised that I didn't have what it takes to be a top theological student, but grades had never been that important to me. I only wanted to be known as smart and with-it. "Cool," I guess we would say today.

My summer in Sterling, my ineptitude in visiting the sick, my lame performance from the pulpit—all these made me aware of the gaps in my priestly education. It's not that the Sulpecians didn't know or didn't care about these ministerial functions. But they didn't see them as having priority over our theological and ceremonial training. It would be a lucky young priest who got the kind of experience I got from Father Frank. I looked forward to a continuation.

6

Seminarian Steelworker

As summer approached, I wrote Frank Bonnike, hoping to serve the parish ministry again in a now-familiar place. But I needed to earn some serious money. Frank replied in the affirmative, indicating that he would pull some strings and get me a summer job at Northwest Steel and Wire, a foundry and manufacturing plant in the small town. It would be a real job for real pay.

Amazingly, the string he pulled turned out to be astronomy pal Bob Lundberg, who wrote candidly, "If you intend to sweep floors at the local steel mill, get your application in early. Write Ted Janssen at Northwest Steel and Wire. You'll get the job! If you don't get satisfaction from him, I'll take it up with his boss."

Wow! Even though I didn't date his daughter.

I wrote as directed and a couple of weeks later, Janssen replied, telling me to show up at the employment office when I got to town.

I couldn't wait! My funds would be replenished at union rates.

Monday morning I showed up at the mill, bright and early, and began to fill out forms. Since I had no factory skills whatsoever, Janssen assigned me to the labor pool, available to fill in any empty spot that occurred.

"And get yourself some work boots," Janssen added. "Steel toes."

Facing the Factory

I showed up the next morning at seven a.m., found my card, punched the clock, and headed for the stamping room where 50 machines were engaged in pounding various sizes of nails out of sheet steel. The noise of the stamping room quadrupled as I opened the door, an eardrum-crushing cacaphony.

I reported to the foreman, but I heard nothing, even when he screamed directions right in my ear. He managed, by an emphatic pantomime, to indicate my work, picking up full bins of nails and dropping off empties.

I noticed that none of the regular workers used any kind of ear protection—no such thing as OSHA in those rugged days. I also saw that they talked normally to one another, though I couldn't make out a word. Somehow I got through the day without incident. When my shift was done, I walked out into the afternoon, my ears roaring as if I were still inside. I could hear nothing of the radio, the car engine, the other traffic.

"How'd it go," Father Bonnike asked solicitously when I arrived at the rectory. I pointed at my ears and shook my head. After a couple of hours, the ringing faded and I was able, to my great relief, to hear normally. Agnes, the German housekeeper, who regarded virtually everything that Bonnike and I did as ill-advised, shook her head and muttered, "*Zerstreuter Professor*," her usual appelation for me. But I couldn't hear her that well.

After another couple days in the stamping room, I was relieved to be assigned to the rolling mill, the heart of the operation. More glamorous, more respectable, and much better paid.

My new task was simplicity itself. As the white-hot stock issued from the shaping rollers, now cut into one foot lengths, I would seize every twentieth bar with a long pair of tongs and drop it in a bucket for testing. I was given a special asbestos apron and a helmet with a faceplate and a darkened window. A snap!

As I approached the first bar easing along the conveyer belt, the heat blazing off the glowing bar hit me like the flame from a blowtorch. The apron and the facemask helped, but my workshirt and gloves gave no protection at all from the searing heat. Driven by pride, I snatched the first bar, dropped it in the bucket and backed quickly away from the line of glowing steel. Apparently I was going to earn my "hazard pay" as I began to think of it.

Garbage Detail.

"Pick up those steel drums around the plant, wheel 'em out to the back deck and dump 'em in the truck there." The super stood, one glove on the handcart, and pointed at the drums. Sounded simple enough to me.

I quickly learned that steel mill "garbage" involved a lot of steel, a lot of oil, AND actual garbage—remains of lunches, snacks and so on. Filthy and heavy. Well, just do it.

Drum after drum, I wrestled the garbage onto my handcart, wheeled it to the back dock and dumped it into the truck, gradually coating myself with the oil, coffee grounds, etc. One drum got jammed with half the stuff stuck inside. Nothing for it, I had to get into the truck, waist deep in the filth, embrace the drum and try to shake it out. As I was doing this, another supervisor came up to me and said, "Hey, kid. I seen you around. What's the story? Tryin' to earn some money for college?"

I dropped the drum gratefully and answered, "No, I graduated from college." As the super stared at me, I added, "I'm in the seminary, studying to be a priest."

He shook his head and responded, rather inappropriately, "Well, I'll be God damned." I couldn't think of anything to say to that.

When I got back to the rectory and walked in the door, oily and reeking, Agnes took one look and cried out, *Ach, du Lieber*. Father Bonnike, instructing a couple in the front room, looked up and waved. As I mounted the stairs, I heard the guy ask, "Who was THAT?"

"Oh, that's Jim." Frank answered matter-of-factly, "He's a seminarian, staying here for the summer."—apparently no further explanation required.

Top of the Pay Scale

Seemed to me that my next assignment would be easy as anything.

I sat in front of a fifty foot long roll of steel fencing as it spooled out and into a long, complex galvanizing bath and then rolled up on the other end. When the end of the roll came up, I was to sieze the tail of the last roll, overlap it with the nose of the next roll, thrust a steel rod through the two to hook them together, then sit back and wait for the next hookup. A roll took about eight minutes to run through the bath.

I even had a partner in this simple-minded operation. He sat next to me on the bench, facing another roll of fencing so the two rolls ran side by side. Clumsy at first, I soon got the hang of the procedure, relaxed and began to chat with John, a kid even younger than myself. I made the same assumptions about him as the super had made about me. I guessed that, if he were lucky, he'd be here the rest of his life, moving up throught the seniority ranks, getting bored, getting old, getting fat.

"How long you been here?" I asked, striving to conceal my pity.

"Oh, about three and a half weeks. It's my second summer, though. Best pay in town."

"This just a summer job for you?" I don't know why I sounded surprised, other than my superior assumptions seemed challenged.

"Yes, I go to college during the school year." John spoke modestly but confidently.

"Whereabouts?" I offered, trying to readjust my assumptions.

"Knox College. I'm a math major." Whoa! I knew Knox to be a top small college and noted for its mathematics program. This guy may have been not only smarter than I was, but smarter than I *thought* I was.

Suddenly the tail of my roll appeared and, before I could grab the next roll and attach it, the tail disappeared into the galvanizing bath. I stared into the hot, bubbling brew, feeling no inclination to plunge my hand in after. But now what?

"No problem," John offered calmly. "I'll just hook yours to the end of mine and both rolls will pull through together." And he did that. I was suitably impressed.

"It's why they have two guys on this job, and why the position pays so much. It takes about two hours to drain the system and re-thread the rolls. So it pays to have two guys on the job, although one could do it."

"Yeah, if he was you," I thought to myself. Having established a kind of social equality, we chatted about college and seminary for the rest of the shift. I resolved to avoid classist judgments about my fellow workers. But I never got assigned to that job again, for no particular reason.

Christian Family Movement

Since I normally worked at the mill from seven to three, Father Bonnike found me some evening tasks, parish meetings, instruction groups, training servers, stuff like that.

One Sunday after Mass, he brought me over to a burly younger man standing with his family outside the church.

"Jim, I'd like you to meet Joe Cesarek. You'll be meeting with the CFM group at his house this Wednesday." Joe shook hands with a steelworker grip, then introduced his family: wife and three children, all friendly and welcoming.

"Good to have you, uh....Father?"

"Call me Jim," I said generously, "I'm not a priest yet. I'll see you at the meeting."

Chaplaining the Christian Family Movement group quickly became my favorite pastoral duty at Sacred Heart. The CFM Yellow Book described the chaplain's role succinctly—shut up and listen! A very good message for clergy, who have a tendency to explain, to solve, to go on and on. Well, you know. At the end of the meeting, the manual permitted a brief commentary on the scripture passage. That I could handle.

CFM'ers normally represent the cream of the parish crop, so to speak. Families with children, and frantically busy, they add a weekly two-hour meeting to discuss ways of deepening their faith, intensifying its practice, looking beyond the Sunday Mass and Confession. They had moved beyond easy pieties, wanted truth, challenge, and practical Christianity.

CFM grew out of the Catholic Action Movement, which originated in France in the thirties and there had considerable leftist leanings. Dangerous stuff in the post-McCarthy fifties, but I couldn't find anything in the manual that sprang from *The Daily Worker*. Intense, demanding, seeking for justice, yes, but socialist? Hardly.

Besides, I found myself becoming a bit of a leftist anyway. Rumors of a strike filled the conversations at the mill, and I listened intently. The RC church tended to be strongly pro-union at the time, with a lot of union members filling its congregations. Curiously, I didn't find a single worker who wanted to strike. One worker put it matter of factly. "This strike is all about the union leadership flexing their muscles. We'll never get back the wages we lose."

And the strike came. The day of the strike, working the three to eleven shift, I found myself alone with a broom in the vast 'attic' of the mill, sweeping up collected dust from years of neglect. The attic floor covered about a quarter of an acre. My eight hours of sweeping would only make a small mark in the surface. An exercise in pointlessness, but another day's pay, and my last, as it turned out.

At the end of my shift, I punched out, totally covered in dust and the last worker out of the plant. I passed through the picket lines forming for the strike, scheduled to begin at midnight, nodding to the few guys I knew. The strike would last a hundred and fifty-nine days, possibly the longest in U.S. labor history. I had returned to St. Mary's long before the settlement.

Cooking, Not Cleaning

Now freed from my labors, so to speak, I found myself the go-to guy for every kind of odd thing that came up, and lots of them did. Agnes Mierzwa had retired from the housekeeper position, and Father Bonnike had to make do with me.

"Here's the deal." he said to me, confidentially. "You make breakfast, I'll make lunch and we'll go out to dinner." I didn't have any problem with that. By "going out to dinner," Frank meant "hustling someone for dinner." Having the pastor for dinner was seen as a rare privilege. I didn't have a problem with that either.

We fell into a routine. Up at six. I would open the church at 6:30 for the seven o'clock Mass, set up the vestments, serve the Mass, then return to the rectory, start my reel-to-reel tape recorder, and make breakfast. I listened always to the same tape, a copy of *Joyous Bach*—an album designed to counter the image of J.S. as a heavy and dour German. And it did.

One morning, in mid-cook, the phone rang. The State Police. One of our parishioners had been killed in a car accident. The police wanted Father Bonnike to convey the news to the widow.

I hustled over to the sacristy to tell Bonnike.

I blurted the news, expecting a shocked reaction.

"Thank God." said Bonnike, fervently. "I'll tell you about it later." He hurried back to make his phone call, and I followed, wonderingly.

After he got off the phone, Bonnike told me the story: philandering husband returning drunk from a bender in Chicago; abused and neglected wife with two young kids and no solution for her situation.

"It's a gift from Heaven for her." Bonnike insisted. Who was I to argue? Clearly, I couldn't take things for granted in the humanly complex setting of the parish. When the phone rang, the subject might fall anywhere on the scale from tragic to trivial. Despite the fact that Sacred Heart had less than a hundred families, Bonnike had an activist presence in the community, and many of our calls turned out to be more than routine parish work.

I Do Some Pastoral Work

Frank, appointed Superintendant of Newman, the new central Catholic high school, had his hands full with the multiple daily decisions involving the building. By default, I got to pick up some of the pastoral slack, however unprepared I found myself. This included instructing so-called mixed marriage couples before their wedding. Bonnike's intention—convert the non-Catholic member. Their intention, normally—resist the sales pitch, and that's what it seemed to be, at least in the notes that Frank instructed me to follow.

"These kids come in here," Bonnike told me. "They have no idea what they're talking about. One guy comes in the other day. I asked him what religion he was. He answered, 'Protestant.' I said, 'What kind of Protestant? Baptist? Lutheran? Church of Christ? He had no idea. He just knew he wasn't Catholic."

"He took me right on," Bonnike offered with relish, rubbing his hands. "He said, 'It says in the Bible, call no man Father.' Thought he had me cold.

"What do you call YOUR Father?" Frank challenged.

"Dad," came the surly reply.

"But he IS your father, yes?"

"Well, I ain't goin' to call YOU 'Father.'" The perspective convert stood his tiny, principled ground.

"What ARE you going to call me?"

"Nothin'."

"That's fine with me." Frank had the last word, if not much of a moral victory. I didn't ask him how the instructions came out.

I had no inclination for such advocacy. I possessed neither sales skills nor a sales mentality. I had no desire to persuade the unwilling, indeed, found the whole process distasteful. Bonnike felt, very simply, that everybody should be Catholic, and given the chance, he could persuade them of their error. Compared to most priests, he came off rather successfully at this, and quizzed other priests on their "convert numbers," very much to their annoyance, since his were always much higher.

I followed his outlines gratefully, but toned down the contentiousness and advocacy stuff, presenting the material as "here's what Catholics believe" rather than "here's what you SHOULD believe." With the result that my few instructees expressed no interest in becoming Catholics.

"You don't confront them, Jim." Frank admonished, clearly disappointed in my wimpy approach. "You've got to convince them of the Truth."

I hemmed and hawed, feeling that he was right in principle, but just unable to approach people that way. I even felt awkward about the Church's strict requirements regarding mixed marriages, perceiving the rules as a kind of punitive harassment of the individuals involved.

Pass the Martinis, Please

True to our plan, Frank began to hustle dinners for us, starting with Leona Regan, our secretary. Well aware of our situation, Leona agreed to have us over, but pointed out firmly that it was not to be a regular thing. I've mentioned that Leona had clergy in the family and was not unduly impressed with the breed. This made for a more relaxed situation, since we didn't have to meet any expectations.

"Martini?" Leona asked cheerfully when we arrived.

"Absolutely," Frank replied, with no reference to the vodka brand which had not yet been invented.

"Why not?" I thought to myself, and answered, "Yes, please."

The first sip might have clued me. It seemed harsh and medicinal but, in a spirit of politeness, I continued to sip. Each sip became a little easier. I began to enter into the conversation more readily. Leona topped off my drink, and I began to hold forth with great confidence, pronouncing on matters ecclesiastical and parochial, mocking Bonnike for his on-the-go ministry, subtly revealing my theological superiority.

Bonnike smiled tolerantly at my sallies, but we took our leave early. I was feeling very well indeed—a condition which did not last 'til morning. An unfamiliar headache and a rancid taste in my mouth left me more than a bit humbled.

As I reflected on the experience, I came to realize that the martini, for some strange chemical reason, passed directly from my mouth through my palate and into my brain where the normal cautionary learnings became paralysed. I have had the same experience with subsequent martinis!

The Endless Phone Call and the Ending.

The phone sat on the dining room table between us, but Frank always answered. One morning at the end of breakfast, he picked up, said "Sacred Heart, Father Bonnike," then sat listening, occasionally rolling his eyes. After a couple of minutes, he passed the phone to me saying, "Listen to this."

I heard the voice of an elderly woman with a pronounced German accent complaining bitterly about her room, her landlady, her family and the general state of the world. She did not pause for reply, nor seem to expect one. I listened for a few minutes, then handed the phone back, mystified. Bonnike placed the phone on the table where the tiny complaining voice continued on for more than several minutes. Finally, the voice said, "Hello? Hello….?" then the sound of a hang up.

A bit shocked at Frank's callousness, I asked about the situation. "Just a lonely old lady who needs to talk." Frank acknowledged. "She really doesn't pay any attention to what you say, so I just let her go on 'til she hangs up."

I felt troubled by this, but after a few one-sided conversations with Mrs. Mertz, I began to understand Franks' response. Again, it wasn't my problem, until it suddenly *became* my problem.

"Mrs. Mertz is moving to another place," Frank announced, and added cheerfully, "and you're going to help her pack up." My heart sank at the announcement, but at least it was something I could do. I'd done it for my mother enough times.

"Be there at ten," Frank directed. "She's expecting you."

Expecting she was, but willing she wasn't. Her out-of-town children had made the arrangements. I avoided the issue with her, simply asking her directions about the packing and proceeding without discussing the issue. Somehow we got through it, I preserving a façade of impenetrable cheerfulness. At faking it, I was really making it.

A 'Hip' Infection

"Come in here a minute." Frank called one night as we headed for bed. "I want you to take a look at this pimple."

He stood in his shorts and, without apparent embarrassment, slid them down his leg. I looked at the "pimple." I saw a huge boil glaring at me; red lines extending in every direction, one running half-way down his leg.

"Frank. That's a boil. It's a serious staph infection and it's spreading down your leg. You've got to see a doctor, right away." I rarely spoke with such authority, but I knew boils from personal experience and I knew Bonnike. Denial is also a river.

Reluctantly he agreed and made a call the next morning to a doctor who belonged to our parish, a gynecologist, as it happens.

"You should have seen me," said Frank, upon his return. "There I am sitting there, surrounded by pregnant women. I felt a little conspicuous, to say the least."

Frank was making light of a serious infection, but the doctor, after lancing the boil, laid down the law—antibiotics; bed rest for a week; no sitting on the infected buttock.

That night, we were expected at a gathering of the clergy at Monsignor Burns' rectory. Burns, the pastor of St. Mary's, the big Catholic church in Sterling, had generated a series of stories about himself, and I was eager to see him in action.

"I can't go to that." Frank said, "You'll have to represent the parish."

"What'll I tell them?" I asked. "Everybody will want to know why you're not there."

"Tell them I have an infected hip," Frank instructed. This sounded a lot more dire than necessary, but wasn't exactly untrue. I would do as he told me.

I Represent the Parish

When I arrived at the rectory, the priests at once inquired about Bonnike.

"He has an infected hip." I stated, dutifully.

"Oooh, that sounds serious. How did it happen? Is he in the hospital?" A chorus of concern.

"No, no," I assured them, "only bed rest for a week."

"Wait a minute," interrupted the Monsignor, sharp as a tack. "What PART of the hip is infected?"

"Well," I said, grinning, "It's around toward the rear of the hip."

A burst of laughter followed. "Frank has a boil on his ass." Bonnike was liked among the younger priests, but also envied as a hotshot and a climber. This revelation would bring him down a bit.

Monsignor Burns offered me a drink, but I knew better and settled for a beer. Two young assistants had once visited Burns to pay their respects; he had offered them a drink and, when they agreed, brought them two water glasses filled to the rim with warm bourbon. Out of politeness and fear of offending, the young priests managed to drink about half the bourbon and left the rectory rather the worse for wear.

Another time, Burns's own assistant was driving the monsignor to some clerical affair in his new car. The monsignor pulled out a cigar and fumbled around for matches. With some pride, the assistant said, "No, no, Monsignor. I've got a cigar lighter right here."

He pushed in the lighter, pulled it out and showed the monsignor the glowing end.

"Amazing!" said the Monsignor, who took the lighter, lit his cigar, shook the lighter vigorously and tossed it out the window. No word as to whether they ever found the lighter.

Wrapping It Up

I liked my second summer in Sterling better than the first, but I learned that my natural shyness impaired my interaction with people other than those already disposed to approve me. This might have suggested to me that my anticipated parish ministry would not be easy. The formal stuff I could do, the personal stuff I might try to avoid. I felt proud of my factory work and grateful that I'd probably not have to do any more. And I'd saved up a bit of cash.

I thought that my interactions with the clergy went well. Though I was not technically one of them, I felt more *like* one of them that I did like one of the laity. Though barely a cleric, I already felt 'set apart' and therefore special. That, I *did* like.

1959–60

o o o o o o o o o o o o o o o o o o o o o o o o o o o o o o
"Anything you can do, I can do better….."

—*Irving Berlin*

7

Third Year

Roman Catholic clergy in major orders must observe perfect celibacy, by decree of the Second Lateran Council, convened in 1139 a.d. This decree was reaffirmed by later councils including Trent (1545-63) and the First (and, at that time, only) Vatican Council, (1869-70.) The original decree encoded reforms initiated by Pope St. Leo IX and Pope Gregory VII, attempting to clear up the chaotic state of the clergy emerging out of the so-called 'Dark Ages.' The reforms addressed the problem of priests passing their benefices (property and income) to their children, rather than concerns about their spiritual state or the quality of their ministry. The Eastern Orthodox clergy had always ordained married men, and continue to do so today.

Despite contemporary issues in the Church, such as the precipitous decline of vocations in America and Europe, pedophelia scandals in the U.S. and other countries, and the problems of patriarchy highlighted by the women's movement, the heirarchy and the Vatican have stood fast against demands to modify or eliminate the requirement, supported by various papal writings including those of Paul VI, more recently, by John Paul II and currently, by Benedict XVI.

Back to the Familiar

I returned to St. Mary's for my third year of theological studies secure in my feeling that I now understood the seminary process and could deal with it, one way or another. In addition, my summer experiences in Sterling gave me the sense that I had gained a step or two in experience over my classmates. Classically, I had gone from feeling inferior to feeling superior. What a guy!

Indeed, I felt so strongly about the value of my summer experience that I wrote Bishop Lane, suggesting that he demand of all his seminarians an equivalent opportunity. Unconsciously, I also intended to call myself and my exceptional qualifications to his attention. I might just as well have written, "Hey, Bishop Lane! Look at me!"

In any case, the Bishop did not reply, but he *did* take notice of me, as I learned later.

Father Genovese; Dogmatic Theology.

Father Paul Genovese entered the classroom swiftly, plopped his notes and the text on the table, fired off the opening prayer in rapid, slightly accented Latin, then collapsed into the chair on the dais, and buried his face in his hands. He remained there, unmoving, for a full minute, as we gazed around at one another, wondering if there were something we should do.

Genovese, a new addition to the faculty, constituted an unknown and potentially threatening presence. We had "the book" on most of our professors—that is, the unverified consensus of opinion formed by the students who had gone before us. But no one knew anything about Genovese—conservative or liberal, easy or tough, brilliant or pedestrian. We would have to figure it out for ourselves.

Father Genovese, a tall, slim, Italianate gentleman, already seemed exhausted by his responsibilities. As we waited silently, Genovese finally roused himself, rubbed his face heavily, as if trying to wake up, and then suddenly, in a loud voice, burst into his lecture.

He announced the thesis under consideration, cited the documentation, raises various questions, and then, in an excited and unintelligible burst, rushed through the conclusion at top speed, ending in a near shout. Then he fell back in his chair as if at the end of a fit and ask, exhaustedly, "Are there any questions."

We were stunned into silence. Since almost no one had understood the last burst, we didn't know what to say. Genovese gazed out mournfully at the class for a while, then opened his notes, gazed at them, let his head fall into his hands, and the whole process was repeated.

When the first class was over and we rushed to the steps to discuss the experience—the general tone one of wonder and mystification. What had he said? What was the point he was making?

Another time, Genovese, after an extra-long class-opening face burial, lifted his head, stared at the class with intensity and spoke quietly, but with great conviction.

"Gentlemen, you've got to elasticize your inclinations to pigeonhole."

Who could not agree? But I don't know that we did. It sounded like good advice, but it didn't seem to apply to the class material. Genovese's pronouncement had no context that we knew of, but I saw a lot of students writing it down. And so did I.

Laughing in the Seminary.

Solemn situations often lead to laughter because there is only a thin line between the solemn and the absurd. In the seminary, every ceremony in the chapel was conducted in the highest seriousness. At the same time, a bunch of guys, most of them in their early twenties, are predisposed to laugh when things go wrong. The fact that the faculty deeply disapproved of this response only increased the psychological pressure.

One of the hymns we sang included the phrase "acknowledge duly," used at the end of a line. And the class ahead of us had a member named William Dooley. Someone picked up on the pun and when the phrase came up, he would turn partially toward Dooley and bow slightly, in a solemn liturgical manner. Dooley's face would turn bright red.

Word of this got around very quickly, and more and more guys, both in his section and across the aisle would incline their heads toward the deeply embarrassed and totally helpless Dooley. It may have come to the attention of the choirmaster, because the hymn disappeared from our repetoire and there was no other occasion to "acknowledge Dooley," much to our regret.

A Rare Visitor

Mrs. Mitchell, a woman without fear, leaned far out of the visitor's gallery on a second level over the high altar trying to see her son, seated in the chapel below and well to her left. Her brilliant yellow straw hat, of a spectacular circumference, caught every eye.

And then, as if in answer to prayer, a sudden gust caught it and swept it off her head. It sailed down across the sanctuary and glided to a perfect landing on the other side. We supressed applause. Spider Meyer, as always the Master of Ceremonies, slid smoothly across the sanctuary, picked up the hat as if he did this at every Mass, and disappeared into the sanctuary.

Mrs. Mitchell, a British actress, resumed her seat and smiled dazzlingly. The moment was over.

Her son Tony, a year ahead of me, had some vivid moments of his own. Returning from London for his third year, the airline weighed his baggage and pronounced it to be almost a hundred pounds (or a hundredweight?) over the limit and proposed a stiff additional fee.

Unprepared for this expenditure, Tony picked up his bags and made his way to the men's room. There he unearthed jackets and sweaters and photographic equipment, layered himself to bulging and removed bottles and bottles of Bovril, a vile British beef jelly to which he was addicted. Using shoelaces, he managed to suspend the Bovril around his neck and waist. He returned, swollen and staggering a bit, to another check-in point, made the weight, and jammed himself into a seat, no doubt to the disgust of the passengers next to him.

"A beastly hot trip," Tony recalled, "but oi saved meself abaht fifty pound."

Another time, Tony showed me some photos he had taken of the building. I noticed that they had been hand-printed.

"These are very sharp. Did you print them yourself?"

He nodded, pleased.

"Where?" I asked. "I didn't know we had a darkroom."

"We don't." Tony smirked. "Oi 'ave one. In me closet." The enterprising Brit had stashed his clothing elsewhere and set up a printer in his closet. Shades of Al Lingus, in a way, but a little less pious. To my knowledge, he never got caught. But then, it wasn't specifically against the Rule.

There Goes That Tune Again...

One day in February, the longest-seeming month, as we sat slumped in class, trying to stay awake, a piano tuner began work in the music room at the end of the hall. As he struck one note over and over, someone in the back picked up on it and began to hum, as if getting a pitch. Other guys picked up on it, and soon there was a perceptible hum coming from the back of the classroom—a hum which changed in pitch as the tuner did.

The professor picked up on it and stared at the back of the room, but a humming face looks much the same as a non-humming face. Finally, he simply said "Stop that." The hummers stopped, the non-hummers in the front looked around in confusion, the moment had passed.

The Movies

One night, we packed Prayer Hall to the rafters for a movie screening—the first and only one during my four years. Someone on the faculty—I'm guessing it was the rector, Gene Van Antwerp—had rented *When Comedy Was King*, a compilation of scenes from slapstick comedies of the silent era.

It was perfect for the audience—a bunch of young men trapped in an institutional setting. Every pie in the face, every skidding turn, every pratfall brought roars of laughter. We pounded each other on the shoulders and backs. The laughter reinforced itself. A comic's dream!

The movie ended to cheers and applause. Van Antwerp looked enormously gratified, but he quieted the crowd and said, in his Navy chaplain voice, "Compline in five minutes." It was close to ten p.m., and Compline should have been said at nine.

Spilling out of the prayer hall, we headed for the chapel, pulling on white surplices over our cassocks for the formal chanting of the Office. One of the last skits had featured Laurel and Hardy and a tearaway suit As we poured into the chapel, Jim Hodrick made as if to rip off my surplice sleeve. The guys behind us began laughing, and others began to imitate the gesture. Those already in their pews could see the action and by the time we were all in place, the whole congregation was chuckling, including some of the faculty.

Then the Deacon intoned the beginning of Compline: *Fratres, sobrii estote et vigilate* ("Brothers, be sober and watchful.") and the irony of the line was not lost on the seminarians, many of whom laughed aloud.

A glance at the faculty stalls revealed that some of the faculty were, in the vivid phrase of Queen Victoria, "not amused." I guessed that Van would take some flak for his film choice in the faculty council.

Somehow we got through the service as the mood wore off and, although nothing was said about the incident, no further movies were scheduled for our entertainment.

Musical Memories

My seminary jazz scene took a sharp turn for the better with the coming of third year.

This John Davis showed up, another "guy straight from the world," with a B.A. from Holy Cross and a Master's in Education from Harvard yet. We took to each other immediately, sharing a similar background, outlook, and attitude. Davis, a cigar man, liberally supplied with The Weed by his tobacconist grandfather in Maine, quickly converted me from my pipe to the tasty but deadly cheroots.

Among his several talents, Davis had mastered the keyboard, playing both classical music and jazz with equal facility. A brilliant and humorous improviser, he played the whole keyboard and could take a pop tune and turn it into Mozart, Beethoven, Prokofief, whatever came to mind. On non-glee club nights, we'd hook up in the music room and jam, though my clumsy tenor sax could barely keep up.

I was much taken with the idea of starting a piece in a classical mode, then segueing into jazz. I worked out a little Mozartian riff which suddenly turned into *Surrey With the Fringe*. As I think of it now, I ripped off Paul Desmond and Dave Brubec. Seemed like a good idea at the time.

Though Davis had abundant classical training and a wide pop repetoire, and though he could swing, he knew virtually nothing about the harmonics of cool jazz, the commercially successful alternative to bebop. This gave me something to contribute to our duo in addition to my sax work.

Davis had quarried a barbershop quartet out of the glee club, but they had a very traditional sound. He was so impressed with my seeming understanding of the "modern" sound that he asked me to write a "cool" arrangement for the quartet.

"We'eh really squeah, y'know," Davis offered in his native patois. "I neveh sang that modehn stuff."

"How about *Winter Wonderland?*" I suggested. "I think I could do something with that."

I should have been amazed by my temerity. I had never written a line of music in my life. But I found myself in a "can do" state of mind.

I sat down at my desk the same night, drew a bunch of staff lines with a ruler, and laboriously began to lay out the introduction. After about an hour, I had finished two lines in four parts and liked the way they sounded in my head. I hastened up to Davis' room and slid the paper under his door.

I didn't see him again until the afternoon rec next day. When I caught up to him, I asked what he thought of the music. Poker-faced, he led me to the piano, pulled the two lines out of his sleeve, and played them out without speaking. The music had no meaning whatever. The notes sounded totally aimless.

"That's IT?" I asked incredulously.

"That's it," Davis agreed, with a strange look.

"Play it again." I insisted. It sounded just the same. I began to laugh, as did Davis. Soon he had his head on the piano, shaking helplessly. I wasn't far behind. Whenever we cooled off, Davis would play the piece again, and we would dissolve. I don't know what happened to the music, but I have never again attempted to arrange anything.

The Rev. Mr. John "Eighty-eight Keys" Davis, in a moment of repose.

All That Jazz.

"I hear you guys have a jazz band."

The speaker—a short, blond, first year man, name of Paul Santyr. We did have a jazz band! As a result of our performance at the Gaudeamus the previous year, the jazz band became institutionalized among the various social activities of the seminary

"That's right. You a player?"

"Drums."

"Great." I said, "We need a drummer. Our drummer was ordained last spring. You any good?" Who was I to ask, the weakest player among the remains of last year's band? But Santyr didn't know that yet. I loved jazz and carried on about it to all who would listen. So someone pointed me out to Santyr.

We made arrangements to get together during evening rec, Santyr set up his drums and we began to jam. One tune made it clear that Paul was our new leader. An excellent drummer and a pure jazz man, Santyr breathed life into the organization, and we became a driving, hard-swinging group.

Part of the attraction of jazz for me sprang from images of the jazz scene—a visual realization of my secret longing to be a beatnik. Arriving a generation too late and far too emotionally cautious to commit to the Beat life, I still felt a romantic attraction to the outsider lifestyle. I read Kerouac and Ferlingetti and Ginsberg, and identified with the cool, though I totally lacked it. But jazz and the big sax fitted my idealized picture of myself, and the realities of my life and commitments made little impact on that picture.

Speaking of pictures, there is a photograph somewhere of me, dressed as a beatnik, with a pointy, wispy goatee, dark glasses, beret, and blowing on my sax to a fare-thee-well. Charlie MacKay took the photo and actually got it printed in *The Voice*, which circulated among thousands of the graduates of the ancient institution. *The Voice* faculty advisor probably got some letters on that one, along the lines of "what has the seminary come to in our time…?"

Anyway, the band began to practice more earnestly, read real charts and acquired what we regarded as an authentic sound. We petitioned the rector, who granted us the opportunity to give a concert.

We played in the basement theatre; a stage at one end and a large, unadorned room with extremely live accoustic possibilities. Students packed the place, ready for some action. We blew our brains out for an hour to enthusiastic applause and cheers and a standing ovation at the end.

As the response continued, I turned to the sweating Paul, still hunched over his drums and said, "Paul, we got to do an encore."

Paul shook his head. I couldn't believe it.

"Come on," I said, "we owe them one." Paul simply shook his head again and said, "I can't." He had been drumming on the last number holding both sticks and maracas in his hands, and the maracas had worn the skin between his thumbs to the point where both hands were bleeding.

Appalled, I turned to the audience and waved them off. They quieted and we packed up, shaking our heads over the condition of Paul's hands, and amazed at his commitment.

The next day, we gathered eagerly in the practice room to listen to the tape. Bad. When bad *was* bad. Worse than bad: uneven tempos, false starts, wrong notes—a whole catalog of mistakes. Our musical egos crawled under a rock somewhere, and we swore to work harder and pay more attention.

The musician-pundit Mason Williams once posed the conundrum: "To have a tape of our whole lives, and then not have the time to watch it." With all due repect for Williams' inspired absurdity, I'm mighty glad not to have a tape of my whole life. I'm pretty sure that it would be very much like the tape of our jazz concert. One time through—plenty.

Paul Santyr, too much of a jazz man for the scene, left the seminary after one year; Cornelio Parado was ordained; and the remainder of the band failed to coalesce into another aggregation. Maybe memories of the tape continued to haunt us. But Davis and I continued as a duo through the end of my deacon year.

Particular Friendship

The Rule discouraged duos. Davis and I had much in common beyond the jazz playing. We shared a taste in music, a love of tobacco, a dry sense of humor, memories of our recent and secular college experiences. Davis came from a small city in Maine not that much different from Elgin.

So we practiced together and when we weren't practicing, we often walked together. And attracted faculty notice! I got the word from my confessor, Ray Brown.

"Some of the faculty have commented that you and John Davis spend a lot of time together," Father Brown observed, rather neutrally.

My blood ran cold. I knew instantly that he referred to the dreaded "particular friendship" indictment. The case against particular friendship was presented as a violation of the spirit of community. Particular friendships excluded others, and therefore should be avoided. Never the least suggestion of improper affection, but everyone knew what lay behind the prohibition.

"No, no," I protested, profoundly uncomfortable with a sense of the unspoken. "We play jazz together. That's it."

"There's more to it than that." Ray insisted mildly. "You walk together a lot, and just the two of you."

"Well, I'll look into it," I promised. I felt shaken, both because I had never been called on anything before, and because I heard the suggestion of an inappropriate relationship. I would have to tell Davis, the first-year man, and I'm sure he would take it the same way as I.

"We can't go walking together all the time," I told Davis, bluntly. "The faculty have called me on particular friendship and I've got to do something." I felt like I was saying, "We've got to start seeing other people." Weird.

"That's nonsense." Davis protested.

"I agree," I responded, "but we've got to do something about it."

We did, and it turned out awkward, of course. Davis felt offended, and I was the author of the offense. We began 'seeing other people,' time went by, and Ray Brown reported no further objections from the faculty. Just doing their job, I guess.

The Medium is the Message

The outside world came little into our sheltered lives. I have mentioned how eagerly we sought the worn and scattered pages of the Sunday *New York Times* when sections would find their way to the jakes. Apart from that, we had no news, no radios, no magazines, no television.

But things began to relax slightly under the new and easier regime of Father Gene "Brass Ass" Van Antwerp, who had spent much of his priestly career as a navy chaplain and knew rather more than most Sulpecians about the lives and attitudes of young men. Not that we were exactly the same as a bunch of navy recruits, but maybe not that much different, either.

One electronic wall came crashing down in 1959, under the impetus of Catholic Jack Kennedy's campaign for the presidency. The Kennedy campaign, dogged by accusations of "popery," made Democrats out of many of us and a very silent majority of the rest.

At any rate, under vigorous pressure from the deacon class, Van was persuaded to permit watching the news during the evening rec, not every night (lest it be habit forming) but maybe three times a week. Television being addictive, as we now know, the privilege was extended, after intense pressure, to one entertainment program following the news.

To provide the necessary regulation and protect us from the lurid diversions of 'fifties' television, a so-called TV deacon was appointed and a faculty member designated to pre-approve or even select the program we might watch. Talk about *in loco parentis*!

Father Canfield and Jack Benny

The arduous duty of monitoring fell to Father John Canfield, a new member of the faculty, and generally unknown to my class. As I recall, he taught Dogmatic Theology to the First Year class and was reputed to be paralyzingly dull and quite indifferent to the liberal/conservative conflicts going on. In any case, one memorable evening, the TV Deacon had selected an appropriately serious and newsworthy program—possibly an NBC White Paper report on some national issue—when Father Canfield showed up in the rec room and took his place among the group of watchers staring through a cloud of cigarette smoke at the large black and white set.

It took a few moments for him to realize the time and what he was watching, then he called out, "Where's Jack Benny?" The TV Deacon said that he had chosen the NBC program because of its importance and relevance to our concerns.

"I want to watch Jack Benny!" insisted Father Canfield. "I marked it on the schedule, and I want to see it. Switch it on." He didn't stamp his foot, but he might as well have.

The TV Deacon silently stepped to the set and switched on the Benny program, then in progress. As the seminarians watched with growing attention, Benny presented a series of sexy sketches, with lots of double entendre jokes, and lovely young women dressed as lightly as the times permitted. Father Canfield writhed in his chair, but by making such an issue of his choice, he would lose face by canceling. The group watched in silence till the end of the show.

I don't know how the whole event was represented to the rector, but in any case, it was the last time that the Jack Benny show appeared on the rec room set.

Boarding the B & O.

Father Spider Meyer, always an early riser, stared unbelieving at his wall clock. The time had just jumped ahead three minutes. He looked at his own watch and then back at the wall clock, connected to the central clock system. Once again, the clock jumped ahead three minutes. By the time he had thrown on a cassock and headed downstairs to the central office, the clock would be a full twelve minutes ahead of the rest of the Eastern Seaboard.

"What the hell's going on here?" Meyer's stage whisper filled the empty office, but the open wall clock and the chair underneath it told him all he needed to know. However, Spider's noisy footfalls down the marble steps of the central staircase had warned the perpetrators and they had fled.

By this time, Meyers had already figured out what was going on. Christmas vacation would begin this morning right after breakfast and the train riders would be desperate to make their connections in downtown Baltimore, a chancy twenty-five minute cab ride from the seminary. Some enterprising spirits who understood the interconnected clock system had slipped into the office before six a.m. and advanced the controlling clock in a series of jumps to give themselves a little edge in making the train.

Not a party to this plot myself, I would nevertheless benefit. The Baltimore and Ohio had one passenger train a day for Chicago, leaving at 8:57 a.m., in the days when the railroads prided themselves on being to the minute. I had never missed the train, but I surely didn't want to spend an extra day in the seminary, and we had to buy our tickets in the station.

The midwestern deacons had made an appeal to the rector for a few minutes grace in view of the inflexible B & O schedule. But the B & O's inflexibility mirrored the rector's own. He gave the classic response: "If we make an exception for one or a few, we'll have to make it for everyone." It must be written in Latin somewhere.

So the morning of departure sizzled with tension. Our bags packed and lined up in the front hall, we were set for instant departure. Cabs had been arranged and would be lined up at 8 a.m. But the seminary schedule proceeded in its relentless manner—six a.m. rising, 6:30 meditation, 7:00 Mass followed by the liturgically anomalous "thanksgiving" Mass (all Masses are Eucharistic celebrations. Eucharist means thanksgiving. A liturgical redundancy!)

Breakfast at 8 a.m. Tradition held that we were free to go at the *Tu autem* which ended the grace. At that moment, a roar went up. Those of us who were trying to catch cabs grabbed rolls from the table and fled down the halls, peeling off our cassocks, grabbing our bags and finding our rides. Chaos erupted out of order. We loved it.

"Round trip to Chicago. Coach. And the clergy discount, please." We didn't get into any technical discussions about the degrees of my clerical status.

"$42.50."

I pushed my money through the iron wicket, glancing nervously at the track to see if the train was moving. But once again, I had made it.

Free Again

Basically, I liked riding trains, and I certainly liked vacations, which gave me a chance to renew all those relationships which I thought of as home.

We certainly must have looked a bit odd on the train in our black suits. Maybe taken for Amish, or Catholic seminarians. In any case, people rarely spoke to us, fearing some sort of religious pitch or other. It didn't bother me a lot, being basically a shy type anyway.

Once, in the lounge car, a gregarious salesman type gestured at our group and said to me, "You guys belong to some religious organization?"

"Yes," I answered, "We're seminarians. Studying to be priests." I was all ready to explain the seminary structure and point out our elevated rank in the structure, but he merely said, "Oh." and turned away. Stuff he didn't need to hear.

If we had a group, we talked, played cards, read, hit the lounge car. We could buy *beer*! Actually, during my first year, I had made a pledge not to drink and I didn't. But the pledge didn't survive all the way to the summer, and second year, I passed up the pledge.

By four in the afternoon, the need for something else to do became palpable. At the first announcement of dinner, we hastened to the ining car. I remember vividly that the B & O served a green salad with or without bleu cheese. Most of the guys hated bleu cheese; I loved it. The cheeze came in a wooden bowl intended for the table of four.

"Take mine," said Dempsey, making a face. "Mine, too," added Jack Melloh, from Wisconsin. Mike McKenna merely nodded assent. With enthusiasm, I heaped my greens with four generous servings of bleu cheeze chunks. By the end of the meal, I began to feel that I had overdone it with the cheeze. Indeed, my digestive system continued to remind me of the meal for the rest of the trip.

More riding, more reading, more cards, and it was time to hit the hay. For a couple of hours, we tossed and turned in our hard old coach seats.

"I've got an idea," said Dempsey. "Let's go up in the observation car. The seats are better there, and they recline way back." And we did that, staring for a while at the blackness rushing by, then plumping our pillows and settling back.

Just after dropping off to sleep, I felt a heavy hand hitting the back of my recliner. "No sleeping in the observation car." The disapproving voice of the car attendant caused me to jerk my seat up.

"Not sleeping," I muttered stupidly, "Just dropped off for a minute." I turned again to stare out at the rushing blackness. The conductor left; we dropped our seats back, fell asleep and in about twenty minutes, repeated the whole business. What is it about a uniform that turns a human being into an arrogant authoritarian jerk? And wasn't I wearing a kind of uniform? Uh, oh.

Dempsey and I gave up and headed back to our coach seats. I don't know what kind of sleep we got, but it wasn't much.

Flirting with Heresy

Hot news from the bookstore—an unlikely source. Some faculty member, probably Norris, had approved the acquisition of Teilhard de Chardin's controversial (and published postmortem) *The Phenomenon of Man*, a highly praised but bitterly disputed exercise in speculative thinking.

Chardin, a Jesuit and a highly respected scientist, postulated that the earth possessed (or was evolving toward) a consciousness which transcended the individual awareness, and would finally result in a direct connection with the divine.

I won't get into the details, because I'm not one of the thirteen people on earth who understand Chardin. Chardin's thinking precursed (a word?) the 'Gaia hypothesis' so popular in the seventies. I'm not sure what the "intelligent design" folk might think, other than to note that Chardin's vision stood at the opposite pole from fundamentalism.

Anyway, the bookstore had copies of *The Phenomenon of Man* under the counter and sporting a plain brown paper cover. Only those who knew could ask for it. The bookstore clerks (seminarians) were not permitted to speak of it, but they would sell you a copy. About $15, as I remember. They flew from under the counter, reeking with the allure of the forbidden.

I loved the forbidden as much as the next guy, but I wasn't willing to pony up a solid fifteen dollars for it. I figured I could check out the library's copy before anyone else. If the library dared order it. As it turned out, they didn't.

Chardin, seven years in the grave, earned himself a *monitum* (warning) from the Holy Office in 1962. This boosted sales and gave him a kind of countercultural theological cachet which continues, more or less, until the present day. How it may have affected his immortal soul, we can only speculate, if we are so inclined.

More Heretical Leanings

The deacon class invited auditions for the fall play—a musical! *Brigadoon*, in fact. A small group of malcontents arose at once, pointing to an editorial in the Davenport *Messenger*, a respected Catholic newspaper. The editorialist inveighed against the 'reincarnation subtext' of the plot, wherein a Scottish village under an enchantment, reappears for a day once every hundred years. A local Catholic college was performing the popular musical, and the *Messenger* feared for the faithful exposed to the insidious message implied in the plot.

Well, come ON! I loved the stage version, seen in summer stock and even the awkward movie version with Gene Kelly in the lead role. 1954, I think it was.

Anyway, a bunch of musical types from the Glee Club tried out. Jack Melloh, fresh from a leading role in the Mozart *Requiem,* nailed the part of Tommy. I made it into the chorus. I can't remember how we handled the female roles; as best I can remember, a narrator carried us over the romantic elements.

One specific fragment remains. We choristers were required to appear to be talking in the background during scenes, but could make no sound. What to say. Someone suggested that we exchange the silent phrase, "You suffer much." For lip readers, it appeared that we were saying: "You son of a bitch." We loved it.

The show ran to a packed house and thunderous applause. No theological objections raised; not even questions regarding the appropriateness of the choice. The deacons had pushed the envelope and we would push it further next year.

A More Spirited Reading

My turn had come! Spiritless Reading currently featured Walter Ong's *The Image Industries,* a dissection of current popular culture by the brilliant and offbeat Jesuit theologian. The head reader handed me the text and indicated the chapter I would read.

In the current chapter, Ong took on Mickey Spillane, and his phenomenally popular Mike Hammer detective series. The sex, the violence and the cynicism, uniquely raw and direct for the time, had boosted Spillane to the peak of popular notoriety.

To illustrate his points, Ong quoted a long and vivid closing passage from *I, The Jury,* in which Hammer, deceived, beat-up, betrayed, confronts the voluptuous blonde who has done him in. Covered by Hammer's .45, she gives him one last sexy kiss. Mike blasts her in the guts with the automatic. As she slumps to the ground, dying, she gasps, "Mike, how could you?"

"It was easy," sneers Hammer, concluding the story with a bang.

Needless to say, I held the avid attention of every single listener in the room, including Bull Noonan, the vice rector.

"Nice reading, Jim," someone complimented me snidely after dinner.

"What can I tell you," I responded, innocently. "It was easy!"

Seminary Sanctuaries.

I'm not talking about Quasimodo screaming from the high altar of Notre Dame, or even Benjamin Braddock in *The Graduate* swinging the cross to save himself and Elaine from the charging wedding guests. I'm talking about safe places where the faculty rarely or never came. Places where we could congregate away from the structure of the schedule, where we could, well, hang out.

The music room, the *Voice* room, the bindery and of course, the jakes provided opportunities for guys to gather away from the isolation of their rooms, especially during the Great Silence, which grew oppressive. I found my own sanctuary in a more conventional way.

Library Workroom

"Why don't you come work for us in the library?" The speaker, John Varley, a third year man, had charge of the operation, and recruited carefully for his workers. We shared a dining hall table for the time, and Varley felt amused by my observations. As far as I could tell, he picked workers for the library staff based on their entertainment value.

By way of passing time in the seminary, various volunteer opportunities were available. Bookstore, library, well…maybe that was it. Anyway, the library seemed like a good gig in my mind.

St. Mary's Seminary library: theology books and plenty of them.

"You'll find it interesting," Varley promised. "I can tell you're a book guy." I *was* a book guy, but I didn't know how Varley could tell. And somehow, I had never worked in a library.

"I'll think about it," I hedged.

"Come on by and take a look." Then Varley threw in the kicker. "You can smoke in there."

Aha! A more and more dedicated pipe smoker, I found it hard to sit at my desk for long periods without smoking. (For that matter, I found it hard to sit at my desk for long periods WITH smoking. Father Dukehart had been right; I liked to be doing stuff!)

That very afternoon, I made my way there. The library workroom occupied a large square space behind the stacks. It held a number of carrels for the catalogers to work in and a large table in the center for more general work, as well as shelves, lots of shelves. And piles and piles of books.

As I opened the door, I confronted a surprising scene. Jim Hodrick, a classmate, lay on his back on the worktable, his legs waving in the air, desperately attempting to recreate a yoga position called The Plow, in which the legs are lifted over the head and brought straight down to touch behind the head.

Hodrick, game but substantially overweight, flailed his legs around without approaching the ground. A bunch of guys had been trying out positions from a new book by Caleb Deschanel called *Christian Yoga*. Now they cheered on the hapless Hodrick with useless offers of advice.

"Relax, Jimbo. Focus. Pay attention to your breathing." Hodrick was having difficulty breathing at all! After Hodrick crawled off, gasping, I said, "Hey, let me have a try."

I peeled off my cassock, glanced at the illustration in the book, hopped up on the table and assumed The Plow. Being skinny and limber, I could hold the position with a modest effort. When I returned to the horizonal, I felt surprisingly refreshed. To a moderate round of applause, I dismounted, just a bit red-faced from the effort, and joined in the socializing. The library workroom seemed like a scene I could get into.

I even bought the yoga book, and began doing the exercises in my room. I thought doing yoga to be extremely cool, ecumenical, and it felt good. An excellent trifecta!

That night, after dinner, I hooked up with Varley, told him I'd like to work there and got on the schedule. It became my home away from home in the sem.

More Sanctuaries

Other places served the same function for others. The craft type of guys gravitated to the book bindery, mysterious with heavy pieces of equipment for stitching, gluing, binding and pressing the books.

The *Voice* room on the fourth floor of the building, cluttered with desks, papers, books, bulletin boards and files, looked more or less like every press room I had ever been in. I felt at home there, too, and I had a buddy on the staff. But I had done that magazine scene for four years at Notre Dame, and didn't want to get drawn in. Besides, the guys on the staff had me whipped intellectually and I knew it.

John Jones, studying for Rockford, and two years ahead of me, served as Editor. We had stuff in common. He had done Notre Dame time, and originated from Dixon, Illinois, just up the road from Sterling, where I had spent two summers. Smart, committed, liberal, a bit sardonic about the system, Jones and I hit it off right away. He invited me to review books for the magazine, and I added that activity to my collection of strategies for avoiding study.

Apparently, a few of the younger professors conducted soirees for likeminded students, but I never made the cut. I think even Willie O'Shea held court for some of the more intensely liturgy-minded guys.

The Infirmary and the Bookbindery provided other clubby settings, but not for me. Key to all the hideaways: not a lot of guys knew or cared about them. They provided little communities "in the know" or so we liked to feel.

Vuestra Merced!

"Why is "*usted*" written '*Vd.*'?" My question sprang not from my desire to learn, but to slow the progress of the Spanish class and thus hide my insufficient preparation. Mr. Fanelli, an elderly Italian gentlement and the only lay member of the seminary faculty, saw through my transparent strategy, but could not keep from rising to the bait. Courtly and pious, he loved the intricacies of language and the opportunity to explain.

"The 'Vd' represents a shortening of the phrase, *vuestra merced*, a polite form of address in old Spanish. Why did you want to know, particularly now, Mr. O'Brien?"

"Oh, I just wondered." I offered lamely. Charlie MacKay quickly took up the cause.

"What's the really polite form of greeting someone?" He asked. It had nothing to do with the lesson.

"*Gusta me mucho a encontrarse con Vd.*" Mr. Fanelli replied, "But no one uses it any more. It takes too much time." He spun off into a little wistful homily about the passing of social graces (as we all hoped he would,) then sternly picked up the text and said, "Gentlemen, no more stalling." The five of us opened our books and stared at the faintly familiar exercise.

Spanish? Lamely remembering my grandiose attempt to acquire a theology degree *and* a knowledge of Spanish, I realized that I had better make some attempt at complying with the bishop's expressed wish. Charlie MacKay tipped me off to the class.

"It's being offered once a week, for an hour, by this Italian guy," MacKay offered, always with the inside knowledge. "There'll be four or five of us in the class. Should be a snap."

"*Gratias.*" I replied coolly, using up a good part of my Spanish apart from the names of foods.

Once a week for an hour, taught by a non-native speaker may not be the best way to learn a language, but somehow I have managed to retain enough of *la lingua Espana* to fake my way through the rudiments of conversation and order *pequito vino* if absolutely necessary. However, I would get my comeuppance the following summer, as you shall hear.

Sex and the Single Seminarian

It wasn't that we didn't talk about sex in the seminary; there just wasn't much to talk about, was there? We all knew that we had taken or would soon take solemn promises of celibacy. (*Not* vows, by the way, only members of religious orders take vows.) This promise would occur for most of us at the end of our third year when ordained to the rank of sub-deacon. This ordination, as we well knew, conveyed only obligations rather than powers or privileges.

The going gag among third year guys about to take the big step was a bit subtle. As subdeacons, we promised to practice "perfect chastity." As deacons, we would promise to practice "more perfect chastity." Fat Jack Atkinson of Tennessee would wonder, "What had we been missing out on all summer?"

The virtually unspeakable issue of homosexuality hovered in the background. The word, or even its vulgar variants, was rarely spoken. Nonetheless, we knew that each class had a group whose vocal stylings, affectations and preoccupations might have suggested that they were, in a phrase of the time, a little "light in the shoes". We had a kind of vague understanding that a small sub-community existed within the larger class. Of course, "they" knew, but we could only assume.

Only once in my four years was the forbidden topic broached publicly, and then by accident. Most of us remembered Van's blurt while explaining the Rule against entering other seminarian's rooms. Clearly the faculty WAS afraid of homosexuality.

Heterosexual sexuality was rarely alluded to, even jokingly. We heard no locker room talk of girls at all.

One time, talking with Charlie McKay, who seemed to know all, I made the observation that many seminarians seemed to have very strong mother figures or widowed mothers, like myself.

"Surprise!" said McKay, ironically. "You never noticed that? Think about it. It'll tell you a lot about the priesthood."

And think I did. And the more I thought about it, and the more I thought about the many priests that I knew and my fellow seminarians, the more I noticed that they seemed to fear women. Women represented a threat, not merely to the priest's virtue, but somehow to the priest's person. Because, I suspect, attraction to a woman represented a betrayal of mother's powerful love. I guess a Freudian would call it an "unresolved Oedipal complex" because that's the way they talk.

Women as Threat

As preparation for pastoral life, we received plenty of warnings about the dangers of women.

"Always keep your desk between you and any woman," counselled Father Brennan.

"Watch out for the nice ones," warned Father Falcone, "You don't fall for the floozie but for the organist."

Father Van Antwerp put it with typical military vigor and reductionism, "There's your mother and my mother, and then there's all the rest of them." I wondered if Father Van had any sisters.

In the ministry and exposed (so to speak) to women in real life, most of us grew up and overcame our unreasoning fear of women. Then another problem raised its head. With the emotional isolation of the ministry, with the supply of needy, attractive, available women often drawn to to if not downright challenged by the roman collar, with the opportunities for special and private access, many priests gave in to their needs; sometimes with great moral agony—sometimes with enthusiasm, and sometimes permanently, not unlike myself.

Others retreated into a crusty hostility, barely masked by civility, and fortified by an abundance of macho anti-women sayings and attitudes and by the masculine sub-society in which they moved.

With homosexual priests, a variety of patterns doubtless emerged, but I remained unfamiliar with that world. I just didn't think about it much.

As for pedophilia, the horrific scandal now sweeping the headlines and shaking the church heirarchy as never before, the isolated seminary life offered no opportunities. Certainly the subject never came up in classes.

When I first learned, many years later, that a seminary schoolmate had been arrested and convicted in Minnesota after a long clerical career largely devoted to preying upon children, I couldn't imagine it. I knew Jim Porter fairly well, and never noticed anything strange about him. Naive as I was, I didn't even find it strange that Porter had engaged in his obsession over twenty or more years with no meaningful intervention by his bishop. When unmasked, he received a transfer from his northeast diocese to the unthinkable wilderness of Minnesota.

We later learned that the transfer approach became standard practice, either within the diocese or, in extreme cases, to another diocese. Only in the present time are we learning of the complicity of the heirarchy in concealing, protecting, transferring and otherwise enabling this evil, all in the name of "protecting the people from scandal". But who was protecting the children?

To my mind jumps the phrase "conspiracy of silence." The whole of American society contributed to the conspiracy. Sexual matters were rarely discussed, and only in broad abstractions or tittilating innuendo. If "normal" sex was taboo, "deviant" sex was infinitely more so. Alfred Kinsey's monumental *Sexual Behavior in the Human Male*, 1948, had opened the door to such discussion, but I hadn't read it, nor did I know anyone who had.

Trays for the sick

One exception existed for the "no visiting rooms" rule: meal trays for the sick. Guys *did* get sick, either actually sick or at least, sick of the routine. Happened both ways for me. I don't remember all the details of the procedure but somehow, word got to the administration, the nuns prepared trays and someone brought them to the rooms.

Ideally, a good buddy would put in to bring your tray. This became the occasion for a convivial visit. Smoking permitted, the occasion provided a relaxed setting for a one-to-one chat. Of course, the visitor missed his own rec period, so you found out who your friends were.

But not always. One day, David Turchik put in his name to take a tray to Tom Schutte who had hurt himself in some game or other. If Turchik—short, blond, cherubic—represented a certain gay style, Schutte stood at the other end of the spectrum, aggressively athletic, openly homophobic, eager for confrontation.

If Turchik was the last guy Schutte wanted to see bringing a tray, Schutte's room may have been the last place Turchik wanted to be. His service stood as an act of moral courage. Later word had it that Turchik confronted Schutte openly about his homophobia, tellingly suggesting that maybe his aggressive stance might be an unconscious mask for something else. Only Turchik and Schutte know the truth of this, but we noticed that Schutte dialed down his attitude on the subject, for which we were all grateful.

A Call from Judy

Hanging out on the front lawn one afternoon, I saw David Carey coming toward me, calling my name.

"O'Brien. You got a telephone call."

Uh oh. Telephone calls—a rarity. We had one ancient wooden phone booth for all 300 of us. Was my mother in trouble again?

"Who's calling?" I asked Carey, suppressing the anxiety in my voice.

"Some girl named Judy Green. Who's she?" Perfectly like Carey to ask a personal question, and perfectly like me to answer it.

"Judy Green? From New York?" I said, incredulously.

"I don't know where she's from, I just took the call. Who is she, anyway?"

I had met Judy the summer before on a limousine ride to Tanglewood from New York city. Seated together, we fell into a pleasant conversation, hoped to meet at the music festival, exchanged numbers. I never saw her again. I met George Nesbit as planned and got taken up with the Pittsfield scene. At once point, I proposed calling Judy, but George discouraged it, rightly. So why *did* I take her number?

I finished telling Carey the whole mini-story as we mounted the front steps.

"Well, I just wondered." Carey said snidely. "I found your address book and saw her name in it. Actually, there was no call. Here's the book."

He got me good.

Golf, or Something Like It.

With new table assignments, I found myself sitting next to Harry McMahon, a deacon whom I didn't know at all. At the first *Tu autem*, which allowed us to talk, he initiated our relationship with an unusual opening question. "Do you golf?"

As it happened, I did, or at least, I thought of it as golf. I began working at a local golf course in Elgin during my sophomore year in high school, and continued there summer after summer until I went off to the seminary.

My training at the game had been rudimentary. Standing on the first tee of Villa Olivia, my high school classmate, Rich Conrad, who had played before, showed me how to push the tee into the ground, balance the ball thereupon and step back.

"Now spread your feet apart, take your driver, and swing at it like hell."

I did that. Not surprisingly, the ball remained undisturbed. I didn't even come close. As I recovered my balance, Conrad said, "That's all right, just take another swing." And so I did. On the fourth or fifth swing, I managed to hit the ball, topping it down the fairway about 60 yards.

"There you go," said Conrad, triumphantly, and stepped up to the tee himself. He took a correspondingly huge swing, struck a towering slice which sailed off to some distant fairway and we were off.

And so we continued whenever we could find the time. As an employee of the course, I didn't pay, whch was one of the main attractions for me. And I began to strike the ball with greater regularity although I could never predict the direction or the length of any given shot. A good score on any hole was "under ten," and I didn't always manage that.

Later that summer, I was playing with the jeweler where I worked at my day job. Stan, a good golfer, managed to play without comment for about three holes and then finally said, "What the hell arc you doing?"

"I dont know," I said, honestly.

"Put your feet together, keep your head down, keep your eye on the ball, keep your left arm straight, don't take such a big swing."

I tried to follow his advice, feeling awkward, crippled, inept. But somehow I managed to strike the ball and it went, to my amazement, straight down the fairway through the air, maybe 150 yards. It was the best shot I had hit to that point. Clearly I had stuff to learn.

I became an enthusiastic if marginal golfer in the years which followed and answered Harry McMahon in the affirmative. "Yes, I golf."

"Great," said Harry. I'm trying to get a few guys together and set up a kind of course on the front lawn, over toward the entrance." Somehow, Harry had persuaded the rector to approve this operation, perhaps with the argument that a lot of priests played golf and this would contribute to the fraternity of the clergy. Or whatever.

Always up for a new project, I got on board and we created a kind of weird course along the edge of the great front lawn, about six or seven holes in length with no tees and no greens, only a starting point and a flag stick to shoot at. I think we more or less conceded the putting.

I can't say much for the course, other than that no one was killed. I seem to remember that we had a kind of tournament, but I didn't win it. Nonetheless, Harry and I became kind of golfing buddies. He had worked out a deal to play at the Baltimore Country Club and I wasn't going to pass up that scene.

Hole in One?

Fourth hole—a medium par three. I plucked out my borrowed two wood and swung with enthusiasm. A towering shot, straight down the fairway. One bounce and onto the green. The ball rolled toward the hole and…….disappeared.

"Waaaaaaaaa….." I screamed, quickly losing the country club cool I was affecting. No one contradicted. Somehow unable to control my enthusiasm, I trotted down the fairway, clubs jouncing wildly in my bag. The foursome trailed after. I ran onto the green and…..saw my ball. It had rolled into the shadow of the flag, about three feet from the hole. A great shot, but no hole in one. I can't even remember if I made the putt, I was so disappointed.

I've had many memorable moments on the golf course, most of them embarrassing, but none quite like that. And I've never made a hole in one. Probably just as well; I'd *never* stop telling that one.

A visit to Woodstock

Not, of course, Woodstock, New York, then unknown in popular culture. The Woodstock in our area featured the Jesuit theological college, its faculty studded with the sharpest minds in an order famous for its sharp minds, and other things.

We didn't have a lot to do with the Jesuits. Jesuits belong to a religious order and take vows of poverty, chastity and obedience. Diocesan priests don't. Standard mantra among diocesan priests: Religious make vows of poverty; diocesans practice it. Nonetheless, we certainly knew about Woodstock and when the chance to visit came up, I jumped at it.

Harry McMahon had made some golf connection, and we were invited to play at the seminary's well-kept nine-hole course.

"See if you can borrow a better set of clubs," Harry recommended. "You'll play better with a matched set."

I didn't really agree with him. I loved each individual club in my collection, patched together from various sets and occasional garage sale purchases. I remember specifically a wooden-shafted two-iron which must have been fifty years old when I started playing. As I occasionally remarked to guys who would comment on my clubs, "Bobby Jones never used a matched set."

And they would inevitably reply, "You're no Bobby Jones." My game supplied the evidence. At any rate, I figured it might be cool to play with a good matched set. I already knew where I might borrow one.

We had a priest living with us, apparently sent to do penance for some infraction. Maybe he was 'drying out.' We didn't know. I DID know that he had a fine set of clubs and boldly, I approached him and borrowed them. He must have felt that he couldn't say no to anything.

"Take care of them," he cautioned. "It's a matched set." I already knew that!

The Jesuit seminarians welcomed us and showed us around. It seemed very like a country club to me. Individual rooms offered all the comforts; couches, radio, Hi-Fi, even TV sets. I mentioned this opulence to our guide.

"You got to keep in mind that we're here for thirteen years," the young Jesuit pointed out. "It's a long time. You guys are out in four."

He had it right. We knew about the extended Jesuit course of study. We shut up about the rooms.

Had a great round on the course; brought back the clubs; discovered that I had somehow lost the seven iron. With a sinking feeling, I called Woodstock; no one had found the club. I returned the club to the generous priest, making lame promises I couldn't keep about hunting for the club. I didn't offer to replace it, because I couldn't afford it.

"Don't worry about it," the priest said, unconvincingly. "I never use the seven." Right. I guess he felt it was part of his penance, and a severe part of it at that.

A visitor from the West.

One afternoon, I got an unusual message. The Rockford seminarians would assemble in the visitor's parlor to meet their guests. What?

We duly gathered, to encounter Father Art O'Neill and Father Bill Joffee, sent by the bishop to meet with us and, I guess, to look us over.

Art O'Neill would never have put it that way. A pastor from Freeport and editor of the diocesan newspaper, *The Observer*, and a St. Mary's graduate, Art embodied high-energy priesting, but didn't take himself all that seriously, or so I thought. His quick, sardonic wit pleased me and my interest in the paper pleased him. I even wrote a letter to the paper once, praising some piece or other. Wryly, O'Neill answered, "Even when you're trying to be complimentary, you manage to embarrass me. I was on vacation when that piece ran."

Father Art O'Neill, Editor of *The Observer*

    I wrote a lot of letters in those days. I needed a sense of connection to the outside world, and I wanted to be noticed. Normally shy and retiring in company, behind my portable Smith Corona I celebrated my multiple opinions by sharing them with anyone who might listen.

    To my knowledge, I alone among the Rockford seminarians wrote to the bishop, sharing (as I thought) my unique perspective on the function of the diocese. The bishop always replied to my letters, sometimes perfunctorily, sometimes through the Vicar General, but never did he suggest that I had overstepped my place, although I now suspect I had.

I knew I was calling attention to myself and hadn't planned on any particular consequences, but I learned in this meeting that my non-plan was working.

The Plan I Didn't Know I Had.

O'Neill's assistant editor on *The Observer*, Bill Joffe, a young priest on the rise, took me aside at some point during the visit. I didn't know Joffe, but I liked his message.

"The bishop has plans for you," Joffe murmured portentously. Some part of me doubted the story, but much of me wanted to believe.

"Here's how it will go." Joffee went on, clearly relishing his insider status. "You'll be appointed to a Rockford parish, so the Bishop can keep an eye on you. If he likes what he sees, he'll ask you to write a weekly column for *The Observer*. If he likes what he reads, he's going to appoint you to my position, and I'll be sent off to J school. After a year, I'll replace O'Neill as editor."

"Wow," I observed coolly. "I guess I'll just have to wait and see." I wasn't sure that these things would come true. I sensed a lot of "ifs" in the scenario. But it was fun to speculate.

As it turned out, Joffee had it right, with the exception of one detail. When I replaced him, he got sent back to a parish. Filled with bitterness, Joffe didn't speak to me for a full year, until I got the same treatment.

I Get an Appointment

The visit excited my imagination. I wanted to be "special" and it looked like the bishop would satisfy my wish. Whether I would be up to the job never crossed my mind. I began to chart my own future, starting with my appointment as Editor of *The Voice*. Surely my journalistic background at Notre Dame would make me a top candidate.

As it turned out, I wasn't quite *that* special, at least in the eyes of the seminary faculty.

At the end of the year, after consulting with the individuals involved, the rector would announce appointments to various special positions in the functioning of the seminary. For us, it was sort of like making the law review staff in law school—a lot of extra work, but a great line on your resume', not that we *had* resume's.

Head Reader topped the prestige chart. The Reader had to be prepared to fill in at the dining hall pulpit at a moment's notice, if the regularly scheduled preachers were, for some reason, not to perform. Head Readers typically had excellent preaching voices and the ability to sight-read Latin flawlessly. I did not qualify.

Head Sacristan, an infinitely demanding position, required close work with the dreaded Father "Spider" Meyer, the faculty ritual specialist. By dint of huge application of time and study, one became familiar with the vast array of minutiae which made up the Roman Ritual—vestments, vessels, procedures, rites, liturgical calendars, the organization of sacred space, and so on. The candidate typically exhibited both interest and aptitude for this kind of detail. I never considered myself threatened in the least with this appointment.

Editor of *The Voice* ranked high on the appointments list. The quarterly publication of the seminary, mailed to alumni and bishops all over the country, carried (and promoted) the prestige of St. Mary's.

When appointment time came, I received my call to the rector's office, invariably an anxiety-producing summons, even if some honor might be the outcome, but facing Van Antwerp didn't measure up in threat to the steel-rimmed gaze of Father Laubacher.

"Sit down, Jim." I sat. I'd never had any official encounter with the new rector.

The rector lifted a sheet of paper, glanced at it and said, "We've decided to offer you the position of Head Student Librarian. It's a new position, but John Varley assures me that you can handle it."

I sat, dumbfounded. I was flattered and disappointed at the same time. I floundered around, then said, "Gee, Father, I was kind of hoping to get *The Voice*."

A totally inappropriate response, not to say outrageous. I had no say whatsoever in the matter. Van Antwerp stared at me for a moment, then said, "That slot has been filled. Do you want the Library?" His voice had acquired a faintly military ring.

I didn't realize that the *Voice* post went to a seminarian of outstanding theological as well as journalistic skills. My college background in journalism counted for nothing in my selection. Picking up on Van's tone, I quickly agreed that I would take the position and do my best.

"Very well. Keep the appointment to yourself until it is announced publicly." the rector said dismissively, implying that my very best would meet the minimum standard. I removed my foot from my mouth and eased on out the door.

Head librarian! A bit of a surprise. I didn't think of myself as a Librarian. I had worked for a time in the library work room, primarily because it offered the opportunity to socialize and to smoke my pipe, when the rule otherwise forbade these activities. The library workers also got first crack at the newest stuff ordered by the library, which we much preferred to our standard texts.

Nonetheless, I shared the news with mingled pride and irony, even though it ranked not so highly. Van's admonition "keep it to yourself" equaled "whistling in the dark" in the seminary's gossip network. Word on the appointments made the rounds within twenty four hours of the meeting with the rector.

Wrapping it up

I'm coming to an uncomfortable learning about myself. I didn't want to be just any priest; I wanted to be special; to be noticed; to be recognised. And, without clearly intending it, I had gotten my wish. The bishop had special plans for me.

Now secure in the seminary setting, I would be one of the "players" without the actual need to prove anything. I didn't get *The Voice*. I wasn't smart enough. But I'd lord it over the Library Workroom, pipe and ego firmly in place.

8

Summer in Prison: St. Charles School for Boys

Ducker Mulcahy and I waited eagerly to observe the intake interview to be conducted by Dr. Ross, the staff psychologist at St. Charles School for Boys, a euphemism for the medium-security juvenile prison in Illinois.

The small room, institutional to a fault, barely had room for the three of us plus the inmate. We sat close enough to play cards.

"Won't it bother the prisoner if we're sitting here during the interview?" I asked Ross.

"Not at all," Ross assured me confidently. "He has no idea what to expect, and he'll be scared to death. He wouldn't notice if you wore clown suits."

Surely an odd analogy, but Ross, Jewish and long-experienced, could not be intimidated by the presence of Catholic clergy, particularly guys as green as we were.

Dr. Ross was the only member of the prison staff that the inmates feared. "Because," as one inmate earnestly confided, "It don't make no difference what you say, or even if you don't say nothin. Ross knows!" We waited to see a soul stripped before us.

Like many of the prisoners, the subject of the interview was twelve, black, underfed, fatherless, a product of inner city Chicago and busted for car theft and a string of priors. His eyes were wide and round, and his strategy for dealing with Ross—deny everything, even his name.

"I ain't sayin'," he muttered over and over, trying to control the shaking in his voice.

Ross Puts His Foot Down

Ross, a stocky man of average height and additionally equipped with an enormous gut, made an imposing sight for the kids, who had seen a lot of authority figures in their short lives, but nothing like Ross. At the time we observed him, he was suffering from an attack of gout, and his right foot was heavily wrapped with Ace bandages.

When our sample inmate sat down in the indicated chair, Ross swiveled his desk chair around, leaned forward and placed his gout-wrapped foot directly on top of the terrified boy's sneaker. The kid glanced at his pinioned foot but said nothing and made no attempt to remove the foot. He remained thus restrained during the interview, which severely limited his ability to squirm around, which he clearly wanted to do.

Ross, impassive behind his well-trimmed beard, glanced down at his folder, flipped through a few sheets and looked up calmly at the scared but defiant black kid.

"You and your friends saw this car, decided to go for a joy ride, got caught. That right?" His voice was quiet, firm, relentless.

"I ain't sayin."

"Somehow the cops figured out that a 12 year old black kid driving a Caddie didn't quite figure." He paused and looked up. "Or you that bad a driver?"

The kid bristled slightly, his pride touched, and muttered, "I kin drive!"

"And probably not the first time, either." Ross's voice was non-judgmental, even faintly admiring.

"Yeah," the kid said, feeling safer. "We took a few rides. A lotta rides." He slid a little more upright, but his foot remained pinned to the floor. He glanced fleetingly at the foot, but decided to do nothing. Ross asked a few more questions, then dismissed him and turned to his desk.

The kid rose hesitantly, as if the dismissal might be some kind of trick, gave us each a sliding glance of assessment, then headed for the door, knowing that the guard waited outside.

When the interview was over, Ross wrote briefly on the intake sheet, then read us the diagnosis: "Given to impulsive, unreflective behavior, with low impulse control." Ross added wryly, "I should get that made into a rubber stamp. It describes about 95% of the population." He paused, then asked, "Any questions?"

"Why did you put your foot on top of his?" I ventured. "Is that to establish your authority, or what?"

Ross stared at me for a moment, then laughed aloud. "I had no idea I had my foot on his. It's all wrapped up and I didn't feel a thing. Maybe I should do that all the time." So much for the secret technique. But I could imagine the kid describing his interview to his roommates, adding to Ross's legend.

Father Jim Molloy

When I arrived in St. Charles, Illinois a week earlier, I met for the first time my boss for the summer, Father Jim Molloy. Father Bonnike had recommended me to him, and he signed me on, sight unseet. Molloy, a cheerful, rotund priest in his mid-forties, had been chaplain to the Boy's School for some years since Bonnike had left the post. Also in residence at the modest brick chaplain's residence—Donald "Ducker" Mulcahy, a seminarian a couple of years junior to me, but more experienced at the Training School, since he had served there the previous summer.

I felt nervous about the prison job, but also excited, since I would be paid as a state employee and would earn, for the three months, about a thousand dollars, more than my salary as a priest for my first year after ordination. Despite my steelworker earnings, I remained measurably poor and I would have unusual expenses when preparing for ordination. I determined to face up to the demands of the situation, whatever might be ahead of me.

I met a lot of priests during my two summers in Sterling, but St. Charles stood at the opposite end of the diocese, and Molloy did not serve in the parish ministry, so I didn't know him, nor he me.

Apparently Bonnike had recommended me highly, however, and I got a welcoming reception. Certainly, Molloy wanted the company. During the year, he lived alone in the chaplain's house on the campus of an upscale girls' boarding school, Mount St. Mary's. Molloy served as a chaplain for the Dominican nuns who ran it in addition to his work at the prison.

I knew the Mount, in a way. When I was in high school, we "knew" that the privileged girls there wore white gloves and silk stockings and had nuns who checked their prom shoes for reflectivity. At any rate, the girls didn't stay around in the summer, just as well for my newly celibate state.

In those days, the term "obese" served as an insult rather than a diagnosis. So I won't use it for Jim Molloy. Rotund will have to do. Molloy, concerned about his weight, dieted religiously, relying on a current diet drink called Metrecal, which came in little cans, tasted vaguely malty and cost plenty. Molloy could afford it—paid by the state at a rate roughly twenty times that of the parish priesthood. But the Metrecal didn't seem to help.

Molloy talked about his diet at length to anyone who would listen, until, at one clergy gathering, listening to the priest complain, a colleague suggested acidly, "Jim, you're supposed to drink that stuff *instead* of the meals, not along with them." It didn't change Molloy's strategy, but he stopped talking about Metrecal.

Father Jim Molloy—poster boy for Metrecal.

A Chaplain's Assistant

My duties at St. Charles training school were ill-defined—instruction, counselling, assisting at religious services, record-keeping. As chaplain and a state employee, Father Molloy was entitled to two assistants, and that's what he got. Nobody much cared what we did. Nobody had any expectations that our work would help anything. It was just "the system."

We celebrated Mass there every Sunday. The problem here involved the question of Communion. Many non-Catholic boys (as we called them in those days) came to the Mass because more interesting stuff went on than in the Protestant service, and of course, they wanted to take Communion, which they were not entitled to do. I served Mass, but I didn't know the population, so as Father Molloy passed down the altar rail giving out the host, he keenly scrutinized the face of each boy, and also what the boy was doing. If the boy seemed clueless about the procedure, Molloy would just move on to the next without giving him Communion.

I don't remember any particular incidents at the Boy's School Mass, but Ducker, who served for Father Molloy at the Girl's Prison in Geneva, had many stories, all of them embarrassing. The girls were way tougher, on the whole, than the boys, because the courts made every attempt to keep the girls out of the system. If they got in, they were usually hardened, sexually experienced and definitely horny. Seeing a tall, blond, good looking young man, they were overt and unrestrained in their attempts to get contact with him, or, if impossible, to embarrass him by graphic sexual references. Ducker would never respond, but he typically turned bright red, which provided his harassers with some degree of satisfaction. I never visited the Girl's Prison, and never felt deprived either.

Ducker Mulcahy and I had a subtle status war going on. Although I was his clerical senior, a full-fledged Sub-Deacon in Major Orders while he was……..not, he had a full previous summer of experience at the Training school and with Father Molloy. I flaunted my Notre Dame Alumnus status, knowing that he had done college in the seminary. But basically, he was a nice guy and we got along well.

Meeting the Inmates

At the Training School, I found myself assigned a group of counsellees, not that I had any expertise to offer, but as I indicated, nobody had any expectations for me, and I could live up to that. I mentioned to Father Molloy that I knew a little Spanish, and so I got the Mexican population by default.

I remember a kid named Rodriquez, a genuinely dangerous gang type, who seemed completely intimidated one-on-one in a religious setting. He had almost no English and I had very little Spanish, most of that tourist-book Spanish, rather than Catechism book Spanish.? *Quiere una taza de te?* (?Do you wish a cup of tea?) did not seem particularly helpful teaching the Ten Commandments. Nevertheless, Rodrigues and I plowed through the Commandments and he learned them. I never had any sense that he thought they applied to him.

Michael Quinn, a big older kid on my list, had IQ-tested at 167, well up in the genius range. An anomaly in a population of sub-average testers, he violated an axiom of the prison system and the justice system as a whole: only the stupid get caught.

A Chicago north-sider, Michael, on his second tour of St. Charles, understood the system as well as the warden. As I talked to him, it seemed clear that he saw the pattern of his life ahead. A bleak picture, for sure.

"Here's what'll happen, Father." Michael said candidly. (Inmates called us "Father" because they knew we were something, at least not guards. It was just simpler, if not canonically correct. We had good standing with the inmates because we had the power to get them out of stuff, or, at least, out of the deadly routine, which carried a high value. Also we carried matches.)

"I got parole coming up," Quinn went on. "They'll send me home; I'll go to school. I'll be bored to death, because I know all that stuff. Some guys will be planning a job, and they'll tell me about it, and I'll say 'No, no, that's not the way to do it.' I'll work out a plan for them; I'll get sucked in on it, and sooner or later I'll be busted again."

Michael seemed OK with the inevitability of it. I found it chillingly hopeless. In fact, hope was a rare quality to find anywhere in the system. I began to understand Father Molloy's harsh comment after a frustrating day: "They should take these kids out, line 'em up and shoot them. It would be an act of mercy." Then I had protested, but now I had a different perspective.

Quinn was smart, tough, street-wise, prison-wise. Also well aware that, at 16, his next prison trip would be to the adult prison, probably Joliet. He wasn't yet tough enough for that.

Just a Little Boy

Speaking of tough, we had one quite young boy, I remember him being ten, serving his third tour of St. Charles. Gene Stumley (not his real name), his mouth foul, his gaze hard and his fists always ready. Prison-wise but not prison-smart, he had been ruled uncontrollable and stood on the brink of transfer to the maximum security prison. After whatever precipitating incident, he had been locked in solitary—a small square room with nothing in it but a toilet bowl. No bed, no sink, no blanket, nothing. Inmates would use anything they could wrench free to express their rage, frustration, desperation, despair.

Stumley requested attention from the Chaplain's Office and Molloy told me to take it.

When admitted to see Gene, I expected to hear a long foul-mouthed rant against the guards, the boys, the system, especially the rat who had turned him in. Instead, I found a frightened little boy, desperately seeking comfort, knowing there was no way out and no way back. He didn't want a chaplain. He wanted a mother to hold him. And he would never get that. Stumley had heard plenty about how tough Maximum was, and how a small boy stood no chance. But the warning hadn't been enough to keep him straight.

I said what I could, but he knew far more about the whole system than I did, and I didn't offer much help. I could give him a cigaret, and that was about it. And he seemed pathetically grateful. After a little while, they came to take him away, and I looked after him, helpless and shaken.

Not the Highest Card in the Deck

All the inmates didn't get as hardened as Gene. A particular favorite of mine was Jerry Mondova, a big, dim kid also doing his third term at St. Charles. First sentence followed a string of car thefts, absolutely standard. The second term resulted from a classic Mondova operation. Out on parole and desperate for funds, Mondova had acquired the parts of a cast-off handgun. Lacking the assembly screws, he managed to cobble the parts together with scotch tape and produced something with the general appearance of a weapon.

Thus armed, he marched into a small grocery store in Chicago and took up a position near the cash register. The owner, an older man, was stocking shelves and, seeing that Jerry had nothing to buy, continued to do so. After a few nervous minutes and getting no attention, Jerry pulled out his gun and rapped on the countertop. The gun fell to pieces, the owner turned and began shouting and firing tin cans at Jerry, whatever he could reach. Jerry fled the store and ran directly into the arms of an approaching policeman. Busted.

Jerry Mondova did his time again, made parole and very quickly fell into familiar ways. One evening, in the money and having come by a supply of marijuana, he toked up pretty good and, feeling fine, strode down the street, jumped into a taxi and gave an address. Only then did he notice that the driver was wearing a police uniform. Somewhat impaired, he had jumped into a police cruiser, which transported him directly to the station. His passage through the court system and back to St. Charles was equally swift.

I got to know Jerry because I was training him and another boy to serve Mass. Jerry was going to be around for a while, so the training wouldn't be lost. Molloy would need servers when Ducker and I returned to the seminary in about a month.

Don't Mess with Roger

Roger, another server trainee, looked and acted like an angel. Blue eyes, blond, curly hair, unblemished skin, a calm and quiet manner, Roger seemed far from the prison stereotype. I didn't see how he could survive without becoming sexual property to the older boys. But nobody touched Roger.

One time, when Roger didn't make the class, I asked Jerry Mondova if Roger had a hard time from the other boys.

"Hey, man.....oh, sorry, Father....I mean. NOBODY mess with Roger. Roger he crazy. Roger kill you. Roger set you on FIRE! NOBODY mess with Roger." Mondova's face and eyes backed up his conviction.

Turns out that Roger burned churches. A pyromaniac, Roger's quiet, calm manner and angelic looks just made him all the scarier. So nobody mess with Roger. The word was out.

I had another counselee (we didn't say "client" in those pre-Carl-Rogerian days) with a high IQ, who had shot his father. With no rap sheet and no Chicago connection, he didn't fit the prison stereotype. I asked him about the shooting.

"I see you shot your father in the eye with a 22. What were you trying to do, Matt?" I asked him, keenly probing.

"I was trying to kill him." Matt looked at me, impassive. Ask a stupid question.....

"And how do you feel about that? Are you sorry?"

"Yes. I'm sorry I didn't kill him." His voice flat, his gaze level, his sincerity obvious, Matt must have wondered what was my point. Well, I surely didn't know, but I wasn't going to mess with Matt.

Most of our inmates came from the hard streets of Chicago, most from broken homes, most were black, and they had long rap sheets and previous records of incarceration, foster home placement, system intervention. Nothing the system provided addressed their needs. Most would become adult criminals; many would grow out of it after two or three prison incarcerations, decide it wasn't worth the aggravation and settle down into some dead-end job. Some would become career criminals. Most would die young of bullets or dope. Nothing I did would make the slightest difference. I began to appreciate the terrible weight of Molloy's job.

A Break from Prison Life

We had occasional breaks from the dispiriting prison work. Molloy, a convivial sort, would gather priest friends for an evening tipple on Friday evenings—weekends being busy times for parish priests.

"Pay attention to Bill Donovan," Molloy advised me. "He's one of the smartest guys in the diocese, and a great preacher, too. He was on the way up, for a while."

"What happened?" I asked.

"He let the bishop know what he thought about things, and that put a lid on his career." Now he's the pastor of a small parish, and that's all he'll ever be."

Part of me hated the notion of politics and careerism in the Church, and another part of me longed to get in the game. I found Monsignor Donovan to be sharp, clever, ironic and at peace with himself and his sidetracked career in the Church. I determined to have him preach at my First Mass.

A Picnic Appearance

A call from the Chancery office ordered me to the Wisconsin resort town of Lake Delevan. The third year theology students for the Diocese of Rockford—six of us—would gather to comport ourselves with the Bishop and several priests of the diocese.

With great reluctance, I tore myself away from my prison duties and drove up for the picnic. Dempsey and Allemand would be there; also Tom Coughlin, a third year theologian at St. Paul seminary, whom I had known in high school. I can't remember any other classmates, but I do remember the photographer doing the work of the Catholic journalist—covering the Bishop.

I remember the cutline vividly, since it was quoted to me repeatedly by my classmates. It said, "'It seems to me, Bishop...' says James O'Brien, as the following listen with some amusement." And here's the proof:

Summer in Prison: St. Charles School for Boys 219

Bishop Loras Lane listens, tolerantly, I presume, as I hold forth. Ed Allemand, Father Charles McNamee and Tom Coughlin find themselves present.

Clearly, I used the occasion to air my views on the conduct of the diocese, and show the Bishop what a hotshot I was becoming.

Recto Tono, Please

The Mother Superior at the Mount surprised us one day by requesting a High (or chanted) Mass for the Feastday of their Founder, St. Dominic.

Anxious to show off my Gregorian skills, I agreed to solo on the complex chants of the Proper. But, halfway through the long long chanting of the Introit, Molloy growled from the alter, "*Recto tono*, please."

I quickly put a lid on the fancy chanting and we proceeded at the normal pace.

"Sorry, Jim, but we would have been there till noon." My sensitive artistic soul assuaged, I had to agree with him. Besides, it was nearly time for me to head back to St. Mary's.

Wrapping It Up

As a fledgling Sub-Deacon, I now had a taste of clerical lifestyle of a more conventional kind than Bonnike's busy, activist rectory. St Charles provided an easy, relaxed life, with the comforts of booze and television and the occasional stroking of the male ego. I found it easy to get used to, seductive even, though boredom hovered just around the corner.

My experiences at the Training School haunted me, as they still do. Prison gave me a glimpse of the dark underbelly of American society, although the prison system provided a highly structured and protected vantage point. After passing through the gates on the first day, I never again for a moment felt threatened or endangered. But the pervasive hopelessness which toned the scene wore heavily on me, though the absence of authority (AND responsibility, AND skills) consequently did not burden me with guilt for my lack of achievement.

I had made good money, better than at the steel mill, and I had a fund of dramatic stories for the guys back at the Big House. The seminary, I mean.

1960–1

"Look out, world, here I come........."

—*Jule Styne and Bob Merrill*

9

Deacon Year

The fourth (and for most, the final) year of theological studies was known as the deacon year, as seminarians normally received ordination to the rank of Deacon at the beginning of the year. This rank, dating back to the first century of Christianity, conveyed genuine clerical status and powers (strictly limited, of course) which included the right to give Communion and to preach from the pulpit. Deacons went out from the seminary to preach in a few parishes in Baltimore, including the other branches of St. Mary's and in the nearby Baltimore Cathedral.

Willie O'Shea knows all!

I arrived at the front steps of the seminary for my deacon year in a manner more conspicuous than prudent. My cousin Carol, a tall, willowy brunette on vacation from Smith College, swung the top-down yellow convertible into a parking place directly in front of the building (and directly below the rector's office). I dug my suitcase from the back seat.

Carol bounded out of the car, wearing a man's white dress shirt (mine, as it happened) tied in front, baring her midriff in a style hot on women's college campuses in the early sixties. She gave me a big hug and an emphatic kiss on the cheek by way of saying goodbye. Although our relationship, though close, was entirely innocent, I began to think it might not LOOK that way. And appearances counted!

I reported in; the rector said nothing, and I began to breathe easier about the situation. Too quickly, as it turned out. After lunch, Father Willie O'Shea, came calling after me in his high, urgent voice. "Jim. Jim O'Brien."

"Yes, father?" Willie had never spoken to me personally. What could this be?

"That girl who dropped you off this morning...." Willie began, and paused. Uh oh. Here it comes. I prepared my explanation.

"Was it Wendy or Carol?" Willie's question stunned me. How could he know of my cousins? How much DID the faculty know about us? And why?

"Carol." I blurted, mystified.

"Oh, well, ok then," Willie went on, satisfied. "I haven't seen them for years and I wasn't sure."

Seeing, and doubtless enjoying my total confusion, Willie explained further. "My mother is Mrs. Bush's cook. I've known the girls all their lives, off and on." Mrs. Bush, my cousins' grandmother, a true Chicago *grande dame* I had met a few times in her highrise apartment on North Michigan Avenue. Although off the hook for my arrival, I still found it amazing that Willie should have this oblique but personal connection with my family.

Some part of me felt a little disappointed at how harmlessly it all turned out.

More Perfect Celibacy

Coming back to St. Mary's, I felt atypically cool and confident. I knew the seminary procedure; I knew my classmates; I had neat summer experiences to share; I had made it through the system, almost. And I would be a Deacon, unless someone raised a last-minute objection. It could happen!

With very few exceptions, most of us would achieve ordination as Deacons, the solemn ceremony to take place at the end of the opening retreat of the year, a little over a week away. Since the rite conveyed rank and privilege without further obligation, it was a highly positive experience.

The office of Deacon had genuine historical and liturgical status dating from the earliest days of the Church. Deacons exercised an official role in the Church liturgy and would preach from the pulpit. Nevertheless, in those days, almost no one outside a seminary saw Deacons in action. We found ourselves squirreled away till our ordination to the priesthood. Almost.

On a strictly rotating basis, we would leave the seminary to serve in solemn ceremonies in a few venues around Baltimore: Paca Street, the philosophy house of St. Mary's; the old Cathedral downtown and the New Cathedral located about three miles away on a huge tract of land.

Breviary Briefs

Deacons recited the Divine Office each day as a requirement of their rank. As sub-deacons, we had acquired breviaries which contained the Latin text for each office service of the year. The recitation (we were required to move our lips, if not to actually speak aloud) took about forty minutes, longer on major feast days, shorter on ferial (ordinary) days.

In those days, people saw priests bent over the breviary, lips moving, deep in concentration. Most priests, busy with many things, found the requirement burdensome and found ways to postpone the recitation until too late to finish.

The Office (literally the word means formal duty) followed the medieval monastic organization of the day. Morning prayers—Matins and Lauds. The hours of the day: Prime, Terce, Sext, None. Evening prayers—Vespers and Compline. In the monastery, the monks chanted the hours in choir. We mumbled the Office privately, walking along the paths or halls, flaunting our advanced status in the heirarchy.

The privilege quickly became a requirement and then a duty and soon an onorous duty. We would ask each other how far along in the Office we were. The classic reply—"I'm over Sext." The lame gag paled quickly.

We discussed the moral issues of the duty in Liturgy class. To skip the Office—a sin. How serious? Depended on the reason, attitude, awareness, all those things. What if you said the wrong office for the day? *Officium pro Officio valet.* (One office suffices for another.) The words right there in the *Code.* An ethical principle most of us knew by heart.

Could you do other stuff *while* reciting the office? A difficult question. It depended. The classical story had it that a Dominican priest petitioned the Holy Office asking if he could smoke while praying. The Holy Office replied with indignation, "Non permitat."

Hearing of the inquiry, a Jesuit priest initiated his own petition: "Can I pray while smoking?" Impressed with his piety, the Holy Office replied, "Permitat." The story says something about all that Jesuit training.

Of course, the daily reciting of the Office serves as the community prayer of the Church. It serves as a biblical commentary on the feast of the day, composed of psalms, prayers and passages of scripture. But many of us found the daily recitation of a ceremony meant to be chanted in choir more of a challenge to get through than a prayerful experience.

At the heart of the issue: saying prayers is not the same thing as praying. Most of us labored to make the recitation a prayerful meditation on the scripture, but such an effort slowed down the reading considerably and we ended up rushing through the text indifferent to the meaning.

Though we didn't know it at the time, this inevitably produces spiritual atrophy—deadly for the priestly ministry.

Father Hogan

We faced theology class with some apprehension. Father Hogan, a personally affable man, was noted for nothing but the difficulty of his course in dogmatic theology.

Mark Liebler offered a warning. "Wait 'til you guys get Hogan. You'll find out that Norris was easy." Uh, oh!

In class, Hogan sounded highly organized, but we found him hard to follow. He would announce the theological proposition under consideration in the manner of Thomas Aquinas, then drift in another direction. We scribbled notes furiously, trying to follow the trend of his thinking. At the end of the class, he would announce, with mild triumph, "And thus it is that….." and repeat the proposition with which he had begun. It sounded brilliant, but what did all that stuff between the beginning and the end MEAN?

Hogan's 'method' certainly challenged us to study. I would spread out my notes during the evening study period, and try to: a. decipher them; b. organize them; c. figure out what they might mean. It took me about half the semester to realize that Hogan, rather than working forward from the proposition, would ease backward through the history of the thinking, drift around among the various opinions and arrive at the beginning. Once I had figured out the method, I was able to understand the course and my grades improved. But what WAS the course?

Mostly Happy Fellas

A small group of the theatre-minded gathered to plan the offering for the Fall. Our class still boasted lots of musical talent, despite the departure of George Nesbit the previous year, so we decided to choose another musical. I pushed for *The Most Happy Fella*, a Frank Loesser musical barely off the Broadway stage, and still playing on the road. I knew the music by heart.

The story might be a bit of a problem, though. Rosabella, a San Francisco waitress, is wooed by Tony, an Italian winemaker of substantial years. On the way to meet her train, he is crippled in a car accident and Rosabella is met instead by his handsome, drifter foreman, Joe. Turns out that Tony has sent her Joe's photograph, with which she has fallen in love. Tony and Rosabella make love; she conceives; Joe says "I'm outta here." Rosabella comes to love the older, crippled man; he comes to accept the baby. Curtain.

I scoffed at the narrative problems. I could write my way around the plot; we had naturals for the male leads, and besides, I argued, "Look at *Brigadoon*."

Jack Melloh nailed the romantic lead; George Baldino, ethnically equipped, sang the role of Tony, the super-Italian winemaker. John Davis and I offered an aria of Rosabella as a duet, thus presumably taking the gender-identification issues away from one individual. Joe Pease from Harrisburg and accompaniest for the Glee Club, took on the thankless role of director and pianist.

Jack Melloh in a, well..., mellow mood.

The house was packed and the applause thunderous. Just like always.

Father "Spider" Meyer

We all assumed that Father Meyer, the faculty Master of Ceremonies, had a baptismal name, but we didn't know it. Everyone referred to him as 'Spider.' We didn't know why and we didn't want to know. Nor did anybody joke about it. Father Spider Meyer was a man to be feared, and he WAS feared and that was it.

I might add that, in the seminary, the Master of Ceremonies did not introduce speakers; he taught ceremonies—the detailed words and movements which accompanied the sacramental work of a priest. And Spider had standards; perfect memory and absolute precision. Different schools of thought abounded regarding the celebration of the liturgy, but St.Mary's offered only one school of thought and Father Meyers taught that school, with rigor.

Curiously, while Spider demanded precision in the performance of ceremonies, he possessed a remarkably foul mouth, acquired as a military chaplain. He exercised this special skill most notably during solemn ceremonies on Holy Days. Acting as Master of Ceremonies for the service, he would glide smoothly around the high altar, take some unfortunate by the elbow and murmur softly to him, 'Oh, you son of a bitch, get your ass over by the celebrant or I'll kick it there."

And, believe me, we did, fighting the urge to run from the sanctuary and hide. One acolyte, approached by Spider after some blunder, actually did leave the sanctuary and not return. We never asked what Spider said to him.

Apart from being instructed in our roles in the daily liturgy—vesting the priests before Mass, serving them during the Mass, and unvesting them after—we didn't see much of Father Meyers until deacon year. But then we had him in spades, so to speak. Deacons began practicing the many and precise moves of the liturgy of the Mass, and memorizing in Latin the prayers which were said by the priest alone.

Actually, we could have been practicing these all along. But we thought it both presumptuous and pretentious to do this before deacon year. I mean, what if you got kicked out, and wasted all that time on stuff you would never use? So, with the beginning of deacon year, we made space in our rooms to set up a practice altar and begin working on the words and gestures.

Practicing the Mass

The deacon's rooms came furnished with a practice Mass set, which included a chalice and all its vestments; a missal stand, altar cards with the prayers of the Ordinary (recited at every Mass) printed on them in Latin.

I set a six foot plank on top of a bookcase, leaned the three altar cards against the back, placed the missal stand at the right and the chalice—complete with finger-towel, paten, veil, the bursa on top holding the corporal—in the middle. Now to start testing my memory.

Feeling more than a little self-conscious, I picked up the chalice, backed up a couple of steps, walked forward a couple of steps, replaced the chalice, turned and opened the Missal to the Mass for the day, returned to the center (a step away), bowed, turned, took one step back, turned again to the altar and began the prayers at the foot of the altar, making sure that my gestures remained precise and reverent.

I had learned the server responses when I was twelve. I had taught them to class after class of aspiring altar boys (no girls in those days!,) taking the priest's part (and showing off my Latin fluency) as they mumbled the responses. No problem here. Except maybe when Spider Meyer would be watching. I better have a performance reserve.

Finishing, I mounted the imaginary steps, bowed and kissed the altar, turned and, keeping my hands flat, erect and within the width of the shoulders (as if playing a small concertina, very quietly), I greeted my imaginary congregation: *Dominus vobiscum*. (The Lord be with you.)

Already I hated the rigidity and constraint of Meyer's requirements but, warned by the previous deacons, I repressed my desire for expansiveness and proceeded stiffly.

I note that the altar cards provided psychological support only. Woe betide the deacon caught glancing at the cards during Mass exam.

Passing the Mass exam

By the beginning of the second semester, we would be called by Father Meyer, in the order of our presumed ordination dates, to perform for him ceremony of the Mass. You didn't want to be the one they told the stories about.

Celebrating Mass is the primary function of the Catholic priest. All his other sacramental and ministerial functions are secondary. Even his character is secondary.

The precise and elaborate ritual represents an accumulation of prayers and actions which date back two thousand years to the Last Supper, reenacted during the Mass. In virtually every age of the Church, some additional prayer or action had been added to the original, simple command of Jesus—"Do this in memory of me."

The ritual involved silent prayers, prayers aloud, readings from the scripture (all in Latin, of course) and precisely proscribed actions. And, for Spider Meyer, precise, exact, rigid, tight, militaristic, perfect, all meant the same thing. If he could have his way, every seminarian celebrating the liturgy would look like a mirror image of every other. The fact that we were tall, short, fat, thin, moved differently, felt differently, meant nothing to Spider. The suppression of the individual was his goal, and indeed, maybe one goal of ritual itself.

Spider, a military man, knew the purpose of drill—to achieve precision, and to bond the individuals into an unthinking, responsive unit. Spider's point of view was anathema to the liberals, who wanted, among lots of other things, to have a beautiful, flowing, engaged, celebratory, human experience, which called attention to what a terrific guy the celebrant was. I meant to say, an experience which engaged and uplifted the congregation.

In the meantime, we had to pass the Mass exam, and we had to pass it Spider's way.

A Very Effective Teacher

In his soft and deceptively gentle voice, Spider would murmur the old Navy axiom, "there are four ways of doing something: the right way; the wrong way; the navy way; and my way." And Spider's memorable coda: "And oh, you sons of bitches better do it my way."

So we practiced the moves in our rooms, controlled our gestures, bowed precisely, murmured our memorized prayers just loud enough for Spider to be able to hear every one.

I had great difficulty memorizing, but fear drove me to the necessary repetitions and the prayers became imbedded in my brain. Even now, I can remember passages that I have not said or read for forty years.

Suscipiat Dominus sacrificium de manibus tuis ad laudem et gloriam nominis sui ad utilitatem Dominum Nostrum Jesum Christum........ Well, I'm losing it, but then, I never had to type it before.

As the spring semester began, Spider would take us in small groups to teach performance of the Mass. This in itself became a highly threatening situation. For example, when not folded or doing something, the hands were to be placed flat on the altar. "Flat" for Father Meyers meant not cupped in the slightest. As a reminder, Father Meyers would smash his fist down on an cupped hand, and the owner of the hand did not dare to move it out of the way. Sadistic? Sure, but *very* memorable.

Another time, A student was having difficulty rendering the solemn bow correctly. After several attempts, Spider told the luckless learner to close his eyes, then struck him solidly in the stomach. As the student doubled over, he murmured calmly, "Yes, like that. Now remember it."

All this served as terrific motivation for the rest of us to practice and practice. As we did so, many of us, particularly of the liberal persuasion, vowed that we would never celebrate with the rigid and graceless moves that we were taught. Once we were ordained and out there, we would do it our own way. But despite that rebellious attitude, I never saw a St. Mary's graduate celebrate in a sloppy way, so maybe Spider was doing his job effectively.

The Peabody Book Shop

John Davis and I took a half-day holiday from the seminary to explore a now-forgotten haunt of literary, swinging Baltimore, the Peabody Book Shop, still hanging on at the threshhold of the sixties. Knowing our forbidden destination in advance, we had skipped our Roman collars, and wore white shirts and black ties. I had gone to the additional length of wearing a crew necked (black) sweater which covered up the tie.

"What'll it be, Fathers?" The elderly bartender leaned on the ancient wooden bar, carved and scarred by decades of students and cool types. Our elaborate "disguises" penetrated in an instant. Somehow, seeing our black overcoats, black fedoras, black suits, black ties, black sweater, the bartender had jumped to the conclusion that we were priests.

I glanced around, fearing that the rector or some faculty member might be there. Paranoia—the natural product of our constantly-watched seminary life. However, the large square room was empty, other than some well-worn tables and chairs and a battered upright piano against one wall. It was, after all, two in the afternoon, not exactly Happy Hour, a term not yet in common use.

Well, I DID know what I wanted. Having seen elegant ads for a new scotch import in the New York Times magazine (a forbidden publication available to us only on the floor of the jakes,) I spoke up confidently.

"I'd like a glass of Chivaas Regale," I announced grandly, "in a snifter glass if you have one."

The bartender stared at me. "You mean Chivas Regal?" he asked, mildly, without changing his expression. Davis turned away and covered his face.

"Uh, yeah." I muttered. I had never heard the brand pronounced. I don't know what possessed me to produce such an elaborate and unscotslike version of the name. One more failure in my quest to appear sophisticated.

A Remembrance of Times Past

The Peabody Book Shop actually served as a used book store in the front, filled with ancient and dusty volumes which could be perused and even purchased from a bored clerk. A long hallway led from the back of the book shop to the large room where we now sipped our taboo drinks.

I recently learned that the Book Shop served as a hangout for the Baltimore literati, in particular, H.L. Mencken, my father's favorite author. In more recent years (the forties and early fifties) it had become a coffee house and jazz room for the very cool, particular grad students from Johns Hopkins. The wooden walls and ceiling of the ancient men's room were elaborately carved with permanent graffiti, more clever than obscene. The only one I remember at this distance in time went as follows:

> "To be is to do." Jean Paul Sartre.
> "To do is to be." Albert Camus
> "Do be, do be, do be." Frank Sinatra.

Back in the bar, we moved to the piano. Davis played jazz and I sang along. Taking my sax would certainly have aroused suspicion at the seminary. We had a couple of drinks, tipped the bartender, and climbed on the bus back to Roland Park. No one came in during the whole two hours we spent there.

We returned, of course, this time more relaxed and wearing our roman collars. The bartender remembered us and gave us appropriate greeting, "Hello, boys."

The Dempsey Drive

"Forget about the train, I've found this fantastic deal." My classmate, Tom Dempsey, called me in the middle of the Christmas vacation to clue me. Dempsey, a Chicagoan whose brother was a cop, had inside information on a lotta things. Who was I to doubt him?

"My brother heard about this airline, they've got this deal, $25 one way to Baltimore leaving from Midway about 6 p.m. We'll be there by eight."

Always eager to save a buck and also to extend my precious vacation by a day, I cancelled my train plans and showed up at Dempsey's in time for his brother to drive us out to the airport, relatively close to Dempsey's south side home.

With specific directions, we ignored the terminal and drove directly to a certain hanger area, sliding easily around the minimal security provisions in this post-war, pre-hijack era. We approached the designated hanger and found……nothing. No lights, no plane, no clue. We circled around for a bit, pointlessly.

"Well, hell," said the cop brother, finally, "He said it was right here. Fantastic deal, though," he added, as a kind of explanation. "I guess we might as well head for home."

No problem for him. But we had to be in Baltimore by nine in the morning, and the rector accepted NO explanations for lateness, not even apocalyptic ones. It was now about nine in the evening. I had no thoughts—nothing but anxiety to contribute.

"We'll drive!" said Dempsey, triumphantly. "We can take my brother's Golden Hawk. I can do 100 on the expressway. They won't touch a cop's brother." I did the math. At 100 mph, no stops, no traffic lights, we could make Baltimore by five in the morning. The price was right.

"Let's go for it." I opined, reserving my calculations and other concerns for another time. For example, Dempsey may have gotten a pass from the Chicago cops, but what about the Indiana State Patrol; the Ohio; the Pennsylvania? If we made it to Maryland, we were home free. I mean, would they bust a couple of seminarians from St. Mary's?

Off we went, loaded with sandwiches and thermos bottles of coffee. The Studebaker Golden Hawk was a powerful sports-configured coupe of the "which way is it going?" era, a car-guy's dream, and capable of 140 mph, although I hoped we wouldn't test the limit. Dempsey's brother laid down one condition: Tom had to do all the driving. Who was I to protest?

Dempsey slammed through the south suburbs often approaching sixty on the deserted streets and when we hit the Indiana tollroad, he cranked it up to 110. Indiana blurred by in the darkness, Ohio too. No cops. A clerk's glance at the toll tickets might have revealed our violation, but no one thought to do that. Finally, in mid-Pennsylvania, about 4 in the morning, Dempsey slid off the Turnpike into some little town and pulled up at a small and ramshackle hotel.

"I gotta get a couple hours of sleep," he muttered. "But hey, don't use our real names when we register."

Why not? I was too tired to ask; also too tired to think of another name. The sleepy clerk took our money, $20, I think; we climbed the stairs and fell into the narrow beds. About four hours later and deeply blurry, we took off for Baltimore, now inevitably late and working on excuses. Dempsey had a vivid imagination. I simply took the position that Dempsey could do the explaining and I would confirm whatever he said.

About noon, we climbed the seminary stairs and reported to Father Van, who stared at our haggard faces, accepted Dempsey's simple explanation, "We missed the plane." and told us to get some rest and not to do it again. Fat chance. No more vacations before ordination.

Kennedy Inauguration

We got to use our third free day from the Apostolic Delegate on January 20th, Inauguration Day for J. F. Kennedy. No question that the seminary community saw Kennedy's victory as a triumph for the Church. Though we didn't discuss politics much, I'm guessing that the majority of my classmates considered themselves as Democrats, particularly after the religious controversies of the campaign.

I vividly remember the night of the election. The rector granted special permission to anyone who wished to watch the returns on the new television and at least a hundred of us crowded around the huge, 25 inch set. Generally, cheering sounded for the Kennedy (projected) victories, groans for Nixon wins. But by midnight, the race continued—too close to call. The rector appeared, shut off the set and sent us to bed.

Next morning the whisper went round meditation. "They're still counting Illinois!"

Illinois? Two time zones east of California? Could Daley be holding up the vote? Certainly Nixon thought so. His campaign challenged the count until the day of inauguration, although he sturdily denied this.

Charlie MacKay, my brilliant and sardonic Sulpecian classmate, invited John Murdoch and myself to attend the inauguration and, coincidentally, to have lunch with some girl friends of his at their apartment in downtown D.C. We could walk over to the Mall, a mere four blocks away.

Girl friends? Women? Uh….well, ok.

The day turned out to be bitterly cold and blizzardy. We gathered in the apartment, and remained glued to the TV set. Nothing untoward occurred, other than our reluctance to brave the storm. Robert Frost's poem blew away, but Kennedy wore no topcoat. We reveled in the brilliant rhetoric of the inaugural address, never asking ourselves what the phrase "We will pay any price in the defense of freedom…." might mean for ourselves and for our country. Almost no one had heard of Vietnam as yet.

MacKay Is Duped

Charlie MacKay hung out a lot in *The Voice* room, a gathering spot for the smart guys and the writers. We felt like insiders. Another younger guy named Jim Andrews, smart, fat, funny, critical, hung with MacKay. One time, a year before, MacKay noticed that Andrews had an ordinary button sewn on his cassock, with blindingly blue thread. Siezing the opportunity, he mocked Andrews for his fashion *faux pas*.

"Well," said Andrews, seriously. "My mother sewed this button on. She's almost blind now, and can't really work with the regular cassock buttons. And she can't tell blue from black. But I'm keeping the button just like it is, whether anybody has a problem with it or not."

"Of course," said MacKay, embarrassed, rebuked and chastened, a rare experience for him.

"That summer," MacKay continued, "I visited the Andrews at their Cape Cod cottage. Mrs. Andrews was gardening when I got there. She straightened and greeted me from some distance. "Hi, Charlie, we'be been expecting you. She wasn't blind at all."

Score one for Andrews

Big Cup

Five months left before ordination; Mass exam to pass; chalice to design; party to plan; invitations, holy cards (not actually holy, but a remembrance of ordination day), a long list of details. I had no experience in any of these areas and no deacons to ask. We *were* the deacons. Much consultation followed with the more socially adept.

The earliest step involved the design and fabrication of my chalice for the celebration of Mass. Not every priest has his own chalice, and every parish church offers several choices. But those of us who embraced liturgical reform could never be content with the elaborately decorated gothic golden chalices which were typical of Roman liturgy since the Middle Ages. We wanted a cup which loudly, albeit symbolically, stated our values (and our implied superiority) to the values of those who came before us. A lot of guys in my time looked to enamel chalices in bold colors. Flashy *and* expensive. Beyond my reach and my taste.

I was ill-equipped to design anything, but I was abundantly supplied with notions which, night after night, I attempted to sketch out on scratch paper in my room during study hours. Among other things, I was unable to create a symmetrical curve, so that every chalice I sketched appeared lopsided.

I knew I wanted a big big cup to symbolise the fact that the chalice was a community cup, although the laity were not permitted to partake of the sacrament under both species at this time. I wanted a silver chalice, hammered silver to imply the product of hands rather than of a lathe or stamping machine. I wanted the handle to be of walnut, rather than precious metal, to evoke the wood of the cross.

By good fortune and judicious solicitation of advice, I came across the name of a French chalice-maker named Louis Jacobi, sent him my design and my thinking, and received back from him a long long letter in French, accompanied by sketches and estimates, and expressing, among other things, a willingness to undertake the task. Fortunately, Jacobi accompanied his letter with an English translation, because my movie French was not at all up to the task.

Voila! My chalice was being made.

The Last of the O'Briens

It must have been during our brief Easter break. Visiting my uncle Frank O'Brien in Washington, I was surprised when he informed me that I would be squiring a young lady during the evening before I left for Baltimore. As a deacon, committed to the practice of perfect celibacy, I found this to be an unusual assignment.

In retrospect, perhaps it wasn't. I constituted the entire male gene pool of the O'Briens, my branch at least. All my cousins being female, my celibacy would represent the end of the line—the last of the O'Briens—at least from a certain, narrow point of view. Despite the fact that my father's family were very very Catholic, I always sensed an ambivalence from them about my vocation, though nothing overt was said. Indeed, nothing overt had ever been said by an O'Brien, on any subject that I can recall.

At any rate, perhaps Uncle Frank decided to provide a tiny test of my vocation, in case I cared to reconsider.

My date, a slim and pretty girl from some exclusive local finishing school, had some glancing acquaintance with my cousins Carol and Wendy. Not exactly my social circle, if I could be said to have a social circle.

Since my uncle proposed to fund the outing, I could think of no reason to refuse, although my spiritual director probably could have. I'd get a chance to hear Gene Bonnike playing a jazz gig in a local club. Probably not the first choice for my date, who shall remain nameless for memory reasons.

We caught the gig; the girl seemed bored; didn't like jazz; no magic there. I took her home—my celibacy and my intentions intact. If Uncle Frank had disappointments, he didn't reveal them, then or later. It turned out to be my last date before ordination, and doubtless just as well.

Preparing for My First Mass

I don't mean practicing the moves of the Mass. By this time, I had passed my Mass exam. I mean planning and setting up the ceremonial elements of my First Mass and the social events to follow. The ceremony would follow by a day the Ordination itself, and would take place in my home parish of St. Lawrence, Elgin.

Apart from Ordination, starring the bishop, (the ordinands getting only feature billing,) the First Mass marked the major social/religious event in a priest's life. Family, friends, favored priests, and the local parishioners who cared to go would gather for the occasion.

First, I had to choose the officers for the Mass. I needed four priests: Deacon, Sub-Deacon, Master of Ceremonies and Preacher. Being asked to serve at a First Mass represented a singular honor. I knew and owed many priests, and many might be disappointed, although they would never say so. Though I gave very careful thought to my choices, I managed to achieve a horrendous social blunder, clumsily rectified at the end.

I wrote to my choices, and received quick confirmations. I wrote up the list and sent it to Monsignor Kennedy in our continuing correspondence. He wrote back, confirming arrangement and added, somewhat stiffly, I thought, "Of course, Jim, the co-celebrants at your Mass will be priests of your own choosing."

Oh, God. I had forgotten to invite Monsignor Kennedy, both my pastor and my repeated benefactor! I assumed he would act as my Archpriest in the solemn ceremony, but I had never asked him. I fired off an apologetic letter, and received a warm response in agreement.

Choosing Monsignor Kennedy as Archpriest was a social "must" but an aesthetic disaster. In this particular form of Solemn Mass, the Archpriest attends the Celebrant at the altar, standing next to him, turning pages, holding back the sleeves of the vestments and so on. The functions are unimportant, the presence is everything.

The Monsignor stood tall—a bulky six feet seven inches and, when fully vested, filled a vast liturgical space. I towered barely five feet ten and tipped the scales at about 125 lbs. The vestments had the effect of emphasizing my long, skinny neck without adding much physical presence. In the comic book language of the time, we became Mutt and Jeff, although most people were kind enough to repress the obvious remarks. I myself never thought of it till I saw the photos of the first Mass.

God Lives in the Details

I knew very little about planning a party. I sent a few invitations for my graduation from college, but they were standard issue, requiring only addresses from me. The First Mass celebration quickly became a full-fledged affair, which meant printed invitations, photos, remembrance cardlets (or Holy Cards, as we called them), menus, reservations, seating charts, all that Perle Mesta stuff.

Many, many deacon hours passed talking about these plans, and the truly clueless among us listened carefully to the *cognocenti*. I had never planned a single seating chart in my life. A menu? Forget it.

Some guys took this stuff more seriously than others. During the previous year, deacon Joe Ruffalo tended to go on and on about the design theme of his various printings. Some wiseacres in his class had enough. They called him Ruff Buffalo, and went so far as to locate an obscure saint called Gaspard di Bufalo, acquired a remembrance card with his likeness, and had printed on the back:

RUFF BUFFALO
Priested
5/60

I still have that card in a book somewhere.

Friends and relatives wrote to accept invitations and often asked for gift suggestions—those innocent days before gift registries. "Pious" gifts seemed appropriate—things like crucifixes, stoles, religious pictures—although money certainly fit the bill for me.

One piece of priestly equipment—little golden (or gold-plated) recepticals to carry the Holy Oil for anointing the sick and dying. They were called oil stocks. One of my classmates suggested 'oil stocks' as an appropriate gift and received 100 shards of Standard Oil! Why didn't I think of that?

Anyway, I made my way down a checklist of stuff, ignoring my studies, but drew a blank on planning the lunch. When, where, what, who, how?

Once more, Monsignor Kennedy stepped up. He volunteered to take on the planning and staging of the First Mass and the luncheon to follow. Or, to be more precise, he volunteered the Ladies Society of St. Lawrence to deal with all this. Good thing. I might have ordered peanut butter sandwiches, for all I know.

The Chalice Show

After Easter, someone arranged to have a display of all the class chalices in the Library. An annual event, I see it now as an exercise in ostentation as well as a public statement of one's liturgical leanings—traditional or contemporary. But, my chalice having arrived and being more than I could have imagined in realization, I found myself delighted to add it to the display.

The enamel chalices clearly took the starring roles. Expensive, completely non-traditional, they proclaimed themselves and their owners. The justification always the same: only the finest to carry the Blood of Our Savior. The same rationale applied to the pastor's Cadillac.

My chalice, though large and unusual in design and material, proclaimed my personal humility, lack of ostentation, willingness to honor workmanship and materials. Or did it? Hmmm.

We circulated around the table, admiring, criticizing, obliquely watching to see if guys took notice of our own chalices, owners identified by name tags. Every chalice was praised to its owners, but we reserved our own judgment.

The chalice display. By some chance, mine is right up front.

The faculty came, too, and often expressed their own opinions as well. I was surprised to see Snuffy Nevins circulating around the table. Surely most of the display offended his sense of the traditional.

By our final year in theology, Snuffy had pretty much faded as a threat to our priestly ambitions, and to us personally. We were all ordained as deacons and there wasn't much he could do to us. Our last chance to bait him occurred with the arrival of our chalices.

My chalice, the only object I have designed in my whole life, had a big, hammered-silver cup, a wooden stem and the base again in hammered silver. It was like no chalice I had ever seen, and I was immensely proud of it.

Knowing that it would irritate Snuffy no end, I sought him out and showed him the chalice, asking him what he thought of it.

"Have you paid for it yet?" he asked. I nodded, mystified. "Well then, it's nice." He wheeled and shuffled away, winner of the last round.

The Seal of Confession

April had come; most of the Mass exams completed; things were lightening up for us deacons. Classes continued, but a distinct sense of pointlessness permeated our studies. There would be no exams; most of us would be called away to ordination before the end of the semester—the date up to our local bishops, who cared nothing about the seminary calendar. And most of us were ready, willing, and eager for the long-anticipated day when we would be elevated to the ranks of the priesthood.

We did have one on-going concern—the Confessional. I mean, not going to it, but sitting in it—being confessors. This was one liturgical function we couldn't, or at least didn't, practice. However, the implacably bland and kindly Father Brennan talked about hearing confessions at some length.

Brennan's mantra—"be kind"—could not be challenged as advice, but didn't seem particularly helpful in the face of our questions and unspoken fears.

The class rang with warnings, however. Never reveal the content of anyone's confession. Instant excommunication would result. Never talk about confessions even in general.

"In fact," suggested Brennan, "Just don't talk about confession at all."

"You'll find," Brennan added, "the ministry is afflicted with little old ladies of the clerical variety, and they love to gossip." The harshest thing I ever heard Brennan say, and it was true enough.

The Seal of Confession, as it was called, referred to the absolute confidentiality of anything said in the confessional. The confidentiality was established in civil law, and widely understood in popular culture. From our earliest years, the Seal formed a dramatic element in Catholic education. We heard heroic tales of confessors who would leave the confession to say Mass, drink the poisoned wine mentioned in confession, then die a martyr to their fidelity.

Sex in the Box

Hitchcock made a film in the early fifties, *I Confess*, based on the premise. It starred Monty Clift as a priest and Ann Bancroft, but the film failed to find a large audience because even Hitch couldn't figure a way to solve the implied romance.

Sexual matters in the confessional produced abundant warnings in class. The normally soft-spoken Brennan spoke with intensity. "Never hear a woman's confession outside the confessional." Who knows what might result?

Our own adolescent experiences suggested to us that much of our confessional material would deal with sex. Brennan produced further prohibitions. "Never inquire as to the details of any material that might be sexual in nature, no matter how vaguely put." Hmmm. If we couldn't understand what the penitent said, how could we know there was anything to forgive? Maybe we could judge from the tone? How guilty did they sound? Not much help from Brennan on this.

Privately, we speculated on what we might face. Our own current confessional experience—as penitents—did not seem useful or relevant. So we came up with hypotheticals.

Hearing Confessions: Theory and Practice

Dempsey's hand shot into the air one day. He launched into an elaborate imaginary confession. "This guy comes into the confessional. He's married but he's cheating on his wife. He loves his wife, but he really loves this other women too. And one of his daughters finds out......" Dempsey paused for a moment, then added, "Hey, Father, this is not ME I'm talking about." A roar of laughter from the class, which had been following the hypothetical like a soap opera.

"Ah, forget it, you guys." Dempsey muttered, his face red at the response.

The only practical advice we could get came from the previous year's deacons, who had been in the field, and occasionally came back to recount their adventures to their former schoolmates.

"Remember that stuff Brennan used to tell us about never hearing a woman's confession face to face?" Mark Liebler, ordained the year before and back for a visit, spoke to a small group of rapt listeners. We nodded eagerly.

"Well, for my very first confession, I'm sitting in the box. I heard someone get in, I opened the slide, and a note comes sliding through the screen. "Father, can you hear my confession in the sacristy? I'm a deaf-mute." A woman's signature on the note.

Filled with conflict and recalling Brennan's dire warnings, Liebler emerged from the confessional, walked into the sacristy, set up a prie-dieu (kneeler) and a chair and keeping rigorous custody of his eyes, received the written confession of the young woman who came and knelt. Making it up as he went along, he wrote a brief advisement, a penance, and handed the note back to her. The whole experience was routine for her, but rattled him to the bone.

Actually, its the only confessional story I remember, but it's a goodie. Shows how different the world would be from our classroom picture of it, or even our own fearful imaginings.

One last unique event in the deacon year's social calendar (such as it was) awaited us, as we awaited it—the deacon picnic!

Deacon Picnic

I'm guessing the picnic came on a Wednesday, so that a minimum numberof classes would be missed. A string of school busses pulled up at nine in the morning, and loaded us aboard, bearing us to some distant country property equipped with a real baseball diamond, a pond for swimming, picnic tables and various forms of sports equipment.

And, could you believe it, beer. Bats, balls, beer, burgers, bugs and BS. An absolute guy scene! Required to have supervision, we invited a couple of our favorite faculty members to join us, the ones perceived as least likely to inform. Dannemiller and Falcone, as I remember. Ray Brown was too intellectual, Van Antwerp, now the rector, too highly placed for such shenanigans.

And shenanig we did. Play, eat, drink, play, eat, drink. I recall nothing specific from the day, although I have a photo of some physical horseplay with Dan O'Conner, who had set aside just enough of his dignity.

The author-to-be grapples Mike McKenna.

"I'm wet and I'm hysterical." O'Brien and O'Connor, years before Mel Brooks!

I think we had a tiny subliminal sense that this would be the last time we would ever get to play as kids. Most of us in our twenties; most of us to be ordained within a month; most of us to be imprisoned (willingly, I guess) within the expectations of "the world."

At any rate, we partied hard, fueled by the unaccustomed beer, and we rolled onto the busses at dusk, most of us rather the worse for wear. We arrived at the seminary with just enough time to shower and suit up for Compline, the last chanted Hour of the Divine Office.

One of our more luckless members would have to begin the service by chanting the opening prayer of Compline: *Fratres! Sobrii estote, et vigilate..* Once again the familiar line would vibrate with irony. The deacon chanter himself clearly had not followed the advise of the psalmist. A very audible sputter of suppressed (and beery) laughter arose from the ranks of the Deacons. Indeed, smiles spread through the full chapel and even among some of the faculty.

The last fling was flung.

Ecce Quam Bonum

As you've noticed, I still have fragments of Latin cluttering my brain, theological and liturgical. But my most vivid Latin memory recalls the gathering of guys on the front steps after breakfast to sing *Ecce Quam Bonum* to the departing deacons as they left to begin their ministries.

Ecce quam bonum, et quam jucundum, habitare fratres in unum. Drawn from the Psalms, the line says: "Look how good and how joyful it is to live as brothers united."

We sang the *Ecce* with vigor and feeling, as the deacons left either singly or in small groups. Dressed in black suits, schlepping black valises, waving and grinning embarrassedly, they paused awkwardly as the full-throated chorus roared the sentimental anthem and the cabbies waited, mystified and probably impatient, for their clerical fares.

248   Making a Priest in the 'Fifties

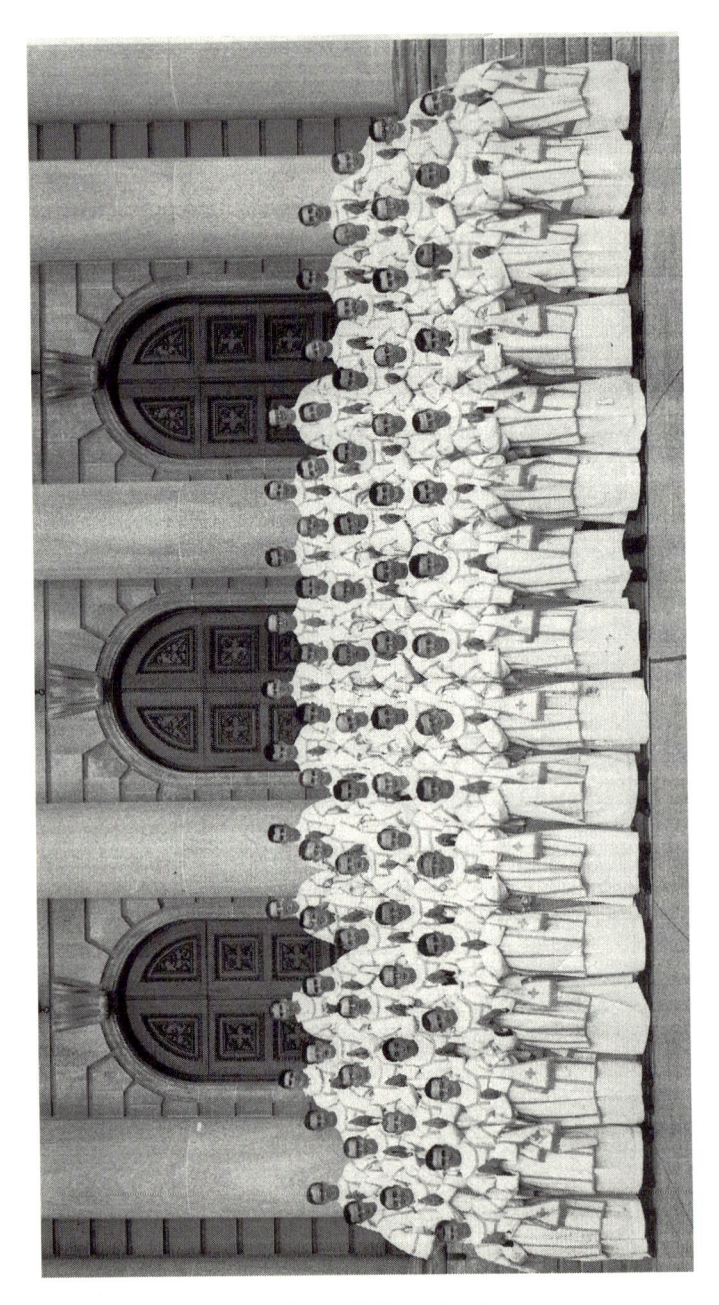

The Deacon Class of 1961, eighty-five strong.

Not everybody got an *Ecce*. The gathering occurred voluntarily, the number determined by popularity and/or notoriety. Well-liked deacons would have upwards of a hundred cassock-clad seminarians ranged up and down the long and wide steps, and the tone of the gatherings was celebratory.

The *Ecce* meant more than simply 'goodbye.' We deeply needed to believe in the sentiment of the psalm phrase. The faculty had drummed the idea of the "brotherhood of the priesthood," into us and exhorted us to live by the principle. The celibate priesthood would be a lonely life and we had to be able to count on the assumed friendship of the other clergy we would encounter.

Most newly-ordained priests eagerly embraced the notion of priestly fraternity, only to be snubbed repeatedly by older clergy, embarrassed by the naivete' and presumption of the new guys. They had no particular interest in any "brotherhood," whether sanctioned by the psalmist or not. But I didn't know that then.

Dempsey and I walked down the front steps for the last time. A glorious day in early May. A gratifying crowd had gathered. We shook hands, got backs clapped, grinned helplessly, then climbed into the car. Our seminary days had ended.

Ite, missa est.

Author Biography

Jim O'Brien grew up in Elgin, Illinois, where he attended St. Mary's grade school, St. Edward High School, moved on to the University of Notre Dame, where he earned an A. B. in Philosophy cum laude. Sent by the Rockford diocese to study at St. Mary's Seminary in Baltimore, he was ordained in 1961, the product of an unbroken twenty years of Catholic education.

In Rockford, he served as parish priest at St. Patrick's, taught religion at Boylan High School and spent a year as Assistant Managing Editor of the diocesan newspaper, the Rockford Observer. Bishop Lane then appointed him Assistant Pastor at St. Joseph's church in Freeport, Illinois and instructor at Aquin High school.

In 1966, Bishop Lane directed him to study broadcasting at Northwestern, where he earned an M.A. in 1967. Bishop Lane then appointed him Diocesan Director for Radio, TV, and Film and chaplain to the motherhouse of the School Sisters of Notre Dame in DeKalb, Illinois and to the Catholic high school there.

Granted a leave of absence from the diocese by Bishop Arthur O'Neill in 1969, O'Brien taught at the University of Miami, received his Ph.D. from Northwestern in 1977, and accepted a position at the College of New Rochelle in New Rochelle, N.Y., where else?

He retired in 1999 as Professor Emeritus in Communication Arts and moved to Madison, Wisconsin, where he coordinates courses in film and writing for the PLATO division of the University of Wisconsin Extention, plays jazz clarinet, and writes his memoirs and those of others.

978-0-595-40853-
0-595-40853-2

Made in the USA